TEACHING AWARENESS IN THE BUDDHIST TRADITION

Teaching Awareness in the Buddhist Tradition

Essays in Honour of Professor Corrado Pensa

EDITED BY

CHIARA NERI AND FRANCESCO SFERRA

equinox

SHEFFIELD UK BRISTOL CT

Published by Equinox Publishing Ltd.

UK: Office 415, The Workstation, 15 Paternoster Row, Sheffield, South Yorkshire, S1 2BX
USA: ISD, 70 Enterprise Drive, Bristol, CT 06010

www.equinoxpub.com

First published 2024

© Chiara Neri, Francesco Sferra and contributors 2024

All rights reserved. No part of this publication may be reproduced or transmitted in any form or by any means, electronic or mechanical, including photocopying, recording or any information storage or retrieval system, without prior permission in writing from the publishers.

British Library Cataloguing-in-Publication Data
A catalogue record for this book is available from the British Library.

ISBN-13 978 1 80050 330 4 (hardback)
978 1 80050 331 1 (paperback)
978 1 80050 332 8 (ePDF)
978 1 80050 379 3 (ePub)

Library of Congress Cataloging-in-Publication Data
Names: Pensa, Corrado, honouree. | Neri, Chiara, editor. | Sferra, Francesco, editor.
Title: Teaching awareness in the Buddhist tradition : essays in honour of Professor Corrado Pensa / edited by Chiara Neri and Francesco Sferra.
Description: Bristol : Equinox Publishing Ltd, 2024. | Includes bibliographical references and index. | Summary: "This book provides important contributions to understanding the teaching of awareness or mindfulness in Buddhism and in related traditions, examined in original ways in a collection of articles that approach this theme from different perspectives: philosophical, philological, exegetic, anthropological, as an aspect of meditative practice, and so on. The volume is dedicated to Corrado Pensa, a well-known Buddhist scholar and practitioner. A valuable feature of this book is the integration of two aspects of the Buddhist tradition, i.e., theory and practice, the volume thereby appealing to both academics and practitioners"-- Provided by publisher.
Identifiers: LCCN 2023001617 (print) | LCCN 2023001618 (ebook) | ISBN 9781800503304 (hardback) | ISBN 9781800503311 (paperback) | ISBN 9781800503328 (pdf) | ISBN 9781800503793 (epub)
Subjects: LCSH: Buddhism--Study and teaching--History. | Spiritual life--Buddhism.
Classification: LCC BQ120 .T43 2023 (print) | LCC BQ120 (ebook) | DDC 294.3/75--dc23/eng/20230213
LC record available at https://lccn.loc.gov/2023001617
LC ebook record available at https://lccn.loc.gov/2023001618

Typeset by S.J.I. Services, New Delhi, India

Contents

Foreword vii
Joseph Goldstein

Preface: Tracing the Path of the Dharma ix
Chiara Neri and Francesco Sferra

Bibliography of Corrado Pensa: Works from 1962–2020 xxiv
Chiara Neri and Francesco Sferra

I. WORDS ON THE DHARMA **1**

1. The Meditative Cultivation of Joy 3
Bhikkhu Anālayo

2. The Concept of *Pariyogāhaṇa* in the Epistemology of the *Paṭisambhidāmagga*: An Immersion in Knowledge and Liberation 14
Giuliano Giustarini

3. Buddhist Awareness as a Means to Unveil the Past and Emancipate the Future: The Buddhist Awareness Camps Project in post-1990 Nepal 29
Chiara Letizia

4. An Unshakeable Awareness: *Siddha*s and *Jīvanmukti* According to the *Mokṣopāya* 58
Bruno Lo Turco

5. Framing the Other: Mindfulness, Photography, and a Reflexive Approach to Comparative Religions 82
Filippo Marsili

6. The Teaching of Awareness in Corrado Pensa's Thought 99
Chiara Neri

7. A Joyful Song Celebrating Buddhist Practice 124
Marta Sernesi

8. Evil According to Buddhism 144
Francesco Sferra

II. THE DHARMA IN WORDS 167

9. The Loveliness of the Ordinary 169
Christina Feldman

10. *Ānāpānasati*: A Brief Introduction 174
Larry Rosenberg

11. Living in Mindfulness and Wisdom 177
Andrea Schnöller

Index of Names 189

Index of Texts (Sanskrit, Pāli and Prakrit) 194

Index of Terms 196

Foreword

Joseph Goldstein

I first met Corrado Pensa in 1976 when he first came to practice at the Insight Meditation Society in Barre, Massachusetts. In the many years since then, we have become good friends and colleagues on this great Dharma journey.

From the very beginning, it was clear that Corrado had a depth of knowledge and a breadth of understanding of many spiritual traditions. This openness to learn from many traditions became the bedrock foundation of his lifelong commitment to liberation, and his unwavering desire to share his wisdom with all those who came to see him. In addition to studying and practicing with a wide variety of teachers, Corrado also undertook his own scholarly research, publishing many books and articles. It's rare to find people who combine the profound path of meditation practice with the rigors of scholarly inquiry. Corrado is such a great exemplar of how these two streams of understanding can flow into one another, enriching both.

An important aspect of the transmission of the Dharma to the West has been the great interest of lay people in practicing meditation, grounded in an understanding of classical Buddhist teachings. And one of Corrado's greatest contributions has been the creation, with other friends, of the Association for Mindfulness Meditation in Rome. This centre has fulfilled the need for a place to support the practice and understanding of laypeople in an urban environment, right in the midst of their daily lives. I had the good fortune to teach in person at the centre and also to connect via Zoom in the midst of the pandemic, and I was inspired by the sincerity and dedication of the Sangha members, who have created a vibrant community of Dharma practitioners.

One of the great intangibles of Corrado's offerings, and one that has made them accessible to so many people, is his wonderful lightness of being, even as he explores ever-deeper insights into the nature of our minds and lives. I'm delighted that this volume is highlighting and celebrating the many contributions of Corrado to the spread of the Buddhadharma in the West. May his life and work continue to light the way.

Joseph Goldstein
May 2022

Author biography

Joseph Goldstein is one of the most important teachers of *vipassanā* meditation; co-founder of the Insight Meditation Society (IMS); and author of numerous popular books, including *The Experience of Insight: A Simple and Direct Guide to Buddhist Meditation* (1976); *One Dharma: The Emerging Western Buddhism* (2002); *A Heart Full of Peace* (2007); *Mindfulness: A Practical Guide to Awakening* (2013).

Preface: Tracing the Path of the Dharma[1]

Chiara Neri and Francesco Sferra

While reflecting on how many things have changed in the last twenty-five years, one may wonder whether children today realize how different their lives would have been just a short time ago. Here, we are mainly considering the enormous amount of information that is now easily accessible through the Internet as well as extraordinary developments in online communication, from e-mail to video calls, from text messages to social media outlets like Twitter and Facebook, just to mention the most common. Our parents most likely had a similar impression regarding us, just like our grandparents had with their children and so on, back over the generations, at least until the first half of the nineteenth century, when changes occurred more slowly and gradually.

Even for our generation, born when mobile phones did not exist, these changes, which allow us to communicate and access knowledge at previously unthinkable speeds, may now seem something quite simple, normal and natural. It is easy for our sense of historical perspective to diminish; we have to think hard to remember that until very recently, communication between people was, so to say, 'artisanal,' requiring more straightforward means and longer times. Contact with other cultures and traditions, let alone engaging with such disparate ways of life, seemed virtually impossible, since very few people could overcome the economic, linguistic and time limitations required.

We lived in a more isolated and seemingly protected world; what was distant seemed exotic to us. Its representation was frequently based on our projections, which were built partly on the accounts of travellers, scholars, geographers, missionaries and merchants, and partly on clichés as well as our imagination and prejudices—but rarely based on direct experience. As a whole, we lived in a world with fewer opportunities.

The last century, particularly after World War II, proved to be crucial in changing our perspective. Today, we can talk and collaborate with people from all over the world, learn about their customs, culture and religion through books, documentaries and reportage. More importantly, we can now do so through direct contact, facilitated by various means of communication and transport, as well as the spread of English as the primary language of intercultural communication.

We must admit that today, Buddhism (and also many other Asian wisdom traditions), along with the countries and cultures to which it has spread, no longer represents a mysterious domain but rather something that we should no longer ignore. This, of course, does not imply that with Buddhism, everything is now clear, nor that everything has been done to spread its understanding,[2] but rather that the tools are now finally available. Asia is no longer the only place where we find accredited Dharma centers, trained and qualified teachers and communities of practitioners who meet regularly and support each other. In America and Europe, we now find a great variety of tools and opportunities for the practice of Buddhism: publications, CDs and audio-visual materials, meditation centers, retreats, etc. This would have been unthinkable until only thirty or thirty-five years ago.

In this regard, we would like to talk about Corrado Pensa and his crucial role in spreading Buddhism in the West, particularly in Italy, both from an academic point of view and as a Dharma teacher. In 1987, together with a small group of practitioners, he founded the *Associazione per la meditazione di Cansapevolezza* (A.Me.Co.), an association for mindfulness meditation. It was mainly inspired by the Theravāda Buddhist religious faith but has also been open to intra-Buddhist and inter-religious dialogue. It is based in Rome and organizes retreats throughout Italy with national and international teachers, and currently has more than a thousand associates.[3] Before exploring his background, let us start with a brief historical overview of the recent dissemination of Buddhism in America and Europe.[4]

For several centuries, the knowledge of Buddhism in the West—especially in Europe and even more so in Italy—was 'academic,' not only because it was conveyed by scholars, but because it was essentially bookish, mediated by written sources: diaries; travel reports; scientific studies; translations; and essays. These sources were often 'second-hand,' that is, compiled based on documents written by others. These were first composed by missionaries and geographers, then by linguists, historians and philologists, and finally by a diverse group of connoisseurs, including scholars but also career soldiers and officials employed in India and other Asian countries; who for a long time were labelled 'Orientalists.'

It was a slow and difficult path, which included people inspired for various reasons, but who were all certainly moved by curiosity and sincere interest. However, for many centuries, one can also say that they were rarely objective in their approach, with only a few exceptions. There were the Christian missionaries who, for example, believed that Buddhism offered an antithesis to their own beliefs, which were surely superior and preferable. Others, on the other hand, sought an authoritative and arcane confirmation of their highly personal doctrines, which resulted in Buddhism being dragged into the general disinterest and suspicion with which their thoughts were received. This was the case, for example, with Julius Evola's (1898–1974) bizarre conception, which suggests that moral sensitivity, *sīla* (Pāli, *śīla* in Sanskrit), is not a value for Buddhists but simply an instrument of the mind of the virtuous, namely a person endowed with virile energy.[5]

In addition, between the end of the nineteenth and beginning of the twentieth centuries, several Asian exponents of living traditions along with Western converts, some of the first transmitters of Buddhism in the West, chose to present it in a language that they considered captivating for the audiences of that time. According to Anagārika Dharmapala (1864–1933), for example, Buddhism would have been ideal for the West since it was a 'scientific religion, [...] a philosophy of life built on a psychological mysticism and a cosmogony in harmony with geology, astronomy, radioactivity and relativity.'[6] He presented Buddhism as a positivist and rational religion, to some extent perfectly in line with Darwin's theories of evolution and free from theology, dogmas and rituals.

These and many other misunderstandings and prejudices, no doubt inevitable in any historical process, have profoundly marked the collective imagination and unfortunately still resurface with insistence today. But there is no need to dwell further on this point. The fact remains that in the first decades of the last century, involvement with Buddhism was limited mainly to an educated and wealthy elite, often disaffected with Christianity and fascinated by new scientific discoveries, but at the same time attracted by the idea of a mystical path aimed at overcoming pain. The preferred approach would remain a theoretical one.

Two closely linked factors have been decisive in developing a more profound interest in understanding Buddhism (and other Asian wisdom traditions) and the practice of the Buddhist path towards liberation. First is the overcoming of what one might call 'philological delirium.' This syndrome led many Westerners educated in prestigious European (British, French, German, Italian and Russian) philological schools to declare to understand Buddhism better than Buddhists themselves. The claim grew out of the fact that they were studying its sources with the 'infallible' methods of ecdotics and linguistics, assuming, quite erroneously, that the written texts, even the most ancient, contained everything there was to know and that their records were always reliable. Accordingly, the living tradition was considered a negligible, degenerate version of true Buddhist teaching. There are precise historical reasons for the genesis of this attitude, which, as well as justifying it, at least partly explain its limits and development, but this aspect will not be dealt with here.[7]

Here, it will be sufficient to highlight the essential steps taken to overcome this phase. First, was a closer relationship gradually established with the exponents of Buddhist traditions; a relationship no longer based on extrinsic, basically colonialist observation, but on trust, confidence and humility. There was a growing conviction that not everything could be explained philologically; that living traditions had a dignity of their own; and that, above all, had much to reveal. This new cultural attitude, which came shortly after the emergence of new directions in the field of anthropological studies, was increasingly aimed at 'field research.' Moreover, since this attitude coincided on a political level with the end of colonialism, it also allowed for a greater receptivity towards contemplative practices, which could be taught by traditional teachers, often charismatic and innovative figures of great depth, such as Achan Chah, Achan Maha Boowa, U Ba Khin, Suzuki Roshi, U Pandita Sayadaw and Chögyam Trungpa, to name just a few of the most prominent.

Contact with these masters was also made possible by the growing ease with which, starting from the 1960s, one could travel to the East, India, Japan and even Southeast Asia. Furthermore, certain historical events and circumstances led to a greater presence of Asian teachers in America and Europe. These were, at times, the result of painful experiences, such as the diaspora created after World War II of numerous Zen masters from Japan, or after the annexation of Tibet by China of Tibetan lamas and tulkus, or exile for political reasons, such as the well-known story of Thich Nhat Hahn.

The second factor that facilitated the development of a more mature interest in Buddhist contemplative practices was the flourishing of a generation of 'receptors.' These were a group of lay practitioners, all born between the end of the 1930s and the beginning of the 1950s, who were either mother-tongue or highly proficient English speakers. They will be remembered as the first masters of Buddhism in the West—the initiators of a new phase in the history of Buddhism, its adaptations and developments. Among these were: Robert Baker Aitken, Martine and Stephen Batchelor, Christina Feldman, Joseph Goldstein, Jon Kabat-Zinn, Jack Kornfield, Frank Ostaseski, Larry Rosenberg, Sharon Salzberg and Corrado Pensa. It is thanks to them, first and foremost, and to so many others who have not been mentioned, that we can speak today of 'Buddhism in the West.'

The academic knowledge of scholars like A. Bareau, E. Burnouf, N. Dutt, E. Frauwallner, L. de la Vallée Poussin, É. Lamotte, S. Lévi, H. Oldenberg, T. W. Rhys Davids, R. Sāṅkṛtyāyana, T. Stcherbatsky and G. Tucci, to name just a few of the greats, had prepared the ground and played a fundamental role in creating a more solid understanding of the Buddhist experience. In the second half of the past century and even today, scholars and researchers have been trying to deepen this understanding on comparative, historical and philological levels. But academic knowledge was not enough, nor would the offer of teachings by the Asian masters suffice, however original and charismatic they might have been—something more was needed.

It would take what we might define as a work of 'metabolization,' carried out by Westerners who—after having received the teachings, understood their preciousness, experienced their fruits as well as the difficulties of putting them into practice—were able to reformulate and transmit their original spirit to others. In other words, there had to be a generation of people, defined earlier as 'receptors,' who were capable of carrying out a cultural integration of the most vital aspects of Buddhism along with the most vital aspects of Western modernity and their own culture of origin, steeped in Christianity and, especially for Americans, Judaism. These 'receptors' also include some Westerners who have become part of traditional monastic communities, such as Achan Anālayo, Achan Braham, Achan Sujato, Achan Sumedho, Philip Kapleau, Houn Jiyu-Kennett, just to mention a few among the most recent.

Among the lay scholars who, like Corrado Pensa, were also 'receptors' and mediators of Buddhism, we may first recall Lance S. Cousins (1942–2015). In addition to being a famous Pāli and Early Buddhist scholar, Cousins founded the Sanatha Trust Association and various meditation centres, which conducted retreats in the UK, USA, and Sri Lanka.[8]

Reformulation and integration, however, do not mean syncretism; in the teachings of the masters mentioned above, there is never an uncritical juxtaposition of doctrines, practices or traditions. Although their language may sometimes be far from the traditional ones, it nonetheless remains faithful on a deeper level. This attitude of cultural mediation, which to be authentic requires an experience of the fruits of what is being mediated, seems to be a crucial point. It reveals an exceptional sensitivity, capacity and charisma that cannot be improvised. In fact, none of the people mentioned above are 'self-proclaimed' Dharma teachers. This is an important aspect that deserves a brief digression.

Thanks to the increased diffusion of English as a lingua franca, one can now read, online and in print, books and Dharma talks by accredited teachers from various countries, consult magazines and listen to CDs with guided meditations and thematic teachings. These are all items produced continuously in meditation centres worldwide and contribute significantly and positively to the deepening and support of the practice.

However, the greater availability of information does not eliminate but paradoxically *increases* the risk of an overly simplified reception of the Dharma. An abundance of information does not imply a critical attitude, which instead requires individual and group study, as well as, of course, verification in the field. The risk is the illusion that, since everything is easily within reach, a single intellectual understanding is enough; with the careful study of a few books, one might even embark on the challenging and very delicate undertaking of spiritual direction. The availability of so much information does not mean that it is more easily transformed into knowledge because, far from being something mysterious and esoteric, it simply requires a prolonged and perhaps unexpected amount of time for its implementation and verification. In other words, it requires the settling, maturation and flowering of the fruits—the letting go of the 'I' and 'mine,' the flow of a spontaneous and objectless compassion, the perception of the fundamental goodness of and interconnection between all things—the emergence of which, in our diverse and complex everyday life, cannot be programmed.

Teaching, therefore, requires a particular 'charisma,' which is sometimes lacking even in people who have progressed on their interior journey; it is not something that develops automatically. This is recognized by the Buddhist traditions themselves, which speak of 'Buddha for himself' or 'Solitary Buddha'[9] to indicate precisely a person who does not show others the way.

When teachers show a lack of self-criticism, pluralism or tolerance, when they do not have a sense of humor and are highly self-referential, and, instead, tend to create addiction and promote the cult of personality, what results is often and sadly the 'sale of the Dharma.' This phenomenon was once defined as 'spiritual materialism,'[10] while recently, we see historicist historians of religions referring to it as the 'market of religions.' We therefore find self-proclaimed masters and even the foundation of different sects (today called 'religious service agencies'), which are more or less linked, very often indirectly, to a historical tradition. Sometimes these sects are in open opposition with one another, competing to acquire followers and prestige, reproducing ancient Asian contrasts in the West, which are often determined more by socioeconomic factors than by ontological or religious views. Along with all of this, comes a resulting misunderstanding and betrayal of the Dharma as well as negative consequences in people's lives.

The above-mentioned 'receptor' masters are not great simply because they have founded Dharma centres or have understood how to exploit the potential offered by recent developments in communication, as mentioned at the beginning of this introduction. They have done much more—they have completed the fundamental work of translating and rewriting Buddhism, which presupposes assimilation, intelligence and originality.

It is based on this *rewriting* that the foundation of the Dharma centres—particularly those, dare we say, in the 'trenches,' that is to say, urban centres, especially those in the big cities—found solid ground. These centres do not propose the practice of a Buddhism detached from time and history, but rather a Buddhism usable by a modern Westerner, a Buddhism capable of responding to one's problems with an appropriate language, but which at the same time is, we repeat, respectful of traditions old and new.

Practicing Buddhism in an urban centre is still a relatively rare opportunity; it becomes sustainable (or at least more sustainable) only if it is not merely an individual path, but a personal path within a group or Saṅgha. The importance of a community and qualified teachers therein is something with which one can hardly disagree. In its absence, it is no wonder that discouragement, doubt and numbness sooner or later take over as these are tremendously natural things from which no one is entirely immune.

Until the 1960s and 1970s, in many parts of the globe, including Italy, meditation centers simply did not exist. Their founders and teacher-guides (often these two figures coincide) are still active. It is worth emphasizing that they are not managers (indeed, some of them perhaps would not make very good managers) but rather people who, with ingenuity, courage, perseverance and, above all, altruism, have been able to give life to an act of historical value.

With this volume, we want to celebrate Corrado Pensa as a scholar and as an extraordinary Dharma teacher. Corrado Pensa began to take an interest in Buddhism when he was a student at the University of Rome. After some initial doubts about whether to pursue Russian literature or Indian studies, he chose to attend the lessons of the great Giuseppe Tucci and then those of Luciano Petech and Raniero Gnoli. In the mid-1960s, he succeeded Tucci as the chair of Religion and Philosophy of India and the Far East (this was, indeed, the title of a chair and not of a faculty as it may seem at first sight). He was only 25 years old, making him the youngest of Tucci's students and the youngest full professor at an Italian University.

A list of Corrado Pensa's publications follows this preface; it is worth noting that he has dealt with a variety of Indian traditions and that some of his contributions on Yoga and Buddhism of the Great Vehicle are still studied and cited by scholars today.

Always interested in spirituality and open to the sense of the sacred, Corrado Pensa had his first Buddhist meditative experience in 1970 at the Zen Center in San Francisco under the guidance of the famous master Suzuki Roshi. His initial contact with *vipassanā* came in 1975, when he went on his first retreat with Jack Kornfield in California. From 1976 onwards, he participated (even twice a year) in extended meditation retreats at the Insight Meditation Society (IMS) in Barre, Massachusetts. Some of these retreats took place biannually and others quarterly. At the IMS, he also took part in *vipassanā* retreats according to the Burmese style of U Pandita Sayadaw, led by teachers from the Gaia House centre in England. Since 1998, following the Kagyu (*bka' brgyud*) Tibetan tradition, he has regularly visited the Awakened Heart Sangha in Wales to practice with the teacher Shenpen Hookham from England.

Pensa is a senior teacher at the IMS in Barre, where he teaches regularly. Together with other IMS lecturers, including Christina Feldman, Narayan Liebenson, Michele McDonald, Larry Rosenberg, Carol Wilson and Fred von Almen, he has conducted various retreats in the USA and Europe (at Gaia House in England and for the Dhamma Gruppe in Switzerland). He also regularly teaches at the Cambridge Insight Meditation Centre (USA).

Let us point out (at the very least) two characteristics of Corrado Pensa. These are also reflected in the spiritual direction of the A.Me.Co., which today he leads together with his wife, Neva Papachristou, co-founder and also a qualified Dharma teacher. The first thing we wish to underline, but only *en passant*, is Corrado's steadfast willingness to work in a team with other teachers. The second is that, although *vipassanā* is his reference tradition, he has always continued to study and practice other forms of Buddhism as well. It is not only the intra-Buddhist openness, which undoubtedly represents a vital and noteworthy aspect of his teaching, but above all, the fact that he continues to put his vocation into play with its ongoing formation, even assuming the role of a student. This should be emphasized since it is rare to find and is exemplary; indicative of a basic attitude aimed at humility and growth.

Even at the A.Me.Co., he has always invited qualified people from various Buddhist traditions to hold meditation courses, seminars or conferences. For example: the Korean Chan courses held by Stephen and Martine Batchelor; conferences on Tibetan Buddhism; Zen Buddhism retreats held by Frank Ostasenski; and, of course, the masters of *vipassanā*, both lay teachers and monks, from various parts of the world.

Another remarkable aspect is that there has been no shortage of non-Buddhist teachers, especially Christians. The retreats held regularly by Father Andrea Schnöller and by Don Luciano Mazocchi have been particularly memorable.

A willingness to teach with others and have others teach, as well as an ongoing intra-Buddhist and inter-religious formation, are potent antidotes to the self-referentiality into which many Dharma teachers and many religious associations have fallen.

To conclude, let us briefly examine some aspects of Corrado Pensa's teaching. We may define one essential element as the 'interreligious openness' mentioned above. Anyone who has attended one of his seminars, retreats, lectures or has read one of his writings will certainly have noticed frequent references to contemplative Christian teachers in both his oral discourse and written texts; and this is not accidental. The basic idea is that of consonance, or in other words, that the things which unite us are more plentiful (and more important) than the things which divide us. The great spiritual traditions universally share an aspiration for the Good of all beings and a conviction of its feasibility; the languages and practices for doing this may be very different, but never in radical contrast.

It is no coincidence that this openness is explicitly mentioned in the A.Me.Co. founding statute itself. The second article specifies that, 'A.Me.Co. is a religious association of Buddhist faith of Theravada tradition in an interreligious spirit [...]. In the universalistic view of Buddhism, meditative practice is understood as a compassionate means aimed at the salvation of all beings.'[11]

Furthermore, this is not pure rhetoric, as is testified by the fact that many people who have come to the A.Me.Co. to practice *vipassanā* come from Christian circles, mostly Catholic. An in-depth study of the practice has led many participants to reconnect with the Christian tradition, seeing it with new eyes, and discovering the fact that contemplation has to do with freedom and not with the betrayal of one's own religious tradition. In short, one tradition does not exclude the other, and both speak to the heart of man.

The other characteristic of Corrado Pensa's teaching we would like to highlight concerns, more precisely, some technical aspects of meditation and spiritual guidance. We are not referring so much to his interviews, where he also draws from, in part, his experience as a former Jungian analyst (having been a practicing psychotherapist for ten years), nor the teaching he imparts during residential retreats, but rather to the lessons given at the meditation courses he conducts at the A.Me.Co. headquarters.

The teachings of the Buddha are not abstractly transmitted by Corrado Pensa but rather through accurate explanations of how to carry out the practice of awareness, both during the sessions ('formal practice') and 'in action,' that is, in daily life. For the latter, he prepares and explains specific exercises that practitioners can carry out during the week and on which they can report later during a seminar session dedicated to questions and answers, which lasts about an hour. Practitioners are invited to actively participate by asking questions, giving impressions and sharing discoveries and difficulties. This session is particularly useful because it allows meditators not only to better understand the Dharma but also to prevent things that are not properly understood from becoming an obstacle on their spiritual path.

In addition to a great passion for the Dharma, the remarkable ability that Corrado has in communicating it is enriched by his many years of university teaching and in-depth training, as mentioned previously. His teachings are compact, clear and numerous; not only does he regularly hold courses at the A.Me.Co. and other centers, especially in the United States, of which there are versions recorded on CD, but he is also the author of several books, numerous handouts and many articles that have appeared in Dharma journals (*Paramita* and *Sati* in particular). In attempting to summarize Corrado Pensa's written production, looking over his numerous articles, one cannot but admire how prolific he was. As revealed by their titles and contents, his early publications were primarily philological, which gave way to academic studies of different aspects of Buddhist teachings. His later works are those of a teacher of Dharma, his thought being clearly grounded in his academic studies.

His early production is oriented towards the study and translation of works dedicated to Yoga and Saṃkhya (e.g. Pensa 1962, 1969a and b, 1972a, 1977, 1978a) and to late Indian Buddhist texts (e.g. Pensa 1961, 1964a). In what we could define as a second phase, Pensa was a true exegete of the Buddha's teaching. Many of his writings investigate aspects related to 'right practice' (e.g. Pensa 1988), such as those concerning right intention (e.g. Pensa 1986a), taking refuge and the precepts (e.g. Pensa 1992b), and developing the perfections (*pāramī* or *pāramitā*) (Pensa 1998), including in particular loving-kindness (*mettā*) (e.g. Pensa 1994b, 1994c) and equanimity (*upekkhā*) (e.g. Pensa 1986a, 1993, 1994a), while not neglecting topics such as problems associated with lay life in the West (e.g. Pensa 1991, 1994e). His work has also often been characterized by attention to interreligious dialogue and, in particular, the search for deep connections between Buddhist and Christian traditions, as we have already pointed out above (e.g. Pensa 1985, 1986b, 1995a, 1995b). There are also many writings dedicated to meditative practice and problems often present at retreats (e.g. Pensa 1973, 1978b, 1987, 1989, 1992a, 1996, 1997a, 1997b), as well as those dealing with the psychological implications of a soteriological path (e.g. Pensa 1974, 1992c).

However, the leitmotif that has characterized his thinking for most of his later life is 'awareness,' *sati* (on which, see Neri in this volume), which, according to Corrado Pensa, represents both the instrument and aim of the Buddhist path (Pensa 1994d). In fact, it is the pivot for the realization of the eightfold path; that is, one cannot proceed on the path without it. This awareness, in turn, rests on three points of support: ethical precepts, meditation techniques and the understanding and investigation of awareness itself (Pensa 1994d: 277ff.). In particular, the third of these elements leads us to a 'disidentification.' It allows us to realize the three characteristic signs of existence: *dukkha, anicca* and *anattā*, that is, suffering or unsatisfactoriness, impermanence and not-self. Thus, awareness becomes a bare perceiving of reality, a wholly realized empty consciousness that vibrates beyond its mystery. The ability of Corrado Pensa to understand and transmit the Buddha's teaching makes him not only a great exegete and 'receptor,' but someone whose own realization has enabled him to bring others to similar achievements.

We met Corrado many years ago, and he immediately made a strong impression on us. We appreciated his qualities as a scholar and as a meditation teacher. We have seen him change over the years, becoming sweeter and more flexible, more and more empathic, less severe (at least we have perceived it that way), with a competence derived from life, study and practice, accompanied by a subtle sense of humour, frankness and kindness which we have rarely encountered elsewhere. He is a person who, as we said, we have seen change for the better (and yes, because even masters improve if they are true masters!); a person who continues to practice and study the Dharma with a child's enthusiasm; and who, in our opinion, shows signs of an increasingly authentic understanding and realization, first of all, by not taking himself too seriously. We believe this is what makes the greats even greater.

Among the teachings that have always helped us and are often found in his writings, there is, first of all, that of awareness as a value in itself and its relationship with trust. Then there is the constant reminder of the ever-present possibility of starting over and of continuously having the practice at hand. These lessons have continually reassured us, instilled us with courage and pushed us to devote ourselves to inner work with greater patience and determination—and it is this which has always been Corrado Pensa's fundamental teaching. For this reason, we decided that awareness was the common thread for this whole volume.

We hope that at least this is clear: that the debt which we, and many others, have towards Corrado Pensa is enormous; that the A.Me.Co. is a very precious gift and that the spiritual journey is also a path of gratitude—and Corrado undoubtedly deserves a great deal of gratitude.

Many of the contributors in this volume are former students of Corrado Pensa who want to pay homage to him because, among other things, he was the first to awaken their interest in Buddhist studies. Other contributors are fellow Dharma teachers who regard him as an inspiring master and friend. This volume is a way of offering Corrado a humble 'thank you' for all he has done for us.

We also want to thank all the contributors to this volume, Neva Papachristou for her kind support, and Luca Piscopo for compiling the Index.

Notes

1 A preliminary Italian version of the bulk of this paper was published by F. Sferra in *Sati* 2012, No. 21/3: 30–43.
2 In fact, often even editions and translations of the primary sources need redoing, as noted for instance by K. R. Norman (1997: 172) concerning the Pāli canon, when he stated that 'Everything that has not been done needs to be done. Everything that has been done needs to be done again.'
3 For the activity of this meditation center, see the association's website: https://www.associazioneameco.it/en/.
4 For more information about the history of Buddhism in non-Asian countries, see Prebish 1979, Bergonzi 1984: 305–396, Halbfass 1988, Baumann 2001, and De Simini 2013.
5 See Evola 1957.
6 Cited in McMahan 2008: 96. Among the scholars who have discussed the connection and the relationship between Buddhism and science, see Cabezón 2003, McMahan

2004, Harrison 2006: 96–97, Lo Turco 2006, McMahan 2008: 89–116, Lopez 2008, Lo Turco 2016.

7 On this topic, see De Simini 2013: 109–114.

8 See Harvey 2015. See also Appleton and Harvey 2019.

9 Pāli *paccekabuddha*, Skt. *pratyekabuddha*, J.Pkt. *patteyabuddha*. They are also called 'Buddhas who do not teach' because they keep awakening for themselves (*pratyeka*) and do not embark on a career of preaching it to others. For some discussions on this topic, see Kloppenborg 1983, Norman 1983, Anālayo 2010.

10 See Trungpa 1973.

11 In the Italian original, the text reads as follows: 'A.ME.CO. è un'associazione religiosa di fede buddhista di tradizione Theravada in spirito interreligioso [...]. Nella visione universalistica del Buddhismo, la prassi meditativa è intesa quale mezzo compassionevole volto alla salvezza di tutti gli esseri.' The statute is available online at the following website: https://www.associazioneameco.it/wp-content/uploads/2017/08/statuto-ameco-atto-notaio-ebner-19-aprile-2012-1.pdf.

Bibliography

Anālayo, Bhikkhu 2010. 'Paccekabuddhas in the Isigili-sutta and its Ekottarika-āgama Parallel.' *Canadian Journal of Buddhist Studies* 6: 5–36.

Appleton, Naomi and Peter Harvey eds. 2019. *Buddhist Path, Buddhist Teachings: Studies in Memory of L.S. Cousins*. Bristol: Equinox Publishing Ltd.

Baumann, Martin 2001. 'Global Buddhism: Developmental Periods, Regional Histories, and a New Analytical Perspective.' *Journal of Global Buddhism* 2: 1–43.

Bergonzi, Mauro 1984. 'Il Buddhismo in Occidente,' in Puech, H. Charles ed. *Storia del Buddhismo*. Bari: Laterza, 305–396.

Cabezón, José 2003. 'Buddhism and Science. On the Nature of the Dialogue,' in Wallace B. A. ed. *Buddhism and Science. Breaking New Ground*. New York: Columbia University Press, 35–68 (1st Indian edition: Delhi: Motilal Banarsidass, 2004).

De Simini, Florinda 2013. *Il buddhismo. Storia di un'idea*. Roma: Carocci.

Evola, Julius 1957. 'Spiritual Virility in Buddhism.' *East and West* 7.4: 319–327.

Halbfass, Wilhelm 1988. *India and Europe. An Essay in Understanding*. Albany: State University of New York Press.

Harrison, Paul 2006. '"Science" and "Religion": Constructing the Boundaries.' *The Journal of Religion* 86.1: 81–106. https://doi.org/10.1086/497085

Harvey, Peter 2015. 'Lance Cousins (1945–2015): An Obituary, Appreciation and Bibliography.' *Buddhist Studies Review* 32.1: 1–12. https://doi.org/10.1558/bsrv.v32i1.28964

Kloppenborg, Ria 1983. *The Pacceka-buddha: A Buddhist Ascetic. A Study of the Concept of the Paccekabuddha in Pāli Canonical and Commentarial Literature*. Kandy: Buddhist Publication Society.

Lo Turco, Bruno 2006. 'Salvare il buddhismo dalla scienza. Osservazioni su una confusione di giochi linguistici.' *Religioni e società* 56: 37–53.

Lo Turco, Bruno 2016. 'Buddhism and modernity: in the margin of Donald S. Lopez Jr. "Buddhism and Science."' *Kriterion* 57.133: 23–343. https://doi.org/10.1590/0100-512X2016N13314blt

Lopez Jr., Donald S. 2008. *Buddhism & Science. A Guide for the Perplexed*. Chicago: The University of Chicago Press.

McMahan, David L. 2004. 'Modernity and the Early Discourse of Scientific Buddhism.' *Journal of the American Academy of Religion* 72: 897–933.

McMahan, David L. 2008. *The Making of Buddhist Modernism*. Oxford: Oxford University Press.

Norman, Kenneth R. 1983. 'The Pratyeka-Buddha in Buddhism and Jainism,' in P. Denwood ed. *Buddhist Studies: Ancient and Modern*. London: Curzon, 92–106.

Norman, Kenneth R. 1997. *A Philological Approach to Buddhism: the Bukkyo Dendo Kyōkai Lectures 1994* (Buddhist Forum, vol. V). London: School of Oriental and African Studies.

Pensa, Corrado 1962. Transl. *Gli aforismi sullo yoga* (*Yogasūtra*). *Con il commento di Vyāsa*. Torino: Boringhieri.

Pensa, Corrado 1961. Ed. and transl. 'Il Bodhavilāsa di Kṣemarāja.' *Rivista degli Studi Orientali* 36: 126–134.

Pensa, Corrado 1964. Transl. 'Il terzo Bhāvanākrama di Kalamaśīla.' *Rivista degli Studi Orientali* 39: 211–242.

Pensa, Corrado 1969a. 'On the Purification Concept in Indian Tradition, with special regard to Yoga.' *East and West*, N.S. 19: 194–228.

Pensa, Corrado 1969b. 'Interdipendenza di purificazione, conoscenza e potere nello yoga in rapporto alla continuità della tradizione indiana.' *Annali dell'Istituto Universitario Orientale di Napoli*, N.S. 19: 1–43.

Pensa, Corrado 1972. 'Observations and References for the Study of the Ṣaḍaṅgagayoga.' *Yoga Quarterly Review* 4: 9–24.

Pensa, Corrado 1973. 'La meditazione: interpretazione, significati, valori,' in G. Tucci *et alii* eds. *Uomo e società nelle religioni asiatiche*. Roma: Ubaldini, 53–65.

Pensa, Corrado 1974. 'C. G. Jung e il sacro: alcune annotazioni,' in E. Castelli ed. *Prospettive sul sacro*. Roma: Istituto di Studi Filosofici 198–204.

Pensa, Corrado 1977. 'Notes on Meditational States in Buddhism and Yoga.' *East and West*, N.S. 7. 1–4, 335–44.

Pensa, Corrado 1978. Transl. *Le strofe del sāṃhkya* (*Sāṃhkyakārikā*). Torino: Boringhieri.

Pensa, Corrado 1978b. 'Meditazione buddhista intensiva: esperienze e riflessioni.' *Conoscenza religiosa* 4: 319–341.

Pensa, Corrado 1985. 'Buddhismo, cristianesimo e dialogo.' *Paramita* 16: 29–34.

Pensa, Corrado 1986a. 'Equanimità e retta intenzionale.' *Paramita* 18: 19–24.

Pensa, Corrado 1986b. 'Il dialogo interreligioso come guida spirituale.' *Paramita* 19: 23–29.

Pensa, Corrado 1987. 'Meditazione sulla gratitudine.' *Paramita* 23: 36.
Pensa, Corrado 1988. 'Note sulla retta pratica.' *Paramita* 25: 7–9.
Pensa, Corrado 1989. 'Riflessioni sui ritiri di *vipassanā*.' *Paramita* 29: 9–13.
Pensa, Corrado 1991. 'Spiritualità buddhista laica in Occidente.' *Paramita* 40: 13–17.
Pensa, Corrado 1992a. 'Uscendo da un ritiro.' *Sati* 1: 23.
Pensa, Corrado 1992b. 'I rifugi e i precetti.' *Sati* 3: 6–14.
Pensa, Corrado 1992c. 'Pratica meditativa e problemi psicologici.' *Paramita* 42: 35–40.
Pensa, Corrado 1993. 'La poesia dell'equanimità (Prima parte).' *Sati* 3: 22–31.
Pensa, Corrado 1994a. 'La poesia dell'equanimità (Seconda parte).' *Sati* 1: 15–25.
Pensa, Corrado 1994b. 'Mettā. Meditazione sulla benevolenza.' *Sati* 2: 4–7.
Pensa, Corrado 1994c. 'Un consiglio sulla mettā.' *Sati* 2: 8.
Pensa, Corrado 1994d. *La tranquilla passione. Saggi sulla meditazione buddhista di consapevolezza*. Roma: Ubaldini.
Pensa, Corrado 1994e. 'La relazione coniugale come via di crescita nel Dharma.' *Paramita* 52: 5–11.
Pensa, Corrado 1995a. 'La spiritualità buddhista dell'accettazione e la spiritualità cristiana dell'abbandono.' *Paramita* 53: 17–23.
Pensa, Corrado 1995b. 'Desiderio d'illuminazione e desiderio di Dio: buddhismo e cristianesimo.' *Paramita* 54: 27–35.
Pensa, Corrado 1996. 'Raccoglimento e investigazione-meditazione Theravāda.' *Paramita* 59: 3–9.
Pensa, Corrado 1997a. 'Meditazione e ansia.' *Sati* 1: 3–9.
Pensa, Corrado 1998. *Corso sulle virtù. Pāramī (1997–1998)*. E. Rafanelli ed. Roma: A.Me.Co.
Prebish, Charles S. 1979. *American Buddhism. North Scituate*. Massachusetts: Duxbury Press.
Trungpa, Chögyam 1973. *Cutting Through Spiritual Materialism*. Boulder, CO: Shambhala Publications.

Chiara Neri, PhD, Honorary Associate in Sanskrit Language and Literature and Indology, University of Cagliari, Italy.

Francesco Sferra, Professor of Sanskrit Language and Literature, University of Naples, 'L'Orientale', Italy.

Bibliography of Corrado Pensa[1]: Works from 1962–2020

Chiara Neri and Francesco Sferra

Books

1962 (transl.) *Gli aforismi sullo yoga* (*Yogasūtra*) *con il commento di Vyāsa*. Torino: Boringhieri.

1967 (ed.) *L'Abhisamayālaṃkāravṛtti di Ārya-vimuktisena. Primo Abhisamaya: testo e note critiche*. Roma: Istituto Italiano per il Medio ed Estremo Oriente (Serie Orientale Roma vol. 37).

1978 (transl.) *Le strofe del sāṃhkya* (*Sāṃkhyakārikā*). Torino: Boringhieri. A revised edition of this translation has been published in Sferra, F. ed., *Filosofie dell'India. Un'antologia di testi*, Studi Superiori 1155. Filosofia, Roma: Carocci editore, pp. 93–141.

1994 *La tranquilla passione. Saggi sulla meditazione buddhista di consapevolezza*. Roma: Ubaldini.

1995 *La consapevolezza ed il suo uso. Corso del lunedì 1995–96*. Lo Turco, B., R. Luongo, and F. Sferra, eds. Roma: A.Me.Co.

1997 *Consapevolezza, comprensione, lasciare andare. Corso del lunedì 1996–97*. Luongo, R. E. Rafanelli, and F. Sferra, eds. Roma: A.Me.Co.

1997 *Introduzione alla pratica del Dharma. Corso del martedì 1996–1997*. De Massimi, O. and R. Marcello, eds. Roma: A.Me.Co.

1998 *Corso sulle virtù. Pāramī. Corso del 1997–1998*. Rafanelli, E. ed. Roma: A.Me.Co.

1999 *Le quattro nobili verità ed altri temi di pratica. Corso del lunedì-martedì 1998–99*. M. Barinci and F. Sferra, eds. Roma: A.Me.Co.

2001 *Osservazioni circa l'investigazione meditativa nell'opera di Achan Maha Boowa*. Roma: A.Me.Co.

2002 *Attenzione saggia, attenzione non saggia*. Torino: Magnanelli.

2002 *L'intelligenza spirituale. Saggi sulla pratica del Dharma*. Roma: Ubaldini.

2004 *Consapevolezza equanime. Corso del lunedì 2004*. Remiddi, L. ed. Roma: A.Me.Co.

2007 *L'addestramento al cammino interiore. Corso 2007.* Remiddi L. and M. Barinci, eds. Roma: A.Me.Co.
2008 *La coltivazione della mente-cuore. Corso 2008.* Remiddi L. and M. Barinci, eds. Roma: A.Me.Co.
2008 *Il silenzio tra due onde. Il Buddha, la meditazione, la fiducia.* Milano: Mondadori.
2012 with N. Papachristou, *Dare il cuore a ciò che conta. Il Buddha e la meditazione di consapevolezza.* Milano: Mondadori.
2018 with N. Papachristou, *Affrettati piano. Il cammino interiore e la meditazione di consapevolezza: una strada per la felicità.* Roma: Ubaldini.

Edited Books

1973 with G. Tucci *et alii*, *Uomo e società nelle religioni asiatiche*. Roma: Ubaldini.
1975 with A. M. Di Nola, P. Boenio Brocchieri, *Sviluppi recenti e tendenze modernistiche nelle religioni asiatiche. Atti del Convegno organizzato dalla Società Italiana di Storia delle Religioni e dall'Istituto Universitario l'Orientale di Napoli* (7–8 aprile 1973), A.I.O.N. Suppl. n. 2 (vol. 35/1), Napoli.

Articles

1961 (ed., transl.) 'Il Bodhavilāsa di Kṣemarāja.' *RSO* 36: 125–134.
1964 (transl.) 'Il terzo Bhāvanākrama di Kalamaśīla.' *RSO* 39.3: 211–242.
1964 'Note di lessicografia Buddhista.' *RSO* 39.1: 61–67.
1964 'Indian Studies in Italy.' In *Indian Studies Abroad*. Indian Council for Cultural Relations, Delhi: Asia Publishing House, 41–48.
1969 'On the Purification Concept in Indian Tradition, with Special Regard to Yoga.' *EW*, N.S. 19.1–2, 194–228.
1969 'Interdipendenza di purificazione, conoscenza e potere nello yoga in rapporto alla continuità della tradizione indiana.' A.I.O.N., N.S. 19: 1–43.
1969 'Le religioni del Tibet.' In Castellani G. S. J. ed., Storia delle religioni, VI edizione, Torino: UTET, pp. 1–37.
1969 'Il rinascimento filosofico-religioso dell'India moderna.' In: Foot Moore G. ed., Storia delle religioni, VIII ed., Milano, pp. 253–259.
1969 'Osservazioni e riferimenti per lo studio del Ṣaḍaṅgayoga.' *Annali, Istituto Orientale di Napoli*, Nuova serie XIX 29: 521–528.
1970 'The conception of man in ancient Buddhism.' In *Men culture and religion. Studies in Religious Anthropology. Homme, culture et religion. Studia Missionalia.* Pontificia Università Gregoriana, 19: 39–54.
1971 'Some internal and comparative problems in the filed of Indian religions.' Studies in the History of Religions (Supplement. to Numen) XIX. Problems and Methods of the History of Religions: Leiden: E. J. Brill, pp. 103–122.

1972 'Observations and references for the study of Ṣaḍaṅgayoga.' *Yoga Quarterly Review* 4, 9–24.
1972 'Some internal and comparative problems in the field of the Indian Religions.' In Bianchi, U., C. J. Bleeker and A. Bausani eds. *Problems and Methods of the History of Religions. Proceedings of the Study Conference Organized by the Italian Society for the History of Religions on the Occasion of the Tenth Anniversary of the Death of Raffaele Pettazzoni, Rome 6th to 8th December 1969*. Leiden, 102–122.
1973 'Uomo e liberazione nel buddhismo Theravāda.' In Tucci, G. *et alii* eds. *Uomo e società nelle religioni asiatiche*. Roma: Ubaldini, 41–51.
1973 'La meditazione: interpretazione, significati, valori.' In Tucci G. *et alii* eds. *Uomo e società nelle religioni asiatiche*. Roma: Ubaldini, 53–65.
1974 'C. G. Jung e il sacro: alcune annotazioni.' In Castelli E. ed. *Prospettive sul sacro*. Roma: Istituto di Studi Filosofici, 198–204.
1975 'L'incontro tra Oriente e Occidente oggi. Problemi e significati con particolare riguardo al Buddhismo e all'Induismo.' In Di Nola A. M. *et alii* eds. *Atti del Convegno organizzato dalla Società Italiana di Storia delle Religioni e Istituto Universitario Orientale di Napoli* (7–8 aprile 1973), A.I.O.N., suppl. n. 2 (vol. 35.1). Napoli.
1977 'Notes on Meditational States in Buddhism and Yoga.' *EW* 27: 1–4, 335–344.
1978 'Meditazione buddhista intensiva: esperienze e riflessioni.' *Conoscenza religiosa* 4, 319–341.
1983 'Riflessioni sull'aridità spirituale in Oriente e in Occidente, in Autori vari, "Liberaci dal male".' In: *Liberaci dal male. Male e vie di liberazione nelle religioni*, Atti del V Seminario Teologico-Missionario su 'Liberaci dal Male,' promosso da Istituto Studi Asiatici e Abbazia di Praglia. Bologna: EMI, 195–212.
1985 'Il lavoro interiore come tranquilla passione.' *Par.* 13: 19–23.
1985 'La congiunzione degli opposti.' *Par.* 15: 15–21.
1985 'L'occidente e le religioni orientali nella prospettiva di Giuseppe Tucci.' *Par.* 16: 19–25.
1985 'Buddhismo, cristianesimo e dialogo.' *Par.* 16: 29–34.
1986 'La via della consapevolezza.' *Par.* 17: 5–12.
1986 'Equanimità e retta intenzione.' *Par.* 18: 19–24.
1986 'Il dialogo interreligioso come guida spirituale.' *Par.* 19: 23–29.
1986 'Krishnamurti o la profondità del presente.' *Par.* 20: 25–30.
1987 'Sulla pace interiore.' *Par.* 21: 9–15.
1987 'Il lavoro interiore costante, una prospettiva interreligiosa.' *Par.* 22: 35–42.
1987 'Meditazione sulla gratitudine.' *Par.* 23: 36.
1987 'Purificazione della mente, amicizia per la mente.' *Par.* 24: 11–16.
1988 'Note sulla retta pratica.' *Par.* 25: 7–9.
1988 'Fede e consapevolezza.' *Par.* 26: 33–37.
1988 'Lo svuotamento interiore come pienezza.' *Par.* 27: 11–17.
1989 'Riflessioni sui ritiri di *vipassanā*.' *Par.* 29: 9–13.

1989 'Religiosità della consapevolezza.' *Par.* 31: 11–15.
1989 'Insegnare la meditazione.' *Par.* 32: 11–16.
1990 'La mente sollecita.' *Sati* 1: 4–5.
1990 'Il gusto del Dharma.' *Par.* 34: 23–27.
1990 'Un piccolo salto evolutivo.' *Par.* 34: 19–21.
1991 'La congiunzione degli opposti nella pratica meditativa.' 'Riflessione sui ritiri di vipassana.' 'Note sulla retta pratica.' 'Il lavoro interiore come tranquilla passione.' 'Desiderio e sofferenza: riflessioni psicologiche e interreligiose.' 'Sulla pace interiore.' In Bonecchi, A. ed. *Psicoterapia e Meditazione*, collana Uomini e Religioni, vol. 56, Milano: Arnoldo Mondadori Editore, pp. 31–62, 259–304.
1991 'Samādhi e Paññā.' *Sati* 1: 9.
1991 'L'attaccamento e la pazienza.' *Sati* 2: 6–8.
1991 'L'impermanenza.' *Sati* 3: 4–9.
1991 'Sull'accettazione.' *Par.* 37: 31–34.
1991 'Narciso e la meditazione.' *Par.* 38: 19–23.
1991 'Spiritualità buddhista laica in Occidente.' *Par.* 40: 13–17.
1991 'Preface.' In C. Joko Beck, *Zen quotidiano. Amore e lavoro*. Roma: Ubaldini, 7–8.
1992 'Uscendo da un ritiro.' *Sati* 1: 23.
1992 'I rifugi e i precetti.' *Sati* 3: 6–14.
1992 'Il Dharma e la fiducia.' *Sati* 3: 16–28.
1992 'Pratica meditativa e problemi psicologici.' *Par.* 42: 35–40.
1992 'Alchimia spirituale.' *Par.* 43: 5–11.
1993 'Il Dharma e la fiducia.' Marcello, R. and C. di Folca, eds. *Sati* 1: 30–43.
1993 'Preghiera.' *Sati* 2: 45.
1993 'La poesia dell'equanimità (Prima parte).' *Sati* 3: 22–31.
1993 'Lo sforzo saggio.' *Par.* 45: 11–16.
1993 'Essere d'accordo con quello che succede.' *Par.* 47: 31–24.
1993 'L'impegno del Dharma.' *Par.* 48: 23–27.
1994 'La poesia dell'equanimità (seconda parte).' *Sati* 1: 15–25.
1994 'Mettā. Meditazione sulla benevolenza.' *Sati* 2: 4–8.
1994 'Un consiglio sulla mettā.' *Sati* 2: 8.
1994 'La concezione buddhista dell'ecospiritualità.' *Par.* 50: 29–34.
1994 'La relazione coniugale come via di crescita nel Dharma.' *Par.* 52: 5–11.
1995 'La consapevolezza calda e unitiva.' *Sati* 1: 6–13.
1995 'Apprezzamento, rispetto e gratitudine.' *Sati* 2: 4–7.
1995 'La spiritualità buddhista dell'accettazione e la spiritualità cristiana dell'abbandono.' *Par.* 53: 17–23.
1995 'Desiderio d'illuminazione e desiderio di Dio: buddhismo e cristianesimo.' *Par.* 54: 27–35.
1995 'Incompetenza, incondizionalità e gioia.' *Par.* 56: 3–8.
1995 'A Buddhist View of Eco-Spirituality. Interdependence, Emptiness and Compassion.' In Thottakara, A. ed. *Eco-spirituality. Perspectives from World*

Religions. Rome: Centre for Indian and Inter-Religious Studies (Spirituality Series 5), 80–96.
1996 'Perché meditare.' *Sati* 1: 4–6.
1996 'A.Me.Co: un'occhiata all'anno di pratica 1996–97.' *Sati* 2: 4–6.
1996 'L'intelligenza spirituale.' *Sati* 2: 30–37.
1996 'Umiltà e libertà.' Comba, A. ed. *Sati* 3: 4–13.
1996 'Raccoglimento e investigazione-meditazione Theravāda.' *Par.* 59: 3–9.
1997 'Meditazione e ansia.' *Sati* 1: 3–9.
1997 'Osservazioni sulla pratica.' *Sati* 3: 3–10.
1997 'La sofferenza centrata sull'io.' *Par.* 62: 3–8.
1997 'Emozioni, consapevolezza, accettazione.' *Par.* 64: 13–18.
1998 'Praticare per ingentilirsi.' *Sati* 1: 13–21.
1998 'Istruzioni per disporsi alla consapevolezza.' *Sati* 2: 3–6.
1998 'Il coraggio della consapevolezza.' *Sati* 3: 3–10.
1999 'Vincenzo Piga e il dialogo buddhista-cristiano.' *Sati* 1: 3–8.
1999 'Vincenzo Piga e il dialogo buddhista-cristiano.' *Dharma. Trimestrale di buddhismo per la pratica e per il dialogo* 1: 92–95.
1999 'Tre angolazioni sulla consapevolezza.' *Sati* 3: 3–10.
1999 '*Preface*.' In G. Harrison, *Nel grembo del Buddha*, ed. R. Mander, Tivoli: Sensibili alle foglie, 5–8.
2000 'Attaccamento ed equanimità. Domande e Risposte con Corrado Pensa.' Marcello, T. ed. *Sati* 1: 3–15.
2000 'Equanimità e fiducia.' *Sati* 2: 3–8.
2000 'L'avversione e la pratica del Dharma.' *Sati* 3: 3–9.
2001 'Osservazioni circa l'investigazione meditativa (*satipañña*) nell'opera di Achan Maha Boowa.' In R. Torella, R. ed. *Studi in onore di Raniero Gnoli nel suo 70° compleanno*, II, Roma: Istituto Italiano per l'Africa e l'Oriente (Serie Orientale Roma 92), 595–616.
2001 'Le relazioni e il Dharma.' *Sati* 1: 3–15.
2001 'Meditazione sulla gratitudine.' *Sati* 2: 3–6.
2001 'A Buddhist view of ecology. Interdependence, emptiness and compassion.' *Journal of Dharma* 261: 36–46.
2001 'Apertura e chiusura di cuore.' *Sati* 3: 3–11.
2002 'La consapevolezza paziente.' *Sati* 1: 3–12.
2002 'La questione della fede nel buddhismo.' *Sati* 2: 3–12.
2002 'Disagio senza avversione.' *Sati* 3: 3–10.
2003 'Il buon animo.' *Sati* 2: 3–8.
2003 'L'urgenza di pratica.' *Sati* 3: 3–7.
2004 'Perdono e promessa. Discorso tenuto a Eupilio e a Pomaia, febbraio-marzo 2004.' Chandra Candiani, ed. *Sati* 2: 3–14.
2005 'L'amore per la pratica del risveglio.' *Sati* 3: 3–10.
2006 'La pace del cuore e gli altri.' *Sati* 1: 3–13.
2006 'Comprendere l'attaccamento.' *Sati* 2: 3–8.
2007 'Sulla motivazione.' *Sati* 1: 3–12.

2007 'Contemplazione della mente e apertura del cuore. Discorso tenuto a Roma il 16 settembre 2006.' *Sati* 2: 3–13.
2007 'La mente custodita.' *Sati* 3: 3–11.
2007 'Preface.' In C. Feldman, *Compassione: ascoltare le grida del mondo*. Roma: La Parola, IX–XII.
2008 'Consapevolezza, emozioni, equanimità.' *Sati* 2: 3–21.
2008 'Aiutare sé stessi, aiutare gli altri.' Barinci, M. and P. Brook, eds. *Sati* 3: 3–11.
2008 'Preface.' In Meadow, J. M., K. Culligan and D. Chowning, *Meditazione cristiana di consapevolezza. Sulle orme di Giovanni della Croce*. Roma: La Parola, VII–X.
2009 'Domande e risposte.' Chironi, G. ed. *Sati* 1: 35–36.
2009 'Coltivare la mente-cuore.' Galuzzi, F. ed. *Sati* 2: 3–18.
2009 'Scegliere ciò che giova.' *Sati* 3: 3–6.
2009 'Preface.' In G. Feuerstein, *Filosofia yoga*, E. Beato ed. Venezia: Marsilio.
2009 'Preface.' In J. Goldstein, *Un cuore pieno di pace. Tracce di spiritualità per il terzo millennio*. Roma: La Parola.
2010 'Praticare con le emozioni.' *Sati* 1: 3–15.
2010 'Semplificazione interiore, ricchezza interiore.' de Ferrari, M. ed. *Sati* 2: 3–13.
2010 'Fiducia e Assoluto.' *Sati* 3: 3–15.
2011 'Consapevolezza ed equanimità.' *Sati* 1: 3–16.
2011 'Il viaggio dall'umiliazione all'umiltà.' *Sati* 2: 5–10.
2010 'Domande e risposte.' Chironi, G. ed. *Sati* 2: 29–34.
2011 'Imparare l'arte della sollecitudine.' *Sati* 3: 6–13.
2012 'Felicità e infelicità. Meditazione guidata.' *Sati* 1: 1–3.
2012 'Ricominciare Sempre.' *Sati* 2: 3–10.
2012 'Fare qualcosa di bello per il Dharma.' *Sati* 3: 5–15.
2013 'L'aspirazione a cercare il Bene.' *Sati* 1: 3–12.
2013 'Riflessioni sulla pratica del Dharma.' *Sati* 2: 3–18.
2013 'Il coraggio e il lasciare andare come fondamento della pratica.' *Sati* 3: 3–9.
2014 'Prendere sul serio la pratica in azione.' *Sati* 1: 6–13.
2014 'Le relazioni e il profondo del bene.' *Sati* 2: 3–11.
2014 'Quattro importanti frutti della pratica.' *Sati* 3: 3–14.
2014 'Preface.' In S. Anselmo, *Il viaggio: desiderio d'infinito. Poesie*. Roma: La Parola, 5–6.
2015 'Trasformare le avversità in occasioni di risveglio.' *Sati* 1: 3–11.
2015 'A cosa serve la pratica del Dharma?' *Sati* 2: 3–11.
2015 'Felicità.' *Sati* 3: 3–21.
2016 'Amore e saggezza.' *Sati* 1: 6–24.
2016 'Amore equanime.' *Sati* 2: 4–14.
2016 'La paura.' *Sati* 3: 4–12.
2017 (with Neva Papachristou) 'L'A.Me.Co. festeggia 30 anni.' *Sati* 1: 3–4.
2017 'Essere amici di sé stessi.' *Sati* 1: 5–14.
2017 'Risvegliarsi alla gioia.' *Sati* 2: 7–9.
2017 'La paura nella luce della pratica.' *Sati* 3: 3–14.

2018 'Meditazione guidata sull'amore.' *Sati* 1: 3–7.
2018 'Riconoscere gli inquinanti.' *Sati* 2: 3–12.
2018 'La meditazione come addestramento alla spaziosità.' *Sati* 3: 3–12.
2019 'Accettazione, comprensione e libertà.' *Sati* 1: 4–14.
2019 'Sulla muditā.' *Sati* 2: 25–28.
2019 'La veglia luminosa.' *Sati* 3: 7–27.
2020 (with Neva Papachristou) 'Mecenatismo, filantropia e generosità nel buddhismo.' *Sati* 1: 27–33.
2020 'Consapevolezza, emozioni, equanimità.' *Sati* 1: 36–56.
2020 'A piccoli passi verso la consapevolezza equanime.' *Sati* 2: 24–35
2020 'Attaccamento e non attaccamento.' *Sati* 3: 23–36.
2020 'Preface.' In G. Giustarini, *La Pratica della consapevolezza: sati nel Canone buddhista pali*. Monterotondo: Fuorilinea, VII–IX.

Reviews

1959 J. Gonda, *Some observations on the relations between «Gods» and «Powers» in the Veda, à propos of the phrase Sūnuḥ Sahasaḥ* ('sGravenage, 1957). *EW* 10.1–2: 121.
1959 J. Gonda, *Stylistic repetition in the Veda* (Amsterdam, 1959). *EW* 10: 1–2, 121–122.
1959 T. de Bary *et alii*, *Sources of Indian tradition* (New York, 1958). *EW* 10.3: 220–221.
1959 K. Kunjunni Raja, *The contribution of Kerala to Sanskrit literature* (Madras, 1958). *EW* 10.3: 221–222.
1959 F. Stark, *Alexander's Path* (London, 1958). *EW* 10.3: 219.
1959 K. M. Varma, *Natya, Nṛtta, and Nṛtya, their meaning and relation* (Calcutta, 1957). *EW* 10.3: 222–223.
1959 Ramakrishnananda, *Life of Sri Ramanuja* (Mylapore, 1959). *EW* 10.3: 229–230.
1960 A. Daniélou, R. Bhatt, *Textes des Purāṇa sur la theorie musicale*, I (Pondichéry, 1959), *EW* 11.1: 48–49.
1960 P. K. Gode, *Studies in Indian Cultural History*, II (Poona, 1960). *EW* 13.1: 60–61.
1960 S. K. De, *Ancient Indian Eroics and Erotic literature* (Calcutta, 1952). *EW* 11.1: 49.
1960 C. Vaudeville (ed.), *Kabīr Granthāvalī* (*Doha*) (Pondichéry, 1957). *EW* 11.1: 50.
1961 W. Pachow, *A Comparative study of the Prātimokṣa* (Santiniketan, 1955). *EW* 12.2–3: 200.
1961 A. Morretta, *Lo Spirito dell'India* (Roma, 1960). *EW* 12.1: 71–72.
1961 V. P. Upadhaya, *Lights on Vedanta* (Varanasi, 1959). *EW* 12.2–3: 201.
1961 J. Gonda, *Four Studies in the Language of the Veda* ('s-Gravenhage, 1959). *EW* 12.2–3: 191–192.

1961 A. Daniélou, N. R. Bhatt eds. *The Gītālaṃkāra* (Pondichery, Istitute Français d'Indologie 16, 1959, XXXII + 232). *EW* 12.1: 72.
1961 Suzanne Siauve, *Les noms védiques de Viṣṇu dans l'Anuvyākhyāna de Madhva* (Pondichéry, 1959). *EW* 12.1: 73.
1961 S. K. De, *Some Problems of Sanskrit Poetics* (Calcutta, 1959); *Aspects of Sanskrit Literature* (Calcutta, 1959). *EW* 12.2–3: 192–193.
1962 P. V. Ramanujaswamy (transl.), *Stories from the Kathāsaritsāgara* (Hyderabad, 1959), *EW* 3.1: 61.
1962 K. G. Pandey, *Comparative Aesthetics*, I. *Indian Aesthetics*, 2nd ed. (Varanasi, 1959). *EW* 13.2–3: 213–214.
1962 E. Conze (ed. and transl.), *The Gilgit Manuscript of the Aṣṭādaśasāhasrikāprajñāpāramitā* (Roma, 1962). *EW* 13.2–3: 226–227.
1963 Satyavrata Singh, *Vedāntadeśika. His Life, Works and Philosophy* (Benares, 1958). *EW* 14.1–2: 113–114.
1963 D. Seyfort Ruegg, *Contributions à l'histoire de la philosophie linguistique indienne* (Paris, 1959). *EW* 14.1–2: 105–107.

Abbreviations

A.I.O.N.	Annali dell'Istituto Universitario Orientale di Napoli
A.Me.Co.	Associazione per la Meditazione di Consapevolezza
EW	*East and West*
Par.	*Paramita: Quaderni di Buddhismo*
RSO	*Rivista degli Studi Orientali*

Notes

1 Although we have endeavoured to track down as many Corrado Pensa's publications as possible, it is highly likely that some have been missed since he published in many diverse venues, academic and non-academic, in print form and in online venues. We have not included the *dhamma* talks that are published in Italian and English in online venues. We are grateful to Giuliano Giustarini and Bruno Lo Turco for all their inputs into this work and Pinuccia Caracchi and Patrizia Micoli for providing us with some references.

Chiara Neri, PhD, Honorary Associate in Sanskrit Language and Literature and Indology, University of Cagliari, Italy.

Francesco Sferra, Professor of Sanskrit Language and Literature, University of Naples, 'L'Orientale', Italy.

Dedicated to Professor Corrado Pensa

PART I

WORDS ON THE DHARMA

Chapter 1
The Meditative Cultivation of Joy

Bhikkhu Anālayo

Dedicato a
Corrado Pensa
in affettuoso ricordo
del nostro incontro personale
a IMS, Massachusetts, tanti anni fa

Introduction

My exploration of the role of joy in early Buddhist meditation builds on a previous study concerned with the related quality of happiness (*sukha*).[1] In that study, originally written as an entry for the *Encyclopedia of Buddhism* in Sri Lanka, I surveyed different types of happiness as well as their gradual refinement during the progress on the gradual path to awakening. Such refinement is based on the fundamental distinction between what is wholesome and what is unwholesome, crucial in early Buddhist thought, and on the clear recognition that nothing is more conducive to true happiness than cultivation of the mind. As the second verse in the *Dhammapada* proclaims, mind is the forerunner of all *dharma*s; hence those who act or speak with a pure mind will be followed by happiness, comparable to being followed by one's shadow.[2]

The *Kandarakasutta* describes a gradual refinement of happiness during different stages of the gradual path. Such refinement proceeds from the happiness of blamelessness (*anavajjasukha*), due to maintaining moral conduct, to the unimpaired happiness (*abyāsekasukha*) of sense-restraint.[3] This in turn leads on to the types of happiness experienced with the deepening of concentration, which are the joy and happiness born of seclusion (*vivekajapītisukha*) and the joy and happiness born of concentration (*samādhijapītisukha*) of the first and second absorption. The peak of happiness is ultimately reached with liberation.

Cultivating Wholesome Joy

The above brief survey of types of happiness has already brought up two cases where joy combines with happiness. These are the first and second absorptions respectively, which are characterized by the coexistence of joy and happiness. In the case of the first absorption, this combination is based on having reached a state of seclusion from hindrances and distraction. With the second absorption, the mind's concentrated condition no longer requires the support of *vitakka* and *vicāra*, two absorption factors that I understand to represent an initial and sustained mental application.[4] Due to no longer needing to rely on these factors, the joy and happiness experienced in the second absorption are fully born of concentration.

The path leading to such experiences operates based on what for early Buddhist thought is a crucial distinction of joy into two types: wholesome and unwholesome. The *Subhasutta* compares the joy of sensuality to a fire that is burning in dependence on fuel, whereas the joy that is apart from sensuality and unwholesome states would be similar to an even brighter fire that does not depend on fuel.[5] Another type of distinction recognizes three types of joy: the worldly joy of sensuality, the unworldly joy of the first two absorptions, and the more unworldly than unworldly joy of reviewing the mind that has been liberated from defilements.[6]

In line with the gradual refinement of happiness sketched above, having established a foundation in morality leads on to the practice of sense-restraint. A discourse in the *Saṃyuttanikāya* explains, in agreement with its parallels, that due to sense-restraint the mind will not be impaired (*abyāsitta*), whereupon joy arises.[7] The terminology used reminds one of the unimpaired happiness (*abyāsekasukha*) mentioned in the *Kandarakasutta.*

The *Saṃyuttanikāya* discourse continues by describing how such joy then leads on to tranquility and concentration.[8] This progression is a recurrent theme in several discourses, so much so that it also forms an integral part of the description of the spheres of liberation (*vimuttāyatana*).[9] A discourse in the *Aṅguttaranikāya* and its *Madhyamāgama* parallel even go so far as to state that the very purpose of joy is to lead to tranquility (which in turn serves the purpose of leading to concentration).[10] The role of joy in such a progression recurs also in the well-known presentation of 'transcendental dependent arising' that proceeds beyond the final link of the standard formula of twelve links.[11]

Joy is in fact one of the awakening factors, those seven qualities whose cultivation leads to liberation. As an awakening factor, joy arises in dependence on mindfulness, investigation-of-*dharma*s, and energy. In keeping with the recurrently described progression just mentioned, joy as an awakening factor leads on to tranquility and concentration. Such joy could be either with *vitakka* and *vicāra*, the two mental factors that characterize the first absorption, or else without these two.[12] This of course does not mean that the experience of joy is only a matter of cultivating tranquility. In fact, in early Buddhist thought tranquility and insight are interrelated dimensions of meditative cultivation, rather than two entirely different modes of practice. The role of joy in the context of the cultivation of insight can be seen, for example, in a verse in the *Dhammapada*. The verse relates contemplation of the five aggregates to the gaining of joy and the realization of the deathless.[13]

Mindfulness of Breathing

In view of the evidently important role of joy in early Buddhist meditation, it comes as no surprise that, together with happiness, joy is also a distinct stage in the type of practice the Buddha himself is on record for having cultivated during a long retreat: mindfulness of breathing.[14] Joy, followed by happiness, stands at the outset of the second tetrad in a scheme of altogether four tetrads, or sixteen steps.[15] The preceding tetrad proceeds through the steps of knowing long breaths, knowing short breaths, experiencing the whole body, and calming bodily activity. It is at this juncture that the meditator proceeds to experiencing joy and then happiness, which then lead on to experiencing mental activity and, subsequently, to calming it.

Before exploring the function of joy as the fifth step in mindfulness of breathing, I would like to mention that the last step in the first tetrad, calming bodily activity, is at times understood to imply a progression up to the attainment of the fourth absorption.[16] However, several discourses indicate that with the fourth absorption the breath is no longer experienced.[17] Yet, the fourth step requires calming the bodily activity while at the same time being aware of inhalations and exhalations. Had the fourth absorption been attained at this stage, such awareness of the breath would no longer be possible.

In fact, the entire scheme of sixteen steps has no explicit reference to absorption attainment. Had this been a chief concern of the canonical instructions, it would have been logical for absorption to be mentioned explicitly. Hence, in what follows, my exploration is based on the assumption that the description of the sixteen steps of mindfulness of breathing should be taken at its face value, in the sense of describing a progressive refinement of *mindfulness* practice, rather than being about different levels of absorption experiences.

The function of joy in this setting is similar to its role in transcendental dependent arising and other such teachings, in that joy serves to lead on to tranquility. In the present case, joy leads in particular to tranquility in the sense of a stilling of mental activity. In fact, several discourses highlight the potential of mindfulness of breathing to bring about a stilling of distracting thoughts.[18]

The principle behind this potential can best be appraised in the light of modern research in cognitive psychology.[19] The relevant findings relate to a basic neural mechanism, acquired during the evolution of species. This mechanism serves to ensure that possible supplies of nourishment will be pursued and potential sources of danger will be avoided. The result is reward-based learning. In short, whenever a particular behaviour has led to the experience of pleasure, which is its 'reward,' this behaviour will be reinforced; we 'learn' to do it again. If the same pattern happens several times, a habit is formed.

The same principle of reward-based learning can also be used in meditation. Positive reinforcement can be brought about through intentional cultivation of joy. This helps to keep the mind aloof from distraction, since in the end distraction is to a considerable degree about searching for something more entertaining than, for example, the boring sensation of the breath.

From this viewpoint, the cultivation of the experience of joy, and the subsequent experience of happiness, can be understood to fulfill a rather crucial purpose in the context of the sixteen steps of mindfulness of breathing. Both serve to support the mind in becoming still, rather than being lost in distracting thought.

This potential is no longer evident once the sixteen-step scheme is reduced to its first tetrad. Such a reduction can already be observed in the early discourses. The *Kāyagatāsatisutta* as well as the *Satipaṭṭhānasutta*, two discourses found in the *Majjhimanikāya*, list only the first tetrad of mindfulness of breathing in their survey of different contemplations of the body.[20] They describe how a meditator withdraws to a secluded spot, sits down cross-legged, establishes mindfulness in front, and then knows long and short breaths, experiences the whole body, and calms bodily activity. The *Madhyamāgama* parallels to these two discourses, with considerable probability representing a Sarvāstivāda line of textual transmission,[21] also have the first tetrad in their survey of bodily contemplations (although not placed first in their listings of such contemplations).[22] They differ from the Pāli versions in that they present just the four steps themselves, without any description of the preliminaries of withdrawing to a secluded place, etc.

A comparative study of the body contemplations in these two discourses in the *Majjhimanikāya* and the *Madhyamāgama* suggests a gradual process of textual expansion, in which various practices related to the body have been added in the course of time.[23]

Expositions of mindfulness of breathing elsewhere among the discourses explicitly identify the first tetrad as an instance of contemplation of the body.[24] Given the concern with the body in the *Kāyagatāsatisutta* as a whole and in the exposition of the first *satipaṭṭhāna* in the *Satipaṭṭhānasutta*, it is quite understandable that mindfulness of breathing should make its way into a gradually expanding exposition of mindfulness practices related to the body and that only the first tetrad was allocated to this category.

The other tetrads of mindfulness of breathing did not make it into the exposition in the *Satipaṭṭhānasutta* (or its parallels). As a net result of this development, the presentation now found in the *Kāyagatāsatisutta* and the *Satipaṭṭhānasutta*, as well as in their *Madhyamāgama* parallels, can easily give the impression that the first tetrad is a stand-alone practice.

A further phase of the same development can be seen in two discourses in the *Ekottarikāgama*, a collection whose Indic original might have been transmitted by a Mahāsāṅghika reciter lineage.[25] In these two discourses, only the first three steps of mindfulness of breathing are found as a practice on their own.[26] Here, knowing the long and short breaths and experiencing the whole body are the only elements in common with the sixteen steps. These three steps occur in combination with attention given to other aspects of the breath, such as, for example, noting its coolness or warmth.

A hint at a still further reduction can be discerned in the *Satipaṭṭhānasutta* which, unlike the *Kāyagatāsatisutta*, has a simile of a turner that illustrates only the first two steps.[27] Although all four steps are mentioned, the simile suggests an incipient tendency to give more emphasis to the long and short breaths only. The same simile occurs in an exposition of *satipaṭṭhāna* in the *Śāriputrābhidharma, an early Abhidharma text of the Dharmaguptaka tradition, whereas in such an exposition in the *Pañcaviṃśatisāhasrikā Prajñāpāramitā* the simile concerns a potter.[28] In both cases, the respective simile comes in the company of just the first two steps; the third and fourth steps are no longer mentioned.

In this way, a tendency reflected in different ways in texts of the Dharmaguptaka, (perhaps) Mahāsāṅghika, Sarvāstivāda, and Theravāda traditions appears to have had the net result of divesting the practice of mindfulness of breathing of a considerable part of its potential to lead to a diminishing of mental distraction. Somewhere along the way, joy was lost from sight.

The tendency to reductionism to the first tetrad continues to the present, evident in the fact that at times publications on mindfulness of breathing only cover the first four steps.[29] The potential of the fifth step to help diminish the mind's tendency to distraction is also lost from sight when the whole scheme of sixteen steps is approached with the assumption that in step four, calming the bodily activity, the fourth absorption is to be attained.[30] From that viewpoint, all that the canonical instructions on mindfulness of breathing have to offer for developing such deep concentration is just the progression through the first tetrad.

As a result, it is not surprising that other techniques had to be brought in to enable meditators to stay with the breath. A prominent example is the idea to employ counting the breaths in order to avoid distraction, an approach to mindfulness of breathing is recommended similarly in a range of later works, such as, for example, Buddhaghosa's *Visuddhimagga* or a meditation manual compiled by Kumārajīva.[31]The degree to which counting becomes prominent in later literature on mindfulness of breathing might well reflect the gradual loss from sight of the potential role of joy.

Conclusion

Joy (*pīti/prīti*) has a central function in the practice of early Buddhist meditation, both in relation to the gaining of deeper concentration by way of the first two absorptions and in the cultivation of the awakening factors that lead up to the breakthrough to awakening. The same importance is also reflected in the scheme of sixteen steps of mindfulness of breathing, where joy (together with happiness) has, in particular, the function of leading to calming mental activity and thereby reducing the mind's tendency to distraction. This role of joy appears to have been lost from sight at a relatively early stage in the evolution of Buddhist thought, due to a reduction of the scheme of mindfulness of breathing to the first few steps in the first tetrad, thereby missing out on the ensuing step: the experience of joy.

Acknowledgment

I am indebted to Bhikkhunī Dhammadinnā for commenting on a draft version of this paper.

Notes

1 Anālayo 2007.

2 Dhp 2, with parallels in the Gāndhārī *Dharmapada* 202, Brough 1962/2001: 151, the Patna *Dharmapada* 2, Cone 1989: 104, the *Udānavarga* 31.24, Bernhard 1965: 415, and the *Karmavibhaṅga*, Kudo 2004: 82; cf. also T 210 at T IV 562a15, T 211 at T IV 583a9, T 212 at T IV 760a21, T 213 at T IV 795c4, and for a detailed study and a survey of parallels Skilling 2007 and Agostini 2010.

3 MN 51 at MN I 346,10+23, a Pāli discourse of which no parallel is known; on the happiness of sense-restraint cf. also Anālayo 2018: 4–6.

4 For a discussion of these two factors and other aspects of absorption cf. Anālayo 2017a: 109–1755, 2019c, and 2020.

5 MN 99 at MN II 203,28 and MĀ 152 at T I 669a12; for a comparative study cf. Anālayo 2011: 577.

6 SN 36.29 at SN IV 235,27 and its parallel SĀ 483 at T II 123b4.

7 SN 35.97 at SN IV 78,28. A Sanskrit fragment parallel, SHT VI 1226.12Vf, Bechert and Wille 1989: 27, has preserved a reference to *[c]ittaṃ na vyāsadyati* as a result of restraint at the eye sense-door. The parallel SĀ 277 at T II 75c26 relates the arising of joy to the mind not being "defiled by attachment", 染著, due to sense-restraint. Another parallel, T 107 at T II 502b24, qualifies the mind that leads to the arising of joy due to sense-restraint as "not dissipated", 不泆, which comes closer to the Pāli and Sanskrit terminology.

8 SĀ 277 at T II 75c27 and T 107 at T II 502b25 proceed directly from joy to concentration, without explicitly mentioning tranquility.

9 DN 33 at DN III 241,9 and its parallels in Sanskrit fragments, Stache-Rosen 1968: 149 (§5.19.c), DĀ 9 at T I 51c7, and T 12 at T I 230c13; on the five spheres of liberation cf. also Anālayo 2009 and Pāsādika 2017.

10 AN 10.1 at AN V 1,15 and its parallel MĀ 42 at T I 485a23.

11 SN 12.23 at SN II 31,31 and its parallels MĀ 55 at T I 491a7 and D 4094 *ju* 50a6 or P 5595 *tu* 54b4; for a study of SN 12.23 cf. Bodhi 1980 and Jones 2019.

12 SN 46.52 at SN V 111,12. The parallel SĀ 713 at T II 191c2 just speaks of joy and its establishing; cf. in more detail Anālayo 2013: 209–212.

13 Dhp 374, with parallels in the Gāndhārī *Dharmapada* 56, Brough 1962/2001: 126, and the Patna *Dharmapada* 61, Cone 1989: 119; cf. also T 210 at T IV 572a20, T 212

at T IV 765c18, and T 213 at T IV 796c4. The *Udānavarga* 32.10, Bernhard 1965: 434, does not mention the deathless.

14 According to SN 54.11 at SN V 326,1, he was on retreat for three months, but according to the parallel SĀ 807 at T II 207a11, the retreat lasted two months.

15 For comparative studies of these sixteen steps cf., e.g., Dhammajoti 2008 and Anālayo 2011: 664–673; 2013: 227– 237; 2016b: 242–249; 2017b: 63–67; 2019a, and 2019b.

16 Ps I 249,1.

17 DN 34 at DN III 290,7 (to be supplemented from DN III 266,9) and its parallel DĀ 10 at T I 57a1; SN 36.15 at SN IV 220,15 (to be supplemented from SN IV 217,8) and its parallel SĀ 474 at T II 121b4; as well as AN 10.72 at AN V 135,3 and its parallel MĀ 84 at T I 561a9.

18 Cf., e.g., AN 9.3 at AN IV 358,16 and its parallel MĀ 56 at T I 491c16; similar indications in other *Āgama*s can be found, e.g., in SĀ 804 at T II 206b16 or EĀ 2.8 at T II 553b8.

19 Cf. Brewer, Davis, and Goldstein 2013.

20 MN 10 at MN I 56,12 and MN 119 at MN III 89,9.

21 Cf. Anālayo 2017c.

22 MĀ 81 at T I 555b10 and MĀ 98 at T I 582c13.

23 Cf. Anālayo 2011: 79–86; 2013: 40–62, and 2019b.

24 SN 54.13 at SN V 329,27 and its parallel SĀ 810 at T II 208a29. In both collections, the same exposition is repeated in subsequent discourses.

25 For a survey of relevant evidence and findings by other scholars see Anālayo 2016a: 172–178 and 211–214. According to Kuan 2017: 446f, an argument by Palumbo 2013 in favour of a Sarvāstivāda affiliation is based on a misunderstanding of a Chinese idiom.

26 EĀ 3.8 at T II 556b1 (a discourse of which no parallel is known) and EĀ 17.1 at T II 582a15, parallel to an exposition of the whole scheme of sixteen steps in MN 62 at MN I 425,3.

27 MN 10 at MN I 56,22.

28 T 1548 at T XXVIII 613b8 (or else 625b24) and Dutt 1934: 205,1.

29 Examples are Gñānārāma 1989, Ariyadhamma 1995/2014, and Johnson 2012.

30 Pa-Auk (no date) instructs to proceed directly from the first tetrad of mindfulness of breathing to mastery of the four absorptions and the cultivation of insight into materiality, by way of the *kalāpa*s, and mentality, by way of the cognitive process, as the starting point for cultivating the insight knowledges. Only after the completion of these stages does he take up the second tetrad of mindfulness of breathing.

31 Vism 278,21 and T 614 at T XV 273a14; for a study of practice schemes related to counting the breaths cf. Deleanu 1992, Dhammadīpa 2009, and Dhammajoti 2009.

Bibliography

Agostini, Giulio 2010. '"Preceded by Thought Are the Dhammas": The Ancient Exegesis on Dhp 1–2.' In Orofino, G. and S. Vita, eds. *Buddhist Asia 2. Papers from the Second Conference of Buddhist Studies Held in Naples in June 2004*, 1–34. Kyoto: Italian School of East Asian Studies.

Anālayo, Bhikkhu 2007. 'Sukha.' In Weeraratne, W. G., ed. *Encyclopaedia of Buddhism* 8.1, 164–168. Sri Lanka: Department of Buddhist Affairs (reprinted in Anālayo 2012).

Anālayo, Bhikkhu 2009. 'Vimuttāyatana.' In Weeraratne, W. G., ed. *Encyclopaedia of Buddhism* 8.3, 613–615. Sri Lanka: Department of Buddhist Affairs.

Anālayo, Bhikkhu 2011. *A Comparative Study of the Majjhima-nikāya*. Taipei: Dharma Drum Publishing Corporation.

Anālayo, Bhikkhu 2012. *Excursions into the Thought-world of the Pāli Discourses*. Washington: Pariyatti.

Anālayo, Bhikkhu 2013. *Perspectives on Satipaṭṭhāna*. Cambridge: Windhorse.

Anālayo, Bhikkhu 2016a. *Ekottarika-āgama Studies*. Taipei: Dharma Drum Publishing Corporation.

Anālayo, Bhikkhu 2016b. *Mindfully Facing Disease and Death, Compassionate Advice from Early Buddhist Texts*. Cambridge: Windhorse.

Anālayo, Bhikkhu 2017a. *Early Buddhist Meditation Studies*. Barre: Barre Center for Buddhist Studies.

Anālayo, Bhikkhu 2017b. *A Meditator's Life of the Buddha, Based on the Early Discourses*. Cambridge: Windhorse.

Anālayo, Bhikkhu 2017c. 'The "School Affiliation" of the Madhyama-āgama.' In Dhammadinnā, ed. *Research on the Madhyama-āgama*, 55–76. Taipei: Dharma Drum Publishing Corporation.

Anālayo, Bhikkhu 2018. 'The Potential of Pleasant Feelings.' *Insight Journal* 44, 1–11.

Anālayo, Bhikkhu 2019a. "Meditation on the Breath: Mindfulness and Focused Attention." *Mindfulness*, 10.8, 1684–1691.

Anālayo, Bhikkhu 2019b. *Mindfulness of Breathing: A Practice Guide and Translations*. Cambridge: Windhorse.

Anālayo, Bhikkhu 2019c. "The Role of Mindfulness in the Cultivation of Absorption." *Mindfulness*, 10.11, 2341–2351.

Anālayo, Bhikkhu 2020. "A Brief History of Buddhist Absorption." *Mindfulness*, 11.3, 571–586.

Ariyadhamma, Nauyane 1995/2014. *Ānāpānasati, Meditation on Breathing*. Kandy: Buddhist Publication Society.

Bechert, Heinz and K. Wille 1989. *Sanskrithandschriftenaus den Turfanfunden, Teil 6*. Stuttgart: Franz Steiner.

Bernhard, Franz 1965. *Udānavarga*. Göttingen: Vandenhoeck & Ruprecht.

Bodhi, Bhikkhu 1980. *Transcendental Dependent Arising: A Translation and Exposition of the Upanisa sutta*. Kandy: Buddhist Publication Society.

Brewer, Judson A., Jake H. Davis, and Joseph Goldstein 2013. 'Why is it so Hard to Pay Attention, or is it? Mindfulness, the Factors of Awakening and Reward-based Learning.' *Mindfulness* 4.1, 75–80. https://doi.org/10.1007/s12671-012-0164-8

Brough, John 1962/2001. *The Gāndhārī Dharmapada: Edited with an Introduction and Commentary*. Delhi: Motilal Banarsidass.

Cone, Margaret 1989. 'Patna Dharmapada.' *Journal of the Pali Text Society* 13, 101–217.

Deleanu, Florin 1992. 'Mindfulness of Breathing in the Dhyāna Sūtras.' *Transactions of the International Conference of Orientalists in Japan* 37, 42–57.

Dhammadīpa, Bhikkhu 2009. 'Two Divisions of Ānāpānasati/smṛti in their Chronological Development.' In Dhammajoti K. L. and Y. Karunadasa, eds. *Buddhist and Pāli Studies in Honour of The Venerable Professor Kakkapalliye Anuruddha*, 567–582. Hong Kong: University of Hong Kong.

Dhammajoti, Bhikkhu K. L. 2008. 'The Sixteen-mode Mindfulness of Breathing.' *Journal of the Centre for Buddhist Studies Sri Lanka* 6, 251–288.

Dhammajoti, Bhikkhu K. L. 2009. 'Two Divisions of Ānāpānasati/smṛti in their Chronological Development.' In Dhammajoti K. L. and Y. Karunadasa, eds. *Buddhist and Pāli Studies in Honour of The Venerable Professor Kakkapalliye Anuruddha*, 639–650. Hong Kong: University of Hong Kong.

Dutt, Nalinaksha 1934. *Pañcaviṃśatisāhasrikā Prajñāpāramitā, Edited with Critical Notes and Introduction*. London: Luzac & Co.

Gñānārāma, Mātara Sri 1989. *Ānāpānasatibhāvanā: Mindfulness of In and Out Breathing*. Transl. Mitra Wettimuny. Mitirigala: Nissarana Vanaya.

Johnson, Will 2012. *Breathing Through the Whole Body: The Buddha's Instructions on Integrating Mind, Body, and Breath*. Rochester: Inner Tradition.

Jones, Dhivan Thomas 2019. "'Preconditions': The Upanisā Sutta in Context." *Journal of the Oxford Centre for Buddhist Studies*, 17, 30–62.

Kuan Tse-Fu 2017. [Review of Palumbo 2013] *Journal of the American Oriental Society* 137.2, 444–448.

Kudo, Noriyuki 2004. *The Karmavibhaṅga: Transliterations and Annotations of the Original Sanskrit Manuscript from Nepal*. Tokyo: Soka University.

Pa-Auk Tawya Sayadaw (no date): *Mindfulness of Breathing (Ānāpānassati)*. Singapore: Pa-Auk Meditation Centre.

Palumbo, Antonello 2013. *An Early Chinese Commentary on the Ekottarika-āgama, The Fenbiegongdelun 分別功德論 and the History of the Translation of the Zengyiahanjing 增一阿含經*. Taipei: Dharma Drum Publishing Corporation.

Pāsādika, Bhikkhu 2017. 'Ancient and Modern Interpretations of the Pañcavimuttāyatana.' *Journal of the Centre for Buddhist Studies, Sri Lanka* 14, 139–147.

Skilling, Peter 2007. '"Dhammas are as swift as thought ...": A Note on Dhammapada 1 and 2 and Their Parallels.' *Journal of the Centre for Buddhist Studies, Sri Lanka* 5, 23–50.

Stache-Rosen, Valentina 1968. *Dogmatische Begriffsreihenim älteren Buddhismus II: Das Saṅgītisūtra und sein Kommentar Saṅgītiparyāya*. Berlin: Akademie Verlag.

Abbreviations

All references to Pāli texts are to the Pali Text Society editions.

AN	*Aṅguttaranikāya*
D	Derge edition
DĀ	*Dīrghāgama*
Dhp	*Dhammapada*
DN	*Dīghanikāya*
EĀ	*Ekottarikāgama*
MĀ	*Madhyamāgama*
MN	*Majjhimanikāya*
P	Peking edition
Ps	*Papañcasūdanī*
SĀ	*Saṃyuktāgama*
SN	*Saṃyuttanikāya*
T	Taishō edition
Vism	*Visuddhimagga*

Author Biography

Bhikkhu Anālayo completed a Ph.D. thesis on the *Satipaṭṭhānasutta* at the University of Peradeniya in the year 2000 and a habilitation thesis at the University of Marburg in the year 2007, comparing the *Majjhimanikāya* discourses with their Chinese, Sanskrit, and Tibetan counterparts. The main focus of his more than 500 publications is on comparative studies of early Buddhist texts. He recently retired from a position as a professor at the University of Hamburg and currently resides at the Barre Centre for Buddhist Studies in the USA, where he spends most of his time in meditation.

Chapter 2

The Concept of *Pariyogāhaṇa* in the Epistemology of the *Paṭisambhidāmagga*: An Immersion in Knowledge and Liberation

Giuliano Giustarini

The Pāli *Suttapiṭaka* and *Abhidhammapiṭaka* mostly deal with the path to liberation as traditionally taught by the Buddha. Through their specific approaches, they state that the goal of this path is achieved by a gradual and yet dramatic shift of the cognitive paradigm, and the path itself is described as a gradual development of cognitive skills and their refinement from obstacles. In this regard, an early exegetical text, the *Paṭisambhidāmagga*, ascribes a crucial role to 'knowing as immersion' (*pariyogāhaṇañāṇa*). The term *pariyogāhaṇa* does not occur elsewhere in the Nikāyas, but it presents strong analogies with wide-spread descriptions of the first-hand knowledge required to eradicate mental defilements. This study aims at exploring the notion of *pariyogāhaṇa*, and at outlining its contribution to the understanding of Pāli Buddhist epistemology.

The *Paṭisambhidāmagga* represents a major contribution in the history of Theravāda thought. It deeply and largely influenced Buddhaghosa's *Visuddhimagga*, which is not only the most famous exegetical oeuvre on the Suttas, but also the Theravāda manual of meditation par excellence. The period of its composition is unclear, and its structure presents clear Abhidhammic features.[1]

The use of the term *pariyogāhaṇa*, or *pariyogāhana* (immersion),[2] in the *Suññakathā* of the *Paṭisambhidāmagga* represents an example of the specific nature of the whole text, for it combines the typical structure and form of the

Suttas (especially of the first four Nikāyas) with the structure and form of the seven books of the *Abhidhammapiṭaka*. The incipit of the text, 'Thus I heard' (*evaṃ me sutaṃ*) emphasizes the direct transmission of the teaching, and therefore it matches an authoritative criterion, the *apadesa*,[3] to test its reliability. In this case, the witness is not Ānanda, the Buddha's attendant (herein the interlocutor of the Buddha) but Sāriputta.

The first passages of the *Suññakathā* overlap with the entire *Suññatalokasutta* of the *Saḷāyatanasaṃyutta*[4] reporting the same dialogue between the Buddha and his attendant Ānanda. Both texts list the sense-spheres and their objects and define each of them as empty of self or of anything pertaining to a self (*suññaṃ attena vā attaniyena vā*). A first difference between the two texts is that the *Suññakathā*, unlike the *Suññatalokasutta*, is introduced by the abovementioned Suttas' phrase, 'Thus I heard,' along with a short account on the circumstances of the teachings (given in the previous discourse of the *Saṃyuttanikāya*). After the synopsis (*uddesa*) of the teachings, the *Suññakathā* presents a *māṭikā*, a list of concepts, that is typically employed in Abhidhamma literature but that might have been 'a flowchart for the composition' of the Suttapiṭaka as well (Gethin 1992: 156); the list is followed by an elucidation (*niddesa*) of the same concepts in detail. This specific taxonomy consists in twenty-five types of emptiness, represented as being empty of characteristics. In particular, here emptiness, in line with the corresponding *Suññatalokasutta*, is the absence of the sense of self and what is related to a self, of the general coefficients of reality (the *saṅkhara*s in an articulated classification), of an inherent essence (*sabhāva*), of general attributes (*lakkhaṇa*), and last of hindrances and defilements that affect the mind and are counteracted by wholesome factors which are empty of them.

Among the types of emptiness examined in the *Suññakathā,* one is related to the immersion (*pariyogāhaṇa*), and belongs in the category of emptiness dealing with hindrances and defilements:

> Immersion into renunciation is empty of desire for sense-pleasures; immersion into non-aversion is empty of aversion; immersion into cognition of light is empty of sloth and torpor; immersion into imperturbability is empty of agitation; immersion into the analysis of the dhammas[5] is empty of doubt; immersion into knowledge is empty of ignorance; immersion into joy is empty of discontent; immersion in the first *jhāna* is empty of the hindrances… immersion in the path to arahantship is empty of all the defilements. This is emptiness in terms of immersion.[6]

In this passage, the term *pariyogāhaṇa* does not explicitly entail a form of understanding. Rather, it refers to methods counteracting specific defilements, hindrances, etc. It is a firm footing in the wholesome qualities that lead to liberation, and understanding is present just as one of these qualities that the mind is established in (the immersion into knowledge, or awareness, *ñāṇapariyogāhaṇa*, as empty of ignorance, *avijjā*). In the commentary on the *Paṭisambhidāmagga*, Mahānāma considers immersion (*pariyogāhana*) as the specific quality of profound understanding (*paññā*), concluding a sequence that contains the following combinations: faith/preparation (*saddhā*/*okappanā*), mindfulness/non-floating (*sati* /*apilāpanatā*), and concentration/firmness (*samādhi*/*avaṭṭhiti*).[7]

In Sutta literature, on the other hand, *pariyogāhaṇa* (or *pariyogāha*, *pariyogāhana*) often implies understanding, as the usage of its contrary form *duppariyogāha* indicates.[8] The lexicon of knowledge employed in the Tipiṭaka ranges from conventional modes of understanding (like recognition, *saññā*) to profound cognitive modes (e.g. *paññā*, wisdom or profound understanding, *ñāṇa*, knowing or awareness, *vijjā*, knowledge) capable of releasing the mind from defilements and, ultimately, from any form of suffering (*dukkha*). These two extremes are detected in the usages of *pariyogāha* too, which can be the ordinary, intellectual knowledge (and its negative form *duppariyogāha* would indicate an inadequacy to grasp the *dhamma*), or modes of investigations intertwined with meditative practices and aimed at final liberation (*vimutti*).

Another example of a negative/privative form of *pariyogāhaṇa* is found in Abhidhamma literature, viz. in the *Puggalapaññatti* and in the *Vibhaṅga*. In both cases the term occurs in lists of defective modes of understanding. In the *Vibhaṅga*, it refers to the sceptical, paralysing doubt (*vicikicchā*), presented as an impediment associated with feeling (*vedanā*) and as an unwholesome factor to be abandoned[9], whereas in the *Puggalapaññatti*[10] it describes a person lacking profound understanding (*asampajañña*), without penetration (*appaṭivedha*), etc.

A form of the past participle of *pariyogāhati*, *pariyogāḷha*, means 'dived into, penetrated into, immersed in' (PED s.v.). In the *Mahāpadānasutta*, the term occurs in a *bahubbīhi* compound to describe a profound understanding of the teachings: 'Those who have seen the *dhamma* (*te diṭṭhadhammā*), reached the *dhamma* (*pattadhammā*), known the *dhamma* (*viditadhammā*), penetrated (or 'dived into') the *dhamma* (*pariyogāḷhadhammā*)....'[11] These qualities are said to be attained by the householder Upāli, a disciple of Nigaṇṭha Nātaputta, when he was converted by a discourse of the Buddha and the stainless eye of the *dhamma* arose (*vītamalaṃ dhammacakkhuṃ udapādi*) in him.[12] The conversion of a disciple of Nigaṇṭha Nātaputta (in this case the general Sīha) occurs with a similar sequence of events and instructions in the *Aṅguttaranikāya*.[13]

In this pericope, the penetration of the *dhamma* is presented as a turning point occurring after a discourse of the Buddha and involves the conversion from a different school.[14] Clearly, the use of *pariyogāhaṇa* and of the compound *pariyogāhaṇasuñña* in the *Suññakathā* refers to a more complex process: the immersion in a wholesome quality or realm corresponds to the deprivation of an unwholesome factor, followed by other pairs through a sort of spiralling ascension to final liberation.

A similar training based on the notion of emptiness is taught by the Buddha to Ānanda in the *Cūḷasuññatasutta* of the *Majjhimanikāya*.[15] In this text, the mind of a meditator is described as withdrawing from various kinds of [re] cognitions (*saññā*): first, this happens by renouncing crowded places and dwelling in secluded forests, where the objects cognized are fewer than in cities and villages. The meditator, after moving the attention away from the cognition still going on in the secluded place, i.e. the forest itself, with trees, mountains, etc., pays attention only to the cognition of earth (*pathavīsaññā*), and then to the single progressive achievements (*samāpatti*), arriving at the baseless (*animitta*) concentration of the mind (*cetosamādhi*). At that point, the meditator realizes that this attainment is still compounded (*abhisaṅkhata*), and then his/her mind becomes free of the three intoxicants (*āsava*): desire for sense-pleasures (*kāma*), becoming (*bhava*), and ignorance (*avijjā*). The liberation attained is expressed by this typical declaration of knowledge: 'Birth is destroyed, the holy life has been fulfilled, what had to be done has been done, there is not going to be further existence.'[16]

The entire process is called 'descent into emptiness' (*suññatāvakkhanti*) and presents at least two close analogies with the *Suññakathā* of the *Paṭisambhidāmagga*. One is in the process of *suññatā*, ultimately tantamount to liberation (*vimutti*), attained in both texts by renouncing obstacles; a difference is in the emphasis in the *Cūḷasuññatasutta* on letting go of partial achievements. The other one consists in the resemblance of meanings of the two terms in the compounds, *pariyogāhaṇa* and *avakkhanti*.

The compound *suññatāvakkhanti* occurs only in the *Cūḷasuññatasutta*. The term *avakkhanti* is often used to indicate rebirth (*gabbhāvakkhanti* is the descent into the womb), and the commentary on the *Cūḷasuññatasutta* glosses the entire compound as 'coming to be into emptiness' (*suññatānibbatti*).[17]

Nibbatti itself is a term typically used in accounts on rebirth, but, in this case, it should be seen just as a transition to the state of emptiness.

In the next paragraph, I will present a term etymologically related to *pariyogāhaṇa* but reminiscent of *avakkhanti* for its stronger relationship with liberation.

Immersion in liberation: *ogadha*

The term *ogadha* is strictly related to *pariyogāha* and *pariyogāhaṇa*, with practically the same meaning: Pāli dictionaries translate it as 'immersed, merging into, diving or plunging into' (PED s.v.), or 'plunged into, immersed (in), included (in), plunging into, immersion' (Cone s.v.).[18] It is often employed in two interchangeable compounds: *amatogadha* (immersion in deathlessness) and *nibbānogadha* (immersion in *nibbāna*). *Amata* is defined as a synonym of *nibbāna* in several texts, including the *Paṭisambhidāmagga*.[19]

The *Paṭhamapācīnaninnasutta* contains the analogy of the Ganges River, which naturally flowing eastwards, representing the monk who, by cultivating the eightfold path, proceeds towards *nibbāna*. The explanation of this inclination is made by describing the properties of each factor of the path as follows:

> And how, monks, is a monk who cultivates and frequently exerts the eightfold path inclined to *nibbāna*, sloping down to *nibbāna*, tending to *nibbāna*? In this regard, monks, a monk cultivates good view, which is merging into deathlessness, destined to deathlessness, ending in deathlessness […] cultivates good concentration, which is merging into deathlessness,[20] destined to deathlessness, ending in deathlessness. This is how, monks, a monk who cultivates and frequently exerts the eightfold path is inclined to *nibbāna*, sloping down to *nibbāna*, tending to *nibbana*.[21]

The compounds *amatogadha* and *nibbānogadha* present some analogies with an expression frequently used to indicate the purpose of the eightfold path, of the recollections (*anussaraṇa*), of the cultivation of moral discipline (*sīla*), and of the practice of the four *satipaṭṭhāna*s: 'for the personal experience of *nibbāna*' (*nibbānassa sacchikiriyāya*). The term *sacchikiriyā* derives from the verb *sacchikaroti*, which means 'to see with one's eyes, to realize, to experience for oneself' (PED s.v. *sacchikiriyā*). When related to *nibbāna*, *sacchikiriyā* emphasises the authenticity of the experience, thus distinguishing it from a mere intellectual achievement.

In the *Kīṭāgirisutta*, *sacchikaroti* expresses the culmination of a gradual progress and is described as a somewhat physical experience:

> Bhikkhus, I do not say that final knowledge is achieved all at once. On the contrary, final knowledge is achieved by gradual training, by gradual practice, by gradual progress. And how is final knowledge achieved by gradual training, by gradual practice, by gradual progress? Here one who has faith [in a teacher] visits him: when he visits him, he pays respect to him; when he pays respect to him, he gives ear; one who ear hears the Dhamma; having heard the Dhamma, he memorises it; he examines the meaning of the teaching he has memorised; when he examines their meaning, he gains a reflective acceptance of those teachings; zeal springs up in him; when zeal has sprung up, he applies his will; having applied his will, he scrutinises; having scrutinised, he strives; resolutely striving, he realises with the body the supreme truth (*kāyena c' eva paramasaccaṃ sacchikaroti*) and sees it by penetrating it with wisdom (*paññāya ca naṃ ativijjha passati*).[22]

Another passage in the same sutta describes the condition of those who are liberated with the phrase 'having touched with the body' (*kāyena phusitvā*).[23] In the *Mahācundasutta*, *kāyena phusitvā* echoes the meaning of *amatogadha*: *ye amataṃ dhātuṃ kāyena phusitvā viharanti*.[24] I offer here two possible translations, one by Bhikkhu Bodhi and the other one by Rupert Gethin. Bhikkhu Bodhi renders the phrase as '[those individuals] who dwell having touched the deathless element with the body' (Bodhi 2012: 919). Gethin (2008: 261) translates it with 'who live having experienced the deathless directly.'

Gethin's translation suggests that *sacchikaroti* and *kāyena phusati* are somehow interchangeable, but his rendering of the instrumental *kāyena* as 'directly' excludes more literal exegeses of the term, like the one given by the commentary to the same passage: 'This refers to the *nibbāna* element, called 'the deathless' because it is devoid of death. Having taken up a meditation subject, in stages they dwell having touched it with the mental body.'[25]

In short, what emerges from the commentary is that it equates *amata-dhātu* to *nibbāna-dhātu* (as expected), offers an interpretation of *kāya* as *nāma-kāya*, and at the same time refers to a meditative progress (*anukkama*) that reaches the *amata-dhātu*. I suspect that the object of meditation is the *amata-dhātu* from the very beginning, and I would alternatively translate the second sentence as follows: 'They abide having seized [the *amata-dhātu*] as a basis for the [meditative] work, they abide having touched it progressively with the mental body.' This slight change reminds of the intentional use of the *amata-dhātu* as an object of contemplation, as it is found in the *Dutiya-anuruddhasutta*. Here the prominent disciple Anuruddha confesses to Sāriputta that, despite his high accomplishments, including a stable and profound concentration, he has not reached final liberation. Sāriputta invites him to let go of those attainments, to move the mind away from them and focus on the *amata-dhātu*. By practicing this way, Anuruddha soon reaches final liberation (expressed by the formula 'birth is destroyed …' seen above) 'having personally experienced it by himself through high knowledge' (*sayaṃ abhiññā sacchikatvā*).[26]

The emphasis on meditation in the commentary to the *Mahācundasutta* may represent a conceptual bridge between meditative attainments and final liberation. On the other hand, the episode of Anuruddha and Sāriputta indicates that meditative attainments become an obstacle if clung to, and this obstacle can be overcome by shifting the focus to the deathless element, namely *nibbāna* itself. Connecting the dots of these passages, we may outline an epistemological approach wherein liberating knowledge is gained by immersion, i.e. it requires a dedication of the practitioner to it; it is fostered by meditative techniques; it is completed by renunciation to sense-experience, including the meditative achievements, and by focusing on the uncompounded, deathless, *nibbāna*.

The interpretation of *kāyena* as *nāmakāyena* clearly refers to the distinction between *nāma* and *rūpa* and defines the realization of *nibbāna* as a mental experience, thus distinguishing it from the use of *kāyena* as a suffusing physical pleasure in the description of the third *jhāna*.[27] Therefore, the occurrence of *kāyena* referred to *nibbāna* seems to aim at describing, rather than a physical experience, a radical and pervasive change beyond a mere intellectual grasping, similarly evoked by the compounds *amatogadha* and *nibbānogadha*.

Penetration by knowledge of the nature of the objects observed

Along these lines, some passages in the commentaries compare the future participle *ogāhitabba* (that should be penetrated) to another future participle, *avacaritabba* (that should be investigated), in order to explain the compound *atakkāvacara* in the following well known expression:

> This *dhamma* reached by me is profound, difficult to see, difficult to understand, excellent, not to be investigated by thought, subtle, to be understood by the intelligent.[28]

The commentaries state that the ultimate truth (*dhamma*) should not (or better, cannot) be investigated, penetrated by thought, but should be investigated by [intuitive] knowledge, or awareness (*ñāṇa*).[29] This distinction parallels the elucidations of the term *pariyogāhaṇa* by its employment with the verb *phusati* (to touch), some of which have been examined above.

This usage of *phusati* in the description of validated experience is also found in the *Pariyogāhaṇañāṇaniddesa* of the *Paṭisambhidāmagga*: here *pariyogāhaṇa* is the penetration of reality, seen in accordance with its main characteristics, and *phusati* is the verb that describes the mode of ascertaining reality in the *pariyogāhaṇañāṇa* itself.

> How does the profound understanding by means of touching correspond to knowing in terms of immersion? He touches form as impermanent, he touches form as unsatisfactory, he touches form as non-self. Whatever he touches, he merges into: the understanding by means of touching corresponds to knowing in terms of immersion. He touches feeling… cognition… the coefficients, consciousness… the eye… decay and death as impermanent, he touches decay and death as unsatisfactory, he touches decay and death as non-self. Whatever he touches, he merges into: the understanding by means of touching corresponds to knowing in terms of immersion. That knowing is in the sense of the known, profound understanding is in the sense of the fully understood. Therefore, it is said, 'the understanding by means of touching corresponds to knowing in terms of immersion.'[30]

The wording here employed to explain *pariyogāhaṇañāṇa* replaces the term *passati* (to see), usually employed in the contemplation of the three essential characteristics of existence, with the term *phusati* (to touch), and equates the abstract form of the latter to *pariyogāhaṇa*, thus contributing further nuances to the meditative lexicon. The description of *pariyogāhaṇañāṇa* in the *Pariyogāhaṇañāṇaniddesa*, in fact, perfectly matches the methods of *aniccānupassanā*, *dukkhānupassanā*, and *anattānupassanā*. In the commentary, Mahānāma connects both *phusati* and *pariyogahati* to the awareness deriving from the practice of insight (*vipassanā-ñāṇa*).[31]

In another passage of the *Paṭisambhidamagga*, the two factors of touching and eye-witnessing are combined to define the figure of the 'body-witness': *phuṭṭattā sacchikarotī 'ti kāyasakkhī.*[32] The interaction of these terms and the meaning of *kāyasakkhi* are explained in the *Kāyasakkhīsutta* as the direct experience through the *jhāna*s, *samāpatti*s, and then the final destruction of the poisons.[33] As in the cases examined before, the commentary glosses *kāya* as *nāma-kāya.*[34]

In the *Suññakathā* of the *Paṭisambhidāmaggapariyogāhaṇa* occurs in the last sequence of the approaches to the wholesome factors counteracting hindrances and defilements. The sequences follow similar patterns: in one, the meditator merges into the wholesome factors and removes the unwholesome ones through four stages of 'emptying' (*suñña*): seeking (*esanā*), grasping (*pariggaha*), attaining (*paṭilābha*), penetrating (*paṭivedha*). Immersion (*pariyogāhaṇa*), instead, is the third and final stage of a sequence that includes choice (*khanti*) and resolution (*adhiṭṭhāṇa*). The culmination of this process is *parinibbāna*, which is the condition obtained after death by one who is 'fully aware' (*sampajāna*). At this point, sense-activity ceases and will not arise again.[35]

Conclusion

Pariyogāhaṇa and its equivalent terms refer to a set of intertwined dynamics. One is an enhancement of knowledge and understanding of the objects observed. Universal characteristics of reality, viz. impermanence, unsatisfactoriness and non-self are detected and clearly scrutinized through a cognitive immersion into the object. Another aspect of *pariyogāhaṇa* is presented as a movement towards liberation and a grounding in it, as efficiently conveyed by the cognate term *ogadha* in its compounds with *amata*- and *nibbāna*-. Along with them, the notion of immersion conveyed by this lexicon provides growing familiarity with the instruments of knowing, so to perform that purification from defilements aimed at *nibbāna*, which at some point may become the very object of contemplation.

In brief, the immersion suggested by the term *pariyogāhaṇa* follows three directions:

1. Towards the object experienced, contemplated, and known (and to the resulting unification of the mind);
2. Towards knowing itself (in its refined forms, as *ñāṇa* and *abhiññā*);

3. Towards liberation, as the ultimate goal of the path and as an object of contemplation as well.

The image of immersion is also significant in the definition of liberation and of that leap of immediate understanding required to attain it. It implies that ordinary knowing is superficial and incapable of penetrating the nature of the objects beyond their mere appearance.

Notes

1 See Law 1933: 65; Norman 1983: 87; von Hinüber 2000: 59–60; Ronkin 2005: 87; Crosby 2014: 37.

2 Rhys Davids-Stede translates *pariyogāḷha* as 'dived into, penetrated into, immersed in' and *pariyogāha* as 'diving into, penetration' (PED s.v.).

3 '*Apadesa* signifies the pointing out or citing of someone as a witness or authority—in this case for some teaching. The four which are cited are the Buddha, a community with elders, several learned monks and just one elder' (Cousins 1983: 2; here Cousins refers to the *Mahāpadesakathā* in the *Mahāparinibbānasutta*, DN 16, CST4 II 187–188, PTS II 123–125, and to the *Mahāpadesasutta*, AN CST4 IV 180, PTS II 167–170).

4 SN CST4 IV85, PTS IV54.

5 In the *Saddhammappakāsinī*, glossing another passage of the *Paṭisambhidāmagga*, Mahānāma says that 'the analysis of the *dhamma*s is the knowledge opposing doubt' (*dhammavavatthānan ti vicikicchāya paṭipakkhaṃ ñāṇaṃ*. Paṭis-a CST4 I 18, PTS I 103). Dhammapāla equates it to the discrimination of the three kinds of *dhamma*s, i.e. wholesome (*kusala*), unwholesome, or neutral (DN-pṭ CST4 I 7, PTS I 133).

6 *Nekkhammapariyogāhaṇaṃ kāmacchandena suññaṃ. Abyāpādapariyogāhaṇaṃ byāpādena suññaṃ. Ālokasaññāpariyogāhaṇaṃ thinamiddhena suññaṃ. Avikkhepapariyogāhaṇaṃ uddhaccena suññaṃ. Dhammavavatthānapariyogāhaṇaṃ vicikicchāyasuññaṃ. Ñāṇapariyogāhaṇaṃ avijjāyasuññaṃ. Pāmojjapariyogāhaṇaṃ aratiyā suññaṃ. Paṭhamajjhānapariyogāhaṇaṃ nīvaraṇehi suññaṃ...pe... arahattamaggapariyogāhaṇaṃ sabbakilesehi suññaṃ. Idaṃ pariyogāhaṇasuññaṃ.* Suññakathā, Paṭis CST4 II 48, PTS II 183.

7 Paṭis-a CST4 II 178, PTS II 522. Of these qualities, *apilāpanatā* is the one that presents the closest analogies with *pariyogāhaṇa*. See Dhs 14, PTS 11 and 1349, PTS 232; Pp 59, PTS 21; Vibh 906, PTS 360 and 935, PTS 373; As 350, PTS 147; cf. Norman 1988: 49–52; Cox 1992: 81; and Gethin 2001: 38–40.

8 See PED s.v. *pariyogāha*, 'hard to penetrate, unfathomable' and *pariyogāhana*, 'plunging into, penetration.' Cf. e.g. the *Khemasutta*, SN CST4 IV 410, PTS IV 376–377: *tathāgato gambhīro appameyyo duppariyogāho seyyathāpi mahāsamuddo.* Transl. Bodhi 2000: 1382: 'The Tathāgata is deep, immeasurable, hard to fathom like the great ocean.' The same phrase is found in the *Aggivacchagottasutta* of the *Majjhimanikāya*, M CST4 II 192, PTS I 487–488; trans. Ñāṇamoli-Bodhi 1995: 593–594: '[The Tathāgata] is profound, immeasurable, unfathomable like the

ocean.' In the *Milindapañha* the analogy of the ocean is used with the same wording to describe prince Vessantara (Mil PTS 283).

9 Vibh CST4 289, PTS 167 and Vibh CST4 557, PTS 255.

10 CST4 60, PTS 21.

11 DN 14, CST4 II 76, PTS II 41.

12 *Upālisutta*, MN 56, CST4 II 69, PTS II 380.

13 AN CST4 VIII 12, PTS IV 186.

14 In the two examples given, the members of other schools (*aññatitthiya*) are Niganthas. In the *Mahāpadānasutta* the same speech is given by the Buddha Vipassī to the prince Khaṇa and his chaplain Tissa (DN 14, CST4 II 76, PTS II 41), and then to a crowd (DN 14, CST4 II 76, PTS II 41). In the *Bhadrakasutta*, by seeing and knowing, and merging into the *dhamma* beyond time, one should investigate the past and the future, and understand that desire is the root of suffering (SN CST4 IV 363, PTS IV 328–329).

15 MN 121, CST4 III 176–184, PTS III 104–109.

16 *Khīṇā jāti, vusitaṃ brahmacariyaṃ, kataṃ karaṇīyaṃ, n' āparaṃ itthattāya* (MN 121, CST4 III 183, PTS II 108).

17 Ps CST4 III 176, PTS IV 152.

18 The cognate term *ajjhogāhati* is used mostly in a literal and not metaphorical way, as plunging into the ocean (*samudda*), the thick of a wood (*vanasaṇḍa*), or a remote place in a forest (*arañña*; DN 3, CST4 I 280, PTS I 101). More figuratively, *ajjhogati* is used to describe the Tathāgata 'plunging into' the eight assemblies (MN 12, CST4 I 151, PTS I 52). In this latter case the commentary glosses *ajjhogāhati* with *anupavisati*, 'to enter' (Ps CST4 I 151, PTS II 34; cf. Cone s.v. *anupavisati*).

19 'Deathlessness has to be thoroughly known as *nibbāna*' (*amataṃ nibbānan 'ti abhiññeyyaṃ*; Paṭis CST4 I 10, PTS I 14–15).

20 Bhikkhu Bodhi translates *amatogadha* with 'has the Deathlessness as its ground' (Bodhi 2000: 1551), and this reading is supported by the exegesis of *nibbānogadha*: *nibbānogadhan 'ti nibbāne patiṭṭhitaṃ* (Spk CST4 III 160, PTS II 336). On the other hand, 'merging into the deathlessness' seems to be more in line with those commentaries that take *ogadha* as a synonym of *abbhantara* (*abhi-antara*), i.e. internal, within, going inside, intimate with (e.g. Ps CST4 I 466, PTS II 370, Ps CST4 II 459, PTS III 439, and Spk CST4 V 514, PTS III 247; see PED and Cone s.v.). It should also be noted that some commentaries offer both exegeses, thus stressing the similarity between them (e.g. Ps CST4 I 466, PTS II 370 and Spk CST4 III 160, PTS II 336). Norman translates the verse *tvañ ca me maggam akkhāhi, añjasaṃ amatogadhaṃ* (Th 168) as follows: 'And do you show me the straight path that plunges into the death-free' (Norman 1997: 23; see p. 24 for Th 179 and 78 for Th 748). Dhammapāla's commentary glosses *amatogadhaṃ* with *nibbānapatiṭṭhaṃ* ('grounded/established in *nibbāna*'; Th-a CST4 180, PTS II 52). In the *Paramatthadīpanī*, instead, Dhammapāla identifies *nibbānogadha* with the eightfold path (It-a CST4 35, PTS 112). Masefield translates the compound *nibbānogadhagāminaṃ* occurring in the *Paṭhamanakuhanasutta* (It 36, PTS 28) with the phrase 'that leads to the firm footing of *nibbāna*' (2000: 29), thus following the same explanation of *ogadha* as *patiṭṭha* offered by Dhammapāla in the commentary (It-a CST4 35, PTS 112). The same stanza occurs in the *Brahmacariyasutta* of the Aṅguttaranikāya (AN CST4 IV 25, PTS II 26) and there Bhikkhu Bodhi translates

amatogadhaṃ as 'culminating in *nibbāna*' (2012: 413). In the *Mūlakasutta* the Buddha tells his disciples that 'all *dhammas* merge into deathlessness, all dhammas end in *nibbāna*' (AN CST4 X 58, PTS V 107). The translation by Bhikkhu Bodhi reads: '[All things] culminate in the deathless. Their consummation is *nibbāna.*' (transl. Bodhi 2012: 1410).

21 *Kathañ ca, bhikkhave, bhikkhu ariyaṃ aṭṭhaṅgikaṃ maggaṃ bhāvento ariyaṃ aṭṭhaṅgikaṃ maggaṃ bahulīkaronto nibbānaninno hoti nibbānapoṇo nibbānapabbhāro? Idha, bhikkhave, bhikkhu sammādiṭṭhiṃ bhāveti amatogadhaṃ amataparāyanaṃ amatapariyosānaṃ...pe... sammāsamādhiṃ bhāveti amatogadhaṃ amataparāyanaṃ amatapariyosānaṃ. Evaṃ kho, bhikkhave, bhikkhu ariyaṃ aṭṭhaṅgikaṃ maggaṃ bhāvento ariyaṃ aṭṭhaṅgikaṃ maggaṃ bahulīkaronto nibbānaninno hoti nibbānapoṇo nibbānapabbhāro.* SN CST4 V 115, PTS V 39. The following discourse, the *Paṭhamasamuddaninnasutta*, offers almost the same example, with the Ganges sloping into the ocean (SN CST4 V 121, PTS V 40). These qualities are also attributed to the five faculties (*indriya*; e.g. SN CST4 V 527, PTS V 232–233).

22 MN 70, CTS4 II 183, PTS I 479–480. Trans. Bodhi 1995: 582–583. The expression *kāyena c' eva paramasaccaṃ sacchikaroti* is explained in the commentary as *nāmakāyena nibbānasaccaṃ sacchikaroti*. We will discuss later the use of *nāmakāya* applied to liberation. See also Tse-fu Kuan 2015: 37, n.18.

23 MN 70 CST4 II 181, PTS I 477. It must be taken into consideration that *kāyena phusitvā* does not refer only to *nibbāna*, but it may indicate the direct experience of the eight releases (*vimokkha*), like in the *Puttasutta* (AN CST4 I V87, PTS II 87), where it describes an attribute of a red-lotus *samaṇa* (on the *vimokkhas*, cf. Giustarini 2016). It also resembles the experience of the third *jhāna*, wherein the meditator, 'mindful and fully aware, experiences pleasure with the body' (*sato ca sampajāno sukhañ ca kāyena paṭisaṃvedeti*; e.g. *Kandarakasutta*, MN 51, CST4 I 13, PTS I 347).

24 AN CST4 VI 46, PTS III 356.

25 Trans. Bodhi 2012: 1761, n. 1345. *Amataṃ dhātuṃ kāyena phusitvā viharantī 'ti maraṇavirahitaṃ nibbānadhātuṃ sandhāya kammaṭṭhānaṃ gahetvā viharantā anukkamena taṃ nāmakāyena phusitvā viharanti.* For the distinction between *nāmakāya* and *rūpakāya*, see Paṭis CST4 170, PTS I 183.

26 AN CST4 III131, PTS I281–282.

27 On the reference of *nāma-kāya*, in the sense of the mental part, to *nāma* in the dyad *nāma-rūpa*, see e.g. the *Mahānidānasutta* (DN 15, CST4 II 114, PTS II 62).

28 *... adhigato kho myāyaṃ dhammo gambhīro duddaso duranubodho santo paṇīto atakkāvacaro nipuṇo paṇḍitavedanīyo* (e.g. *Ariyapariyesanasutta/Pāsarāsisutta*, MN 26, CST4 I 281, PTS I 167).

29 *Atakkāvacaro 'ti takkena avacaritabbo ogāhitabbo na hoti, ñāṇen' eva avacaritabbo* (e.g. CST4 I 281, PTS II 174).

30 *Kathaṃ phuṭṭhattā paññā pariyogāhaṇe ñāṇaṃ? Rūpaṃ aniccato phusati, rūpaṃ dukkhato phusati, rūpaṃ anattato phusati. Yaṃ yaṃ phusati taṃ taṃ pariyogāhatī 'ti—phuṭṭhattā paññā pariyogāhaṇe ñāṇaṃ. Vedanaṃ...pe... saññaṃ... saṅkhāre... viññāṇaṃ... cakkhuṃ...pe... jarāmaraṇaṃ aniccato phusati, dukkhato phusati, anattato phusati. Yaṃ yaṃ phusati taṃ taṃ pariyogāhatī 'ti—phuṭṭhattā paññā*

pariyogāhaṇe ñāṇaṃ. Taṃ ñātaṭṭhena ñāṇaṃ, pajānanaṭṭhena paññā. Tena vuccati phuṭṭhattā paññā pariyogāhaṇe ñāṇaṃ (Paṭis CST4 I 93, PTS I 106).

31 'The expression "he touches" means that he touches, pervades [the object] by the touching which consists in awareness derived from insight; the expression "he merges into" means that he enters [the object] by the awareness derived from insight.' (*phusatī 'ti vipassanāñāṇaphusanena phusati pharate pariyogahatī 'ti vipassanāñāṇena pavisati*; Paṭis-a CST4 I 93, PTS I 334; see also Paṭis-a CST4 I 42, PTS I 46). Mahānāma's interpretation may be inspired by the *Peṭakopadesa*, which equates *pariyogāhanā* to *vipassanā* (Peṭ CST4 69, PTS 133).

32 Paṭis CST4 II 221, PTS II 52.

33 AN CST4 IX 43, PTS IV 451–452. The *Āhuneyyasutta* (AN CST4 X 16, PTS V 23) includes the *kāyasakkhi* in the list of the ten kinds of persons who are worthy of gifts, respect etc., along with *tathāgata*s, *paccekabuddha*s, etc.

34 *Taṃ samāpattiṃ sahajātanāmakāyena phusitvā viharati* (Mp CST4 IX 43, PTS IV 206): 'He dwells having contacted that attainment with the coexistent mental body' (trans. Bodhi 2012: 1833, n.1956).

35 Paṭis CST4 II 48, PTS II 181ff. In the *Kammanirodhasutta* of the *Saḷāyanasaṃyutta*, the old *kamma* is identified with the six sense-spheres (*saḷāyatana*; SN CST4 IV 146, PTS IV 132). This explains how sense-experience exists because of past *kamma*, and in the *parinibbāna* no residual of *kamma* is found. In the sequence of the dependent arising (*paṭiccasamuppāda*), the ultimate source of the *saḷāyatana*s (and of the entire *saṃsāra*) is ignorance (*avijjā*), and when this is uprooted, there is no *saṃsāra*, including sense-experience (*Paṭiccasamuppādasutta*, SN CST4 II 1, PTS II 1).

Bibliography

All references to Pāli texts are to the Pali Text Society editions.

Bodhi, Bhikkhu transl. 2000. *The Connected Discourses of the Buddha: A New Translation of the Saṃyutta Nikāya*. Boston: Wisdom Publications.

Bodhi, Bhikkhu 2012. *The Numerical Discourses of the Buddha: A Translation of the Aṅguttara Nikāya*. Boston: Wisdom Publications.

Cone, Margaret 2001. *A Dictionary of Pāli*. Oxford: the Pali Text Society.

Cone, Margaret 2011. *A Dictionary of Pāli*. Vol. II. Oxford: the Pali Text Society.

Cox, Collett 1992. 'Mindfulness and Memory: the Scope of Smṛti from Early Buddhism to the Sarvāstivādin Abhidharma.' In Gyatso, J. ed. *In the Mirror of Memory*. SUNY: New York.

Cousins, Lance C. 1983. 'Pali Oral Literature.' In Denwood, P. and A. Piatigorsky eds. *Buddhist Studies. Ancient and Modern*. London and Dublin: Curzon, 1–11.

Crosby, Kate 2014. *Theravada Buddhism: Continuity, Diversity, and Identity*. Oxford: Wiley Blackwell.

Edgerton, Franklin 1993; 1a 1953. *Buddhist Hybrid Sanskrit Grammar and Dictionary. Vol. II: Dictionary*. Delhi: Motilal Banarsidass.

Gethin, Rupert L. 1992. 'The Māṭikās: Memorization, Mindfluness, and the List.' In Gyatso, J. ed. *In the Mirror of Memory*, 149–172. SUNY: New York.

Gethin, Rupert L. 2001. *The Buddhist Path to Awakening*. Oxford: Oneworld.

Gethin, Rupert L. 2008. *Sayings of the Buddha*. Oxford: Oxford University Press.

Giustarini, Giuliano 2016. 'Liberation(s): the Notion of Release (*vimokkha*) in the Paṭisambhidāmagga.' *Journal of Indian Philosophy* 44.2: 241–266. https://doi.org/10.1007/s10781-014-9262-3

von Hinüber, Oskar 2000. 2nd ed. *A Handbook of Pāli Literature*. New York–Berlin.

Horner, Isaline B. Transl. 1969. *Milinda's Questions*. London: The Pali Text Society.

Kuan, Tse-fu 2015. 'Abhidhamma Interpretations of "Persons" (*puggala*): with Particular Reference to the Aṅguttara Nikāya.' *Journal of Indian Philosophy* 43: 31–60. https://doi.org/10.1007/s10781-014-9228-5

Law, Bimale C. 1933. *A History of Pāli Literature*. London: Kegan.

Masefield, Peter transl. 2000. *The Itivuttaka*. Oxford: Pali Text Society.

Monier-Williams, Monier 2002. (1st 1899 Oxford University Press). *A Sanskrit-English Dictionary*. Delhi: Motilal Banarsidass.

Norman, Kenneth R. 1983. *Pāli Literature*. Wiesbaden: Harrassowitz.

Norman, Kenneth R. 1988. 'Pāli Lexicographical Studies V. Twelve Pāli etymologies.' *Journal of the Pali Text Society* 12: 49–63.

Norman, Kenneth R. 1997. *Poems of Early Buddhist Monks*. Oxford: The Pali Text Society.

Ronkin, Noa 2005. *Early Buddhist Metaphysics: The Making of a Philosophical Tradition*. London and New York: Routledge Curzon.

Rhys Davids, Thomas W. and Stede, William 1921. *The Pali Text Society's Pali-English Dictionary*. London, Pali Text Society.

Abbreviations

AN	Aṅguttaranikāya
As	Atthasālinī (Dhammasaṅganī-aṭṭhakathā)
CST4	Chaṭṭha Saṅgāyana Tipiṭaka, 4th edition
Dhs	Dhammasaṅgaṇi
DN	Dīgha Nikāya
DN-pṭ	Līnatthapakāsinī I (Dīghanikāya-purāṇaṭīkā)
It-a	Paramatthadīpanī (Itivuttaka-aṭṭhakathā)
Mil	Milindapañha
MN	Majjhima-nikāya
MN-pṭ	Majjhimanikāya-purāṇaṭīkā
Mp	Manorathapūraṇī (Aṅguttaranikāya-aṭṭhakathā)
Paṭis	Paṭisambhidāmagga
Paṭis-a	Saddhammappakāsinī (Paṭisambhidāmagga-aṭṭhakathā)
PED	Pali-English Dictionary (Rhys Davids and Stede)

Pp	Puggalapaññatti
Ps	Papañcasūdanī (Majjhimanikāya-aṭṭhakathā)
PTS	Pali Text Society edition
Sadd	Saddanīti
Sn	Suttanipāta
SN	Saṃyuttanikāya
Spk	Sāratthapakāsinī (Saṃyuttanikāya-aṭṭhakathā)
SN-pṭ	Linatthappākasinī III (Sāratthapakāsinīṭīkā; Saṃyuttanikāya-purāṇaṭīkā)
Th	Theragāthā
Th-a	Paramatthadīpanī (Theragāthā-aṭṭhakathā)
Ud	Udāna
Ud-a	Paramatthadīpanī (Udāna-aṭṭhakathā)
Vibh	Vibhaṅga
Vibh-a	Sammohavinodanī (Vibhaṅga-aṭṭhakathā)

Author biography

Giuliano Giustarini is Lecturer in Buddhist Studies and Pāli Grammar at Mahidol University (Nakhon Pathom) and translator of the Pāli Nikāyas for the Fondazione Maitreya (Rome). His main interests include the *Suttapiṭaka* and *Abhidhammapiṭaka* with their commentaries, and Buddhist philosophy and meditation. Among his recent publications are: 'Notes on the *satipaṭṭhānas* in the Vibhaṅga Mūlaṭīkā', *Journal of Indian Philosophy* 2023, 51: 77–95, and 'Meditative listening in the Pāli Buddhist Canon', *Numen* 2023, 70: 254–285.

Chapter 3

Buddhist Awareness as a Means to Unveil the Past and Emancipate the Future: The Buddhist Awareness Camps Project in post-1990 Nepal

Chiara Letizia

Introduction

In the late 1990s activists belonging to two previously Hinduized ethnic groups of Nepal, the Tharus and the Magars, started to engage in the diffusion of Buddhism among the members of their groups through the organization of Buddhist Awareness Camps (*Bauddha jāgaraṇ praśikṣaṇ śivir*, literally, 'Buddhist awakening training camps'). Fascinated by the increasing and exotic presence of Theravāda Buddhism among these groups in southern Nepal, in 2003–4 and 2007–8 I conducted fieldwork among the Tharu and Magar communities of eastern Terai (Udayapur, Nawalparasi and Rupandehi Districts) (Letizia 2005, 2007, 2014). The kind and welcome invitation by Chiara Neri and Francesco Sferra to contribute to this book in homage to Professor Corrado Pensa has given me the opportunity to look at these old data in a new light and to look more attentively at the discourses on Buddhist awareness among the Tharu and Mahar communities studied. More importantly, Chiara and Francesco's invitation gives me a wonderful opportunity to express my deep gratitude to Corrado for his profoundly inspiring academic and dharma teachings.[1]

A few clarifications must be given from the outset: the notion of 'awareness' used in these camps (*jagaraṇ*, literally 'awakening,' 'consciousness raising') clearly does not coincide with the Buddhist technical notion of *sati* as it can be found in the Pali canon, but, as we will see, includes social, ethnic, political, religious and developmental aspects. None of the activists with whom I worked made any explicit equation between *sati* and the awareness preached in these camps. Moreover, as will be shown in this chapter, some of the 'truths' that, according to these activists, were supposed to be brought to consciousness through this Buddhist awakening were not exactly Buddhist truths, and they were constructed, rewritten, or, to put it more plainly, invented stories. However, these 'invented' stories were generated by real aspirations and they helped to build new social realities and new rituals, and eventually to create the conditions for the diffusion of Buddhist teachings, included the teaching of meditation.

In the first part of the chapter, I give an overview of the historical, religious, and political context that brought the Magar and Tharu urban intellectuals to announce in the 1990s a collective shift to Buddhism for their groups, which had been Hinduized at least since the second half of the eighteenth century. I then focus on the Buddhist Awareness Camps project and discuss the ways in which the notion of 'Buddhist awareness' was used and understood in the discourses of the activists, and the truths that it was supposed to unveil. These discourses appear to be part of the much larger and dominant discourse in Nepal on modernity, social reform, and development, strongly encouraged by the government and by international development projects. The nature of this Buddhist awareness could be seen, at least in part, as a hybridization between two modernist imaginaries, Buddhist and developmental.

'Buddhist modernism' and the reform of Newar Buddhism

Tharus and Magar intellectuals came into contact with Buddhism in the 1990s through the activism of some Buddhist Newars of the Kathmandu Valley, where Theravāda Buddhism had been introduced as a reform of traditional Newar Buddhism in the early twentieth century.[2] The form of Theravāda adopted by early Newar practitioners had already undergone an important transformation in late nineteenth- and early twentieth-century Ceylon under the impact of colonialism and Christian missionary activity. As a result, Theravāda Buddhism had emerged in its modernist, rationalized, nationalist, and anti-occidental form with a powerful missionary agenda (Leve 2002).

The key factor of these developments was the encounter in 1880 between Colonel Olcott, one of the founders of the Theosophical Society, and the young Don David Hewavitharana, the future Anagarika Dharmapala, a key nationalist figure and the first transnational Buddhist figure who shared the aspiration of returning to the authentic, rational and scientific form of Buddhism, rejecting superstitions and folk Buddhism[3]. In 1891, Anagarika Dharmapala founded the Maha Bodhi Society and laid the foundations of this new form of Theravāda that has been referred to as Buddhist modernism[4] or Protestant Buddhism.[5]

Many characteristics of Buddhist modernism became influential in Nepal, namely the development of Buddhist missionaries; the importance given to Buddhist education and publishing; the portrayal of Buddhism as rational and scientific and the condemnation of 'blind faith'; the popularization of meditation; the importance given to the philosophical teachings and the rejection of ritualistic types of Buddhism; the connection with ethnonationalism;[6]the central role of lay people; the advocacy of social reform; and, finally, the criticism of other religions, in particular Hinduism and Christianity.

The opposition to Hindu norms and structure and the notion that the Buddhist path was a means of social emancipation figured prominently in the discourse of another important protagonist of Buddhism modernism: Dr B. R. Ambedkar, the leader of the Indian Dalits, who as the first minister of Law and Justice of independent India took a leading part in the framing of the Indian constitution. In 1956, Ambedkar publicly converted to Buddhism and converted in a collective ritual 500,000 of his largely illiterate Mahar disciples[7]. Ambedkar choose Buddhism because it was an indigenous religion, born on Indian soil, and because he saw in the Buddha the prototype for the fight against Brahmanism.[8] As we will see, the conversion of Dalits to Ambedkar Buddhism in Maharashtra and the adoption of Buddhism by Tharus and Magars in the Tarai had some points in common: the anti-Hindu elements and the idea that conversion to Buddhism was a tool of freedom from a position of inferiority in the Hindu hierarchy.

Sarah LeVine and David Gellner (2005) have described the contacts between the early Nepalese Theravādins and the Maha Bodhi Society: a handful of Newars visiting India for trade encountered the missionaries of the Mahabodhi Society in Calcutta in the 1920s and '30s and they brought their teachings back to Nepal. The entire first generation of Nepalese Theravādins received their first ordination from the Maha Bodhi Society monks in India. The objectives of the Buddhist Society of Nepal, published in 1951, were for the most part adapted from the Maha Bodhi Society Programme and included the propagation of Buddhism in Nepal through the building of monasteries and the publication of translations of the Buddhist scriptures (Kloppenborg 1977: 307). Buddhist influence in Nepal was not limited to the Maha Bodhi Society but extended to a number of transnational Buddhist organizations, and Nepalese monks and nuns travelled worldwide to study, receive ordination and to strengthen ties with Buddhist institutions.[9]

Modernist Buddhism was introduced in the Newar community as a reform of traditional Newar Buddhism, a distinctive form of Mahāyāna Vajrayāna Buddhism preserved in Sanskrit texts and in esoteric rites conducted by Tantric Buddhist priests (Gellner 1992). Newar Buddhist 'monkhood' has survived as a caste duty passed from father to son, through a Buddhist initiation/life-cycle ritual that allows the members of a high caste of married householders to form a *saṅgha* of quasi-monks attached to a monastery.[10]

Theravāda reformers wanted to 'awaken' the sleeping Newar Buddhists and to lead them to the 'authentic' and 'original' form of their religion. The goal of Nepalese Theravādins was to purify Newar Buddhism from blind faith and folk religion (magical practices, use of meat and alcohol, animal sacrifice and caste distinctions), to reintroduce monasticism and to educate the laity to the Buddhist doctrine and provide them with the translation of Buddhist texts.

Lauren Leve (2002, 2016) has shown that the shift to Theravāda implied the production of a new type of socio-religious subject. Contrasting the practice of *vipassanā* meditation with the traditional practice of animal sacrifice at the festival of Dasain, Leve shows that the former has changed moralities and minds of Newar Theravāda adherents. Unlike Newar Buddhism, which defines *dharma* as the appropriate performance of social relationships (in relation to the family, ancestors and gods) and locates moral authority in society, 'Theravada emphasizes conscious intention and personal insight and invests ethical agency in the individual, conceived as a bounded and autonomous whole' (Leve 2002: 852). Even if they insisted that Buddhism should not be chiefly identified with rituals, Theravādins engaged in a process of 'religious domestication' (LeVine and Gellner 2005: 62–65) and the monks started assuming some functions of the traditional household priests, such as the administration of life-cycle rituals[11], which were short and inexpensive, compared to the complicated, costly and long Newar Buddhist rituals. Also, in accordance with the traditional Newar Buddhist society, the laity had a prominent role in the Theravāda movement, in the administration of the monasteries, in the meditation centres, and in the modernization of Buddhism (LeVine and Gellner 2005: 206–207). As we will see, these two aspects have become central to the diffusion of Buddhism in Tharu and Magar communities, where lay Buddhist activists played a prominent role and even started conducting Buddhist life-cycle rituals.

The context of the diffusion of Buddhism to the ethnic groups

The political context that allowed the contact between the Newar activists and the Tharu and Magar activists was the 1990 campaign for a secular state and the rise of ethnic movements against state Hinduism and the dominance of the Hindu high castes. To understand these developments, some context is required.

The state of Nepal was forged in the late 18th century by the conquest and incorporation by the king of Gorkha of many religiously and culturally diverse polities. To rule this disparate empire, the Shah kings looked to Brahmanical texts and norms and declared Nepal as a 'pure Hindu land' (*asal Hindustan*). During the Rana regime in the 19th century, a national Code imposed Hindu structures and values upon a very heterogeneous population. The ethnic groups (formerly known as 'hill tribes') were slotted into the middle of hierarchy, above the Dalit ('Untouchables'), in a position clearly inferior to the 'high' Hindu castes, whose leadership and dominance was thereby assured. Unification was attempted by imposing a major Hindu festival, Dasain, as the pre-eminent national festival, and by enforcing cow worship. Over time, ethnic groups responded by adopting Hindu practices to seek social mobility and inclusion in the state (Pfaff-Czarnecka 2008, Whelpton 2008).

In this context, Theravāda represented a challenge to the Nepali state, and the early years of Nepalese Theravādins were marked by internal persecution: Ranas assimilated Hinduism to national identity, and aggressively supported traditional Hinduism against modernist reforms, outlawing proselytization and conversion.[12] At various times between the 1920s and 1950s, Theravāda monks were arrested and exiled.

Though successive constitutions never ceased declaring conversion illegal,[13] as the years passed Buddhism found itself in a privileged position compared to other religions like Christianity and Islam, which were considered as foreign and dangerous. Buddhism came to be considered as a sub-sect of Hinduism and, drawing on Puranic doctrine, the Buddha was venerated as an incarnation of Vishnu. At the end of the Rana regime, the situation evolved further: in 1951, Theravāda monks received permission to practise and to preach freely. In 1952 the festival of Buddha Jayanti was recognized as a national holiday, and in 1956 the 4th World Buddhist Conference held in Kathmandu to mark 2500 years since the Buddha's *parinirvāṇa* was attended by B. R. Ambedkar, who delivered his historic speech 'Buddha and Karl Marx.'

The Panchayat regime which followed in the 1960s intensified the unification attempts of preceding Nepalese governments by encouraging an ideology of national identity and rejection of cultural difference. Hinduism was the official state religion, whereas Buddhism, Jainism and Sikhism were being seen as branches of Hinduism. Panchayat nationalism was built on the idea of a shared national identity which homogenized caste and ethnic differences: a uniform population tied by the common bonds of Hinduism, monarchy and the Nepali language at the cost of other languages, religions, and cultures.

In April 1990, the Panchayat System was dismantled in the wake of a People's Movement (*janandolan*) and King Birendra agreed to become a constitutional monarch. Secularism was one of the major demands of this movement, and the Buddhists emerged on the national scene as a major force in the campaign for a secular state. Answering the call of the Nepal Theravāda Buddhist Association, on 30 June 1990 thirty thousand people demonstrated in the streets of Kathmandu to demand a secular state, in the largest political gathering Nepal had ever seen. Theravāda Buddhists were marching for a secular state because they wanted to take Buddhism out of the Hindu fold as an independent religion, and they wanted to be free to express their religion. In fact, 'secularism' (*dharma nirapeksata*, literally 'religious non-alignment'), was not a call for the separation between religion and state, nor a move to banish religion from public life, but 'the institutional instantiation of freedom of religion and religious equality' (Leve 2007a: 94). Secularism was a demand for equal recognition of all religions practised in the country and the abolition of the special state-sponsored primacy given to Hinduism.[14] The ethnic groups in the country, now collectively named *janajāti*, demanded that their distinct cultural and linguistic differences be recognized, denounced the domination of high-caste Hindus in the economic, political, legal and educational spheres, and called for a more inclusive state. This movement contributed to the general ethnicization of politics and engendered a change in political consciousness.[15] The main association established in 1991 to push these issues was the Nepal Federation of Nationalities, (NEFEN, now called NEFIN[16]), an umbrella organization that brought together more than fifty indigenous groups and positioned itself explicitly in opposition to a Hindu identity.[17]

Thus, secularism in post 1990 Nepal 'became a rallying call for multicultural democracy' (Leve 2007a: 84) that brought together Buddhist activists and ethnic activists.[18] The 1990 Constitution recognized for the first time the ethnic, linguistic and cultural diversity of Nepal; however, it still referred to the country as a Hindu kingdom. Strongly disappointed at the failure of their struggle for secularism, some young Newar Buddhist activists were motivated to work on other fronts, namely the proselytization of Janajatis, in part to increase the number of Buddhists in the decennial National Census, which they believed had been kept artificially low during the Panchayat period. They created an association of young Buddhists in Kathmandu (*Yuba Bauddha Samuha*, hereafter YBS)[19] and organized meetings in Theravāda monasteries, where they invited the leaders of the different ethnic groups. Thanks to Taiwanese funds, these encounters brought about the creation in 1995 of the Himalayan Buddhist Education Foundation (HBEF). The mission of this foundation was to provide Buddhist education and to promote Buddhist morality among the different castes and ethnic groups of Nepal.

The Buddhist Awareness Camps

The YBS started the 'Buddhist Awareness Camps' project in 1994 (LeVine and Gellner 2005: 234–235). One of the founders of YBS, Keshab Man Shakya, wrote that the idea of these camps came to him while he was studying in America, when he observed the Wednesday activities and programmes of a local church (Shakya 2006, 2008; Gellner 2019).

These residential camps were directed at all ethnic groups, but here I will consider only the camps organized especially for Tharu and Magar groups, which were the most receptive to this missionization. Held in villages, these residential camps were always organized by YBS in partnership with ethnic associations. The teachings were given not only by monks, but also by lay instructors of the same ethnic group as the participants, in their own language. The instructors did not limit themselves to teaching Buddhist doctrine (the five precepts, the three refuges, the four noble truths and the life of Buddha), but also gave lectures demonstrating the historical link between Buddhism and Tharu or Magar societies, and presenting Buddhism as an agent of progress for these communities.

The Buddhist awareness camp held in Banepa in 1995 is a good example of the synergy between different activists: the monk Aśvaghoṣa taught the life of the Buddha, while the militant intellectual M. S. Thapa Magar, leader of the national association of Magars, gave a speech on Buddhism and the Magar *jāti* ('people'); the Tharu activist Syaram Chaudhary spoke on Buddhism and Tharu society; the Newar activist Gehendra Udas spoke on Buddhism in Nepal; and Lok Darshan Bajracharya, former Deputy Director of the Lumbini Development Trust, talked about Buddhist activities in the international context (HBEF Newsletter 1996). Thus, starting from the religious Theravāda context of the monk's speech, the lectures progressively opened up to Buddhism among ethnic groups in Nepal and finally extended the horizon to the transnational scene.

A pamphlet containing an invitation to participate in a camp organized in Kailali District in 1997 underscored the particular link between the Buddha and Nepal, the universality of Buddhist teachings, and deplored the lack of local education:

> Buddha, the son of Nepal, is not only a Nepalese god; he is the light of the Asian continent. Maybe you know that the light given by the Buddha is not only a guide for Asian people: his light of peace has spread to the whole world. In Europe and in America, Buddhist monasteries have been built and people are studying Buddhist teachings and are leading a happy life following these teachings. However, it is so sad to see that there is darkness under the lamp: we are not progressing, we are caught up in an illusion, we are not leading a peaceful life following the teachings of Buddha. Since we have realized this, we invite you to a camp of Buddhist Awareness (Buddhist Awareness Camp 1997, my translation).

These camps operated until 2001, when the Maoist insurgency caused these activities to stop. They were slowly restarted after the end of the People's War. The camps I attended in 2007 were organized by local activists, without the supervision of YBS.

The appeal of Buddhism for ethnic leaders and intellectuals

In the context of this post-1990 renaissance of ethnicity and movement against a two-century-long process of Hinduisation, ethnic leaders and activists were involved in the quest for and construction of their group's identity, culture, history and language and started writing on their own group (Lecomte-Tilouine 2002, Krauskopff 2009b). The growing fame of Buddhism, both on the global scene and at the national level, made it a worthy alternative to Hinduism (in the 1980s King Birendra made use of Buddhism to declare

Nepal as a 'Zone of Peace'; in 1985, the government of Nepal formed the Lumbini Development Trust; and in 1997 Lumbini was inscribed as a UNESCO world heritage site). Buddhism also had the added advantage of being considered an authentic Nepalese religion, because Lumbini, Buddha's birthplace is in Nepal, and the Buddha was increasingly presented and felt as a symbol of national identity.[20]

For an ethnic group to be recognized as indigenous (using the United Nations terminology and discourse), it was important for it to have always lived in Nepal. However, many Janajāti groups had myths which traced their origins to Tibet or Rajasthan. Proving a group's descent from the Buddha thus helped to prove its indigeneity.[21] Buddhism also appealed to ethnic leaders because it allowed them to express a Janajāti identity by way of negation–the affirmation of being non-Hindu–[22] and to include at the same time a dimension of social emancipation: by adopting Buddhism, they could reject the position of inferiority in the Hindu hierarchy imposed by the State. And according to the tropes of Buddhist modernism, Buddhism was presented as historically and doctrinally set in opposition to Brahmanism and the caste system, and as a modern, egalitarian religion opposed to Hindu rituals and norms perceived as discriminatory and superstitious.

Buddhism, as these ethnic leaders encountered it, offered a notion of salvation identical to that found in Ambedkar Buddhism: conceived not only as the liberation of the individual from the *saṃsāra*, but in social and political terms as liberation from injustice and social discrimination.[23] The modernist ideas connecting the soteriological message of Buddhism with such commitment, combining individual development and social reform, and considering social service as the fruit of meditation and compassion, were the nexus that allowed Buddhism to be included in activists' agendas in their struggle for democracy, social inclusion, and ethnic recognition. The notion of Buddhism as a modern, rational, and progressive religion which proposed liberation from both social backwardness and spiritual suffering fitted well with the emphasis put by many ethnic associations on modernizing, promoting education, and abandoning 'backwardness' (Krauskopff 2003).

This modernist Buddhist message found a fertile soil in both towns and villages where it echoed the projects of development (*bikās*) and social transformation—and their associated discourses—that the Nepali government, assisted by international donor agencies (like the US-funded Villages Development Programs), administered to improve the villagers' life conditions. These projects and policies imposed the ideologies of modernity and social progress that situated villagers in the past or in an inadequate present with respect to the scale of progress, characterized by ignorance, backwardness and lack of understanding (Pigg 1992). These ideologies and the social categories of development were internalized by villagers in the way they saw themselves and other Nepalis. Nepalis experienced modernity through a development ideology that insisted they were not modern (Pigg 1996). As Tatsuro Fujikura has shown, development discourses were discourses of awareness (2011, 2013) regarded as 'leading to new ways of conducting life appropriate to the changing times' (2013: 41). Development discourses labelled the 'underdeveloped' part of the population as somehow lacking in consciousness (*cetanā*). Consciousness in such talks denoted an 'urge to transform oneself and one's environment, precipitated by sudden discovery deep in oneself of a fundamental desire for improvement and progress' (2013: 42).

'Awareness raising programs' were held in many corners of the country on topics including sanitation, saving, family planning, gender equality, or forest preservation. Development fieldworkers would visit villages to convince villagers to build a toilet, to make a vegetable garden, to use a contraceptive device. If they didn't, the development worker would say: 'They have no awareness' and if they did, the development fieldworker would say, 'They gained some consciousness' (Fujikura 2011: 273).[24] People interviewed by Fujikura told him about their 'awakening' (2011: 276): that they had become free by recognizing previously repressed truths, or that they had learned they did not need to blindly follow the way of life handed down to them by their ancestors. The same discourses were heard in Buddhist awareness camps: Buddhist discourse and development discourse referred to the same modernization narrative and to the same notion that a reform of behaviour and consciousness was needed in order to move in a progressive or improving direction.

The leaders of Magar and Tharu associations chose to adopt Buddhism. The first international conference of the Magars, held in the Jhapa District in 1998, declared Buddhism as their religion: a special branch of the Nepal Magar Sangh (the national association that represents Magars in NEFIN), named Nepal Magar Sangh Bauddha Seva Samaj ('Buddhist Service Society of Nepal Magar Association'), was formed in order to deal with Buddhist activities, under the guidance of two Magar intellectuals, M. S. Thapa Magar and Dev Bahadur Rana. For its part, the national association of Tharus, Tharu Kalyankarini Sabha (the association that represents Tharus in NEFIN[25]) created a committee of specialists to conduct research on and to spread awareness of Buddhism in the Tharu community; this committee operated under the guidance of the prominent intellectuals Ramanand Prasad Singh and Tej Narayan Panjiyar.[26]

At the end of each Buddhist awareness camp, the participants promised to spread Buddhist awareness in their home districts. After the above-mentioned camp of Banepa in 1995, Tharus and Magars founded branches of the Buddhist Association in their respective districts. The *Udaypaur Yuba Bauddha Jagaran Samiti* ('Youth Buddhist Awareness Committee of Udayapur') was founded by Tharus in Deuri VDC, in 1996. Its first president, Vasudev Choudhary, came in contact with Buddhism through the Tharu Kalyankarini Sabha and attended the first Buddhist camp in Kathmandu where he met Theravāda monks and nuns as well as the Newar members of YBS. Inspired by Ramanand Prasad Singh's and Tej Narayan Panjiyar's books, he created in his home in Deuri village a Buddhist library. Bringing Buddhism to the Tharus became the mission of his life (Letizia 2016b).

The local branch of *Nepal Magar Sangh Bauddha Seva Samaj* in Rupandehi District was formed in 1999. Its president, Tulsi Regmi Magar, told me that he did not know the first thing about Buddhism at the time of his election. He told me how he had to take temporary ordination in a *vihara* in Butwal in order to study Buddhism, and recalled how the leaders of Nepal Magar Sangh were pushing the local members to attend Buddhist awareness camps at the Kirtipur Vihar in Kathmandu. As we will see, these camps were followed by an intense activism which led to the construction of small local monasteries, attempts to offer substitute life-cycle Buddhist rituals performed by lay officers, and efforts to find evidence of a Buddhist past in Tharu traditions and artefacts.[27]

The shift to Buddhism was not the result of a shift in beliefs: at the beginning it was a nominal and a collective move, made in the context of a campaign for increasing the number of Buddhists in the National Census, and only later did it become a shift in ritual practices. In the past Hinduism was the majority religion in almost all districts of Nepal, but Theravāda activists organized campaigns in order to convince their groups to change these figures.[28] Tharu and Magar activists followed the direction of their respective national organizations to mark their 'religion' as 'Buddhist' in the 2001 national census, despite the total absence of a Buddhist tradition among them.[29] The Buddhist modernist idea of individual responsibility and autonomy of choice contrasted with the collective adoption of Buddhism by the national ethnic organizations, but, as we will see, these notions emerged in the discourses of Buddhist activists nonetheless.

During fieldwork, I heard the story of people who dated their 'conversion' to Buddhism to the date of the official declaration of their leaders, but who only started inquiring about Buddhism afterwards. In Rupandehi and Nawalparasi districts, I visited some Buddhist monasteries that had been constructed with funds collected by the local community, but which then remained dormant while the new Buddhists waited for someone to give Buddhist teachings. If the absence of knowledge of or interest in Buddhist doctrine was not considered an important factor when declaring the collectively Buddhist, two other aspects were considered essential by the activists: first, raising awareness of the 'real' religious past of the group and second, carrying out the transformation of rituals, which will be briefly discussed below.

Revealing a Buddhist past, rewriting history

Both Tharu and Magar intellectuals felt it was necessary to prove that the Buddha himself belonged to their group and that Buddhism was their ancestral religion before they were forced to become Hindu. For both groups, the adoption of Buddhism was presented as a return to origins, a progressive awareness and remembering their Buddhist past (Letizia 2005, 2014).[30]

Magar and Tharu intellectuals wanted to prove their Buddhist past with the help of archaeological and historical data. They produced new histories of origin which ran counter to the previous 'sanskritized' histories and where the upper castes were no longer considered as models to emulate. For example, the Tharu intellectual, Ramanand Prasad Singh, refused to acknowledge the previous myth of the Rajput origin of the Tharus and affirmed their Mongolian origin instead. According to him, the name of 'Tharu' would derive from 'Sthavir,' the name of the elder disciples of the Buddha, sin which case the Tharus would be the descendants of Buddha's clan, the Śakya. This theory was presented as the 'true story' of the Tharus (Singh 1988).[31] This new story mirrors the previous myth about the provenance from Rajasthan and serves the same function of providing a prestigious origin, but in addition affirms the autochthony of Tharus (Krauskopff 2009b: 260).[32]

Another important Tharu intellectual, Tej Narayan Panjiyar, affirmed the Buddhist past of the Tharus and wrote that they found refuge in Kathmandu in order to escape the persecution of Brahmans in the region where the Buddha was born (Krauskopff 2009b: 262), establishing a parallel with the myth of origin of the Newar Shakya Buddhist caste.[33] Conversely, a Magar intellectual, M. S. Thapa Magar, traced in his book a complicated history to demonstrate that Buddha, Ashoka, and the Licchavis were Magars and postulated a Mongolian origin for all of them (Thapa Magar 2002).

A noticeable characteristic of these stories is that they operate a reification of ethnic categories and consider Magars and Tharus, respectively, as socially uniform groups. The reference to an original Buddhism (and sometimes to a common ancestor, the Buddha), contributed to the effort of the ethnic leaders to constitute a common identity, erasing the remarkable differences (cultural, linguistical, social) between different groups scattered in the country which shared the same ethnonym. Tharus of the eastern Tarai and Tharus living in the far west were culturally and linguistically very heterogeneous,[34] but as Tharu activist Ramanand Prasad Singh recalls: 'We used to go from one district to another to inform others about their own common origin' (Guneratne 1998: 761). Similarly, Kham Magars living in the western part of the country did not share any cultural features with Magars of eastern Nepal, but Buddhist activists told me that they had started visiting their Far Western counterparts, contributing to the creation of an imagined belonging.

Gisèle Krauskopff remarks that these 'rewritten stories' use the traditional register to produce their truth: the mythology of an original Buddhism is based on a Hindu model of origins, where religious identity is defined in terms of genealogy and descent (Krauskopff 2009a, 2009b). At the same time, she notes, these stories produce a modern political discourse, adapted to a contemporary and global context. The intended recipients of these stories written by urban intellectuals and sometimes published in English were not only the members of the group, but a wider national audience constituted by members of other ethnic groups and politicians as well as a global audience of foreign scholars, international ethnic activists and Buddhist institutions. These intellectuals competed with Brahmans on the field of history and erudition, and they looked for national and foreign scholars' endorsement of their stories. As one of these historians, Subodh Kumar Singh, told me in 2007 when I asked him why he was writing in English: 'Because Brahmans have destroyed Nepal's history and even foreign scholars have been influenced by them and don't know the real past. We Tharus must write our own history; otherwise, we will not survive. We cannot let others write our own history.'

Local Buddhist activists actively and relentlessly looked for evidence of the new stories about the Buddhist origins of their group in order to convince the people of their village. To prove that Buddha belonged to Magar or Tharu communities, activists scrutinized the Buddha's life, Buddha statues, or Buddhist artefacts to find traces of Tharu or Magar traditions or language. To quote some of their affirmations: 'We know that the Buddha ate pork meat before dying, and pork meat is the most delicious food for Magars'; 'the jewels of Buddha's mother that you can see on Buddhist statues are identical to the traditional jewels that Tharu women used to wear'; 'I was struck by the similarities between the objects in Lumbini Museum and our traditional artefacts.'

Similarly, they analyzed their own local practices, traditional artefacts, sacred sites to show that they held traces of a Buddhist past, or conversely, that there was no trace of Hinduism in them: 'The mound-shaped earth shrine at the entrance of the Tharu house has the same shape as a *caitya*'; 'in the altars of Tharu houses, one never finds a single Hindu *murti.*' They also pointed to their somatic characteristics and moral qualities as evidence of their natural Buddhism: 'We Tharus are honest and innocent, as we have the nature of the Buddha; we are naturally Buddhist without having the concept of being Buddhist'; 'We Magars have the same Mongolian face as the ancient statues in Sarnath.' To be Buddhist meant to be a descendant of the Buddha, to have the physical traits of the Buddha, or to have the same moral qualities of the Buddha; Tharu and Magar activists were trying to naturalize themselves as Buddhists.

At the same time the quest for evidence of a Buddhist past was presented as a scientific endeavour, archaeological and biological (to the point of quoting the presence of 'similar DNA between Tharus and Lord Buddha'). The discovery of a Buddhist past was presented by the activists as the result of awareness and education, which in turn was seen an opportunity for adopting a religion considered as rational and scientific, discarding superstition and blind obedience to Brahmans and encouraging a responsible attitude, and therefore offering a tool for the modernization and development of their 'backward' group.

In our interview in 2008, activist Rim Bahadur Sris (in Nawalparasi District) explained how he scolded people for indulging in 'superstitious behaviours':

> Why do you believe that goddess Sarasvati gives us knowledge? If you close all your books, and wait for some knowledge from her, do you expect to get it? If you separate a wife and a husband, and ask God for a baby, do you think he will give it? Nothing is impossible, but we need to work hard to obtain what we want, not relying on blind faith or on gods. In this new Nepal, we should understand that one must work and avoid bad actions in order to be happy and successful; Buddha teaches us that

we have to be responsible and not simply believe what we hear, but to experience personally whatever has been taught to us.

Changing the practices and new ritual specialists

As requested by their Kathmandu-based leaders, Magar and Tharu local activists started by addressing the practices of the villagers.[35] First, they asked them to abandon a series of Hindu practices: to stop performing animal sacrifices,[36] to stop calling the Brahmans for the celebration of costly rituals, and to stop celebrating Dasain, Nepal's most important Hindu festival. Dasain commemorates the victory of the goddess over the forces of evil symbolized by the buffalo demon Mahiṣāsura and on the eighth and ninth day of the festival, every Hindu household sacrifices animals (or a substitute). Janajātis interpreted the sacrifices at Dasain as expressions of Hindu high-caste domination and launched campaigns to boycott it (Hangen 2005, 2010: 144–51).

The second ritual step was the attempt to change the life-cycle rituals, by providing Buddhist substitutes. The Brahman was replaced by the Magar or Tharu lay ritual specialist, called *Uapa* for Magars and *Tharu Pandit* for the Tharus. These specialists celebrated cheap and more accessible life-cycle rituals following a Buddhist ritual handbook,[37] and read Pali suttas, translating them into Nepali for the audience. The handbook required some proficiency in reading Nepali and Pali, which explains why these ritual specialists were among the most cultivated people in their village (schoolteachers among the Tharus and retired soldiers among the Magars). Often their home hosted the only library of the village, full of free publications from Buddhist institutions in Taiwan, China or Malaysia, and also of magazines published by Nepalese Theravāda monks. Some of these *Uapas* and *Tharu Pandits* close to Buddhist monks were involved in meditation and in the study of Buddhist scriptures, and sent their children to Theravāda monasteries in the *vihāras* of Kathmandu Valley (Sri Kirti Vihar and Vishwa Shanti Vihar), to receive teachings.[38]

Their Buddhist practice transcended the ethnic group's boundaries: Magar *Uapas* often collaborated with *Tharu Pandits* and offered them their services, they invited Newar lay Buddhists and monks, and maintained links with a wider transnational network of Buddhist education.[39]

Many of these ritual specialists mentioned the difficulties they experienced in spreading their message in villages where Hindu traditions were strong and where festivals like Dasain were important social and cultural community events. For example, problems occurred at times of weddings when only one of the families of the bride or groom was already Buddhist and the other family insisted on having the usual Hindu ritual, or during the funerary ritual of *śrāddha*, where members of the family resisted changes, worried for the wellbeing of the spirit of the deceased and his or her safe transformation into an ancestor. In the words of *Tharu Pandit* Vasudev Choudhary:

> People suffer and they ask me in anguish where are the *piṇḍas* (small rice balls offered to the dead). I reply that to believe that one can recreate the body of a dead person by offering a *piṇḍa* is pure imagination. I tell them to free themselves from these imaginations and that the Buddha has taught us to doubt everything that has not been personally experienced. I tell them that they should concentrate on avoiding doing things that are harmful to others and to themselves, and on doing what is good to themselves and others. There are traditional families that hesitate to change, but when they are told that what they are doing is not really following their ancestors, sometimes they are convinced.

Except for the aspects more linked to ethnic claims, the Buddhist message sounded awkward to the majority of the villagers. They would listen to it because *Uapas* and *Tharu Pandits* were usually respected members of the community. If the person presenting the message to the villagers lacked the necessary authority, he risked being laughed at and marginalized. The news that important scholars had discovered that the Tharus and the Magars were Buddhists was certainly a source of authority. My own presence was sometimes cited in support for the shaky authority of some Tharu *Pandits,* who could show the villagers that the Buddhist cause was even attracting foreigner scholars.

Conveying the teachings through ritual

Where the community had already built a little Buddhist temple (usually called *gumba*), these Buddhist activists could organize the life of the little Buddhist community around it, and thereby created opportunities for some Buddhist rituals and teachings. For example, they invited the community to gather and recite the Five Precepts and the Three Refuges at Purnima and Aunsi (the days of the full and new moon) and at Buddha Jayanti (the festival celebrating the birth, enlightenment and passing away of Gautama Buddha). In a few places, the community began practising meditation at the temple instead of celebrating the Hindu festival of Dasain. Generally, however, ten-day vipassana meditation retreats and daily meditation played a negligible or non-existent role in the lives of the new converts in rural areas in contrast to urban middle-class Buddhist enthusiasts (LeVine and Gellner 2005: Ch. 8; Leve 2017: Ch. 6).

The exhortations and preaching of the *Uapa* and Tharu *Pandits* were usually delivered on the occasion of rituals. The *Uapas* and Tharu *Pandits* themselves said that they were not celebrating 'pure Buddhist rituals', whatever this might mean, but that they were performing them 'half-Hindu, half-Buddhist' in order to be more accepted by the community. They all agreed that these rituals had kept a Hindu structure and that, sometimes, the change consisted simply in replacing the Brahman with a Buddhist priest and replacing the Sanskrit mantra with the Pāli *sutta,* and that sometimes the only hint of Buddhism was the presence of an image of the Buddha in the ritual space.

During interviews in 2008, some Newar members of the YBS involved in the organization of the Buddhist camps expressed concerns about this ritualistic Buddhism with 'too much priesthood': on one hand, they agreed that Janajātis were 'dominated by Hindus' and it was necessary to substitute the rituals; one the other, they worried that Tharu and Magar Buddhists ritual specialists were acting 'like Brahmans' or like the Vajrācāryas (Newar Buddhist Tantric priests), who could celebrate a ritual but would not be able to give dharma teachings. They thought that Buddhism should not be chiefly identified with rituals, but should be seen as a philosophy, a mode of existential inquiry. In other words, their Buddhist modernist ideas (that Buddhism should be about introspection, meditation, and ethical care of the self) conflicted with their own Buddhist activism (which recognized the need to provide substitute rituals to wean their followers away from Hindu practices). During a conversation on this topic with the then President of YBS Triratna Manandhar, I observed that Newar Theravāda Buddhists *themselves* had replaced some Newar traditional rituals with Buddhist rituals of their own devising, and my interlocutor replied: 'we don't do offer a *substitution*: we bring the ritual to the teachings". He was right: for example, the vast majority of Theravāda Buddhists have replaced the traditional *bārha tayegu* puberty ritual for Newar girls with a cheaper ritual that includes Buddhist teaching in its programme (Kunreuther 1994, Hartmann 1996).[40]

Despite these concerns on the part of the activists, I noticed that in a number of instances the Tharu or Magar Buddhist performance of the ritual actions prescribed in the ritual handbook was also accompanied by anecdotes, moral teachings, and elements of Buddhist doctrine.[41] For example, in 2004 during a Buddhist Magar *śraddhā* ritual with a clear Hindu structure, the *Uapa* invited people not to cry and to be aware of the Buddhist truth of *anicca*, the impermanent nature of all things. He then told the famous Buddhist story of Kisa Gotami, a woman who had lost her only child and asked Buddha to help her, and to whom the Buddha replied that he could bring the child back to life if she could bring him a mustard seed from a house where nobody had ever died. She desperately went from house to house, but could not find a single one that had not suffered the death of a family member, and finally, having realized the universality of death, was ordained as a nun and eventually became an *arahant*.

During a camp of training for new *Uapas*, the instructor explained to the participants that a good *Uapa* has to know the Suttas and many Buddhist stories, and should provide Buddhist teachings during the funeral: during the funerary procession, the *Uapa* has to remind the bereaved family about the impermanence of all beings, and at the cremation *ghat*, the *Uapa* should give a teaching from the meditation on the decomposition of the body.

While their structures seem to have remained the same, the rituals were increasingly becoming an occasion for teaching the doctrine and by this fact changing both the nature of the ritual itself and of what was expected by the person attending it: as Leve (2002: 847) has noticed for traditional Newar rituals, 'the moral quality of the ceremony is located in the performance itself,' while the Theravada ritual of Buddha Puja 'is a mnemonic affirmation of moral intention,' an internalization of moral truth that requires obeying the discipline and embracing the Buddha's insights.

Conclusion

Buddhism reached Magars and Tharus through the Theravāda Buddhist revivalism among the Newars of the Kathmandu Valley. The political context that allowed the contact between the Newar activists and the Tharu and Magar activists was the campaign for secularism and the post-1990 rise of ethnic movements against state Hinduism and the dominance of the Hindu high castes. The distinctive form of Magar and Tharu Buddhism presented in this chapter brought together different aspects in its own genealogy: the transnational Buddhist modernist movement, which found echoes in the local modernist ideology of development, the influence of the domestication of Theravāda Buddhism in Newar society, the connection with a wider international Buddhist network, the claims for recognition of the ethnic group's specific identity and indigeneity, the rejection of Hindu rituals that affirmed a socio-political identity in the Hindu state, and the secular aspiration to de-Hinduize the state and establish an inclusive, multicultural and multi-religious Nepal.

Looking at the data, it is easy to identify contradicting values: to pass their Buddhist message to their groups, Magar and Tharu intellectuals and activists employed tools deriving from the dominant Hindu culture: rituals modelled on Hindu structure and the mythology of original Buddhism. This ethnic Buddhism seems to contradict Buddhist universal values. The Buddhist modernist idea of individual responsibility and autonomy of choice contrasts with the collective adoption of Buddhism by the national ethnic organizations, and with the affirmation of a natural or original Buddhism. The affirmation of a Buddhist ancestral past to justify the adoption of Buddhism is at odds with invitations to get rid of the tendency to blindly follow ancestral traditions. Thus, one can find somewhat contradictory messages in the activists' discourse: the activists tell the members of their group not to follow Hindu practices because they should not blindly follow ancestral traditions (and also because by doing so they are not *really* following their ancestors); instead, they invite them to become aware of the truth of an ancestral Buddhism and to adopt Buddhist practices accordingly.

What could be easily pointed at as a set of contradictions is in fact the result of the above-mentioned heterogeneous and complex genealogy of Tharu and Magar Buddhism. The Buddhist awakening and awareness responded to many different registers, claims and needs (ethnic identity, political emancipation, modernity and development, new religious aspirations).

These apparent 'contradictions' stem also from the fact that the awareness of the truth established by the intellectuals and preached by activists in the camps was working as a bridge between the past and the future: an awareness of the past that provided a change of consciousness, allowing political social and religious changes to be brought for the future. Importantly, the intellectuals and activists incarnated this process in their own lives, as they experienced a personal transformation through their endeavours and asserted the positive effect Buddhism had on their societies and on themselves.[42]

At the beginning, the Tharu and Magar shift to Buddhism was a nominal and a collective ethno-political move, but over time it brought about changes in ritual practices that contained the seeds for a deeper transformation of individual knowledge. These ritual transformations and the connection with a larger Buddhist network carried with them the potential to bring about a disconnection from the ethnic preoccupation and anti-Hindu activism so that the practice and proselytization of Buddhism could become a goal of its own (and allow the shift from a response to the question that characterized the renaissance of ethnicity: 'Who are we?' to a questioning of the individual in the Buddhist path).

When I once asked a Newar Buddhist active in the organization of Buddhist Awareness Camps for Janajātis why they were called 'awakening' (*jagaran*) camps, he responded laconically, 'because Nepali Buddhists are asleep.' He surely deplored the lack of Buddhist knowledge in both Newar and Janajāti communities. However, the Buddhists studied here were invited to awaken and to be aware of their foundational past to build their social and individual emancipation in the future.

Notes

1 I had the privilege to meet Professor Corrado Pensa in 1991, as a student of his classes of Eastern Philosophy at the University of Rome La Sapienza, attended by a crowd of enthusiastic students. His courses inspired me (and everybody else) profoundly and opened a world to our young and eager minds, to the point that we often brought friends and relatives to attend and share the joy and the inspiration. I soon attended also Professor Pensa's dharma teachings at A.Me.Co 'Associazione per la Meditazione di Consapevolezza' (Insight Meditation Association) – where we called him simply Corrado. The memories of these years in Rome are the dearest of my life and they sowed the seeds of my successive choices to start conducting research on religions in Nepal and eventually become a professor of South Asian religions. My greatest dream would be to be able to inspire and motivate my students as Professor Pensa motivated my younger self.

2 For the Theravāda movement within the Newar community see Kloppenborg 1977, Bechert and Hartmann 1988, Leve 2002, 2017, Gellner 2002, LeVine 2005, LeVine and Gellner 2005, Gellner and LeVine 2007.

3 See Gombrich 1988, McMahan 2008.

4 Bechert 1990, McMahan 2008.

5 Obeyesekere 1970, Gombrich 1988:174, Gombrich and Obeyesekere 1988: 5–6.

6 The conjunction of Buddhism modernism and Sinhala nationalist movement developed by Dharmapala in Nepal took the form of the conjunction of Buddhism and the affirmation of Newar ethnic identity (Gellner 1986), This conjunction split when Theravāda Buddhist activists started to appeal to Nepalese ethnic groups, which associated Buddhism and the assertion of their own ethnic identity.

7 See Zelliott 1992, Jondhale and Beltz 2004.

8 Ambedkar chose for his conversion the time of Dassehra (leaving Hinduism during the most important Hindu festival) and the year 1956, marking the 2500th anniversary of the *parinirvāṇa* according to the most accepted chronology.

9 Nepal hosted two of the World Fellowship of Buddhists annual conferences. Bhikkhu Amritananda, one of the first Nepalese *bhikkhus*, travelled to Theravāda countries,

to Mongolia and Vietnam, to establish contact with Buddhist institutions that might provide training for Nepalese novices (LeVine and Gellner 2005: 67). Nepalese novices received sponsorships from Buddhist institutions in Burma, Sri Lanka, and later in Thailand and Taiwan as well. These links abroad became essential to the growing order of nuns, who could obtain full ordination from the Foguang Shan sect in Taiwan (LeVine 2005: 64–71).

10 Gellner 1988, Letizia 2000, von Rospatt 2005.

11 Kunreuther 1994, Hartmann1996, LeVine and Gellner 2005: 65, Gellner 2010.

12 Since 1935, proselytizing and conversion have been prohibited under the civil code, which specifically forbade the spread of beliefs that 'ruined the religion traditionally practised by the Hindu community' (Gaborieau 1994: 63).

13 Constitution of the Kingdom of Nepal 2047 (1990): Part 3.19, Right to Religion. The article remained unmodified in the Interim Constitution 2063 (2007); the ban on conversion still appears in the current Constitution of 2015 and in Article 158 of the Criminal Code.

14 On secularism in Nepal, see Gellner 2001; Letizia 2011, 2016a; Gellner and Letizia 2016, 2019; Shneiderman 2018.

15 See Gellner 1997, 2003, Pfaff-Czarnecka 1999, Hachhethu 2003, Lecomte-Tilouine and Dollfus 2003, Hangen 2010, Toffin 2009.

16 After the UN declared 1993 as the year of the Indigenous Peoples, Janajatis started to stress their groups' indigenousness (Gellner and Karki 2008:110). In 2003 the term *ādivāsī*, 'indigenous people' was inserted and the organization's name was changed to Nepal Federation of Indigenous Nationalities, NEFIN (*Nepal Janajati Adivasi Mahasangh*).

17 At level of personal practice, however, many people who self-identify as Janajāti nonetheless identify themselves as practising Hindus.

18 Secularism was also one of the initial forty-point demands submitted by the Maoists to the government before the launch of the 'People's War' in 1996.

19 For the early history of the YBS, as told by its founders, see Smarika 2006.

20 For the politics of Buddhism in Nepal, see Gellner 2018. On the fact that all Nepalis are proud that the Buddha was born in Nepal and on the ways in which this claim is leveraged for divergent political purposes, see Dennis 2017.

21 Other Nepalese groups (and among them many Magars and Tharus) reaffirmed other traditional indigenous religions, like Kirant religion, Bon, shamanism, and 'natural religion' (see Schlemmer 2004, Lecomte-Tilouine 2010).

22 Some activists said that Janajatis were in Nepal before Aryan intruders came to Nepal bringing *varṇa* ideology and Hinduism. On the effort to represent identity in racial terms (opposing Aryans and Mongols) by the ethnic political party Mongol National Organization, see Hangen 2005 and 2007.

23 The idea of 'converting' or 'reclaiming' Dalits for Buddhism, as in India, has not been pushed or adopted as a policy by the Dharmodaya Sabha, the Buddhist Society of Nepal. The Newars, who controlled how Buddhism was represented in the country, accepted Janajātis as fellow Buddhists, but seemed uncomfortable with the idea of a big influx of Dalit Buddhists. Efforts to create coalitions of Janajāti and Dalits may have been impeded by the fact that the category of indigenous peoples excludes Hindu caste groups, which Janajātis argue, are non-natives originating from India (Hangen 2007: 20, 51).

24 For the development programs that aimed at transforming the consciousness of their participants, see also Leve 2007b.
25 For the Tharu Kalyankarini Sabha (Tharu Welfare Society), see Guneratne 2003: 139–188.
26 On the role and activity of these two Tharu intellectuals from Saptari District, who engaged in rewriting the history of the Tharus, see Krauskopff 2009a and 2009b. Both Panjiyar and Singh have passed away, but at the time of my fieldwork their family members continued their work: Ramanand Prasad Singh's son published books on Buddhism and Tharu history (Singh 2006, 2010), while some members of Panjiyar's family supported Buddhist activism in Udayapur District.
27 I have not followed contemporary developments, but a search on the internet reveals that both groups still refer to Buddhism in their self-presentation on websites and Facebook profiles. See among many examples the Facebook page 'Buddha belongs to Tharu tribe' https://www.facebook.com/buddha.tharu/ and the page of the Magar Buddha Sewa Samaj https://www.facebook.com/Nepal-Magar-Buddha-Sewa-Samaj-Kathmandu-Nepal-133158520188401.
28 This census activism is a response to the logic of pro-Hindu state activists, who argue that Nepal should be a Hindu state because 80% of Nepalis are Hindus.
29 The campaign was partially successful (with 25% of the Magars declaring Buddhism as their religion) but the adoption of Buddhism was not the only alternative available: many activists considered Magars as 'nature worshippers,' practitioners of the 'Religion of Nature.' For the opposition Naturism/Buddhism, see Lecomte-Tilouine 2009 and 2010.
30 Ambedkar (1948) recasts untouchables as 'broken men' who converted to Buddhism in A.D. 400 and were ostracized by Hindus, who punished their refusal to return to Brahmanism with the stigma of untouchability.
31 Ramanand Prasad Singh wrote in English, more for a local educated and foreign audience than for the members of his group, but later his writings have been translated into Nepali and widely distributed in the Tharu community (Choudhary, and Choudhary 1997) and also posted on Tharu websites like tharuculture.blogspot.com.
32 Ramanand Prasad Singh's son wrote a book along the same lines entitled *The Great Sons of the Tharus: Sakyamuni Buddha and Asoka the Great* (Singh 2006) and more recently wrote that 'the remnant of the Shakyas and Koliyas is the Tharu community of today, and the culture that was practised during the time of the Buddha is still followed by the Theravadin Tharus. It is the culture that helped to preserve their identity' (2010: 157).
33 Panjiyar translated into Tharu the *Grihi Vinaya*, the moral code for Buddhist lay people, written by Amritananda, one of the first Nepalese *bhikkhus* (Krauskopff 2009b: 263).
34 As Guneratne observes, the Tharus 'share no common cultural symbol, such as language, or religion, or even a common myth of origin on which they might anchor their imagining community' (1998: 752).
35 In an interview in 2003, Gore Bahadur Khapange, an influential politician and at that time president of the Nepal Magar Sangh, told me: 'The Nepal Magar Sangh said that Magars must be converted to Buddhism. Now we must work to implement this decision on the ground. The most important step is to replace the Brahmin. This is

the first duty of the Magars. If we do not change the content of the ritual, it is not so serious, the important thing is that the person celebrating changes.'

36 A very dynamic *Uapa* instructed his Magar Buddhist devotees to not perform sacrifices with arguments that proved to be very effective in convincing the villagers: 'sacrifice is like going to the doctor with a wound on the hand and having the doctor cutting your arm: you want to save your life, but you end up damaging yourself (your karma)'; 'if you really want to offer blood to your god, take some blood from your body with a syringe at the health post and offer it to the statue, in this way you will not take a life and the gods will be happy anyway.'

37 The handbook was written by Dharma Ratna Shakya, a Newar Buddhist scholar and social activist who played a key role in establishing the first curriculum for teaching Buddhism in Nepal (*Pariyatti Siksa*) (Shakya 2003, Gellner 2016). He wrote this book at the request of Janajāti leaders who were eager to change their rituals.

38 The role of these new Buddhist ritual specialists is strikingly similar to that of the Buddhist *pūjāri* of Ambedkar Buddhism in Maharashtra, where in many villages a local person such a schoolteacher who may have done a training course performs simple Buddhist *pūjās* in the *vihāra* and teaches Ambedkar Buddhism (Fitzgerald 1997: 228–229). This being said, at the time of my fieldwork I had no data referring to contacts between the Nepalese Buddhist activists and Ambedkarite ones.

39 The Buddhist Camps were financed with Taiwanese funds, books and ritual objects found in their houses and small monasteries were of Malaysian, Taiwanese and Thai origin. More generally, financial support for the development of Buddhism in Nepal, including the education of Nepalese monks and nuns overseas, was offered by Buddhist institutions from Burma, Sri Lanka, Taiwan and Thailand.

40 A Newar Theravāda monk interviewed in 2008 told me that he was worried by the anthropologist writings incorrectly suggesting that Theravādas were repeating the Vajrācārya (Tantric Buddhist traditional priest) model. He said: "we are not *purohit*. We are not offering substitution of traditional Newar rituals, as you can see by the fact that our rituals are *open* to everybody. We are not making any substitution, but we are just following the tradition of the temporary ordination that you can find everywhere in Theravāda countries".

41 The teachings given during the rituals and the camps were taken from the Buddhist literature that *Uapas* and *Tharu Pandits* receive from the Theravāda monasteries of Kathmandu (for example, Bhikkhu Amritananda's publication of Jātaka stories in Nepali booklets, or the translation by Dunda Bahadur Vajrāchārya of the Pāli canon in Nepali) or from the many free publications coming from Malaysia and Taiwan, in English or Hindi translation.

42 In Kathmandu Valley meditation centers *vipassanā* was presented to the participants both as 'an art of living which frees the mind from negativity' and a 'practice that develops positive energy for the betterment of the individual and the society' (LeVine and Gellner 2005: 218).

Bibliography

Ambedkar, Bhimrao R. 1948. *The Untouchables: Who Were They and Why They Became Untouchables*. New Delhi: Amrit book Co.

Bechert, Heinz 1990. 'Buddhistic Modernism: Its Emergence, Impact and New Trends.' *Business & Economic Review* 14: 93–104.

Bechert, Heinz and Jens-Uwe Hartmann 1988. 'Observations on the Reform of Buddhism in Nepal.' *Journal of the Nepal Research Centre* 8: 1–30.

Dennis, Dannah 2017. 'Mediating Claims to Buddha's Birthplace and Nepali National Identity.' In Udupa, S. and S. McDowell, eds. *Media as Politics in South Asia*, 176–189. London: Routledge.

Fitzgerald, Timothy 1997. 'Ambedkar Buddhism in Maharashtra.' *Contributions to Indian Sociology*, N.S. 31.2: 226–251. https://doi.org/10.1177/006996697031002003

Fujikura, Tatsuro 2011. 'Discourse of Awareness. Notes for a Criticism of Development in Nepal.' *Studies in Nepali History and Society* 6.2: 271–313.

Fujikura, Tatsuro 2013. *Discourse of Awareness: Development, Social Movements, and the Practices of Freedom in Nepal*. Kathmandu: Martin Chautari.

Gaborieau, Marc 1994. 'Une affaire d'État au Népaldepuis deux siècles: le Prosélytism Echrétien et Musulman.' *Archives des sciences sociales des religions* 87.1:57–72. https://doi.org/10.3406/assr.1994.1455

Gellner, David N. 1986. 'Language, Caste, Religion, and Territory: Newar Identity Ancient and Modern.' *European Journal of Sociology* 27: 102–48. https://doi.org/10.1017/S0003975600004549

Gellner, David N. 1988. 'Monastic Initiation in Newar Buddhism and Hinduism.' In Gombrich R. F. ed. *Indian Ritual and its Exegesis*. Vol. 2.1, 43–112. Bombay: Oxford University Press.

Gellner, David N. 1992. *Monk, Householder, and Tantric Priest: Newar Buddhism and its Hierarchy of Ritual*. New York: Cambridge University Press.

Gellner, David N. 1997. 'Ethnicity and Nationalism in the World's only Hindu State'. In Gellner, D. N., Pfaff-Czarnecka, J. and J. Whelpton, eds. *Nationalism and Ethnicity in a Hindu Kingdom: The politics of culture in contemporary Nepal*. Amsterdam: Harwood.

Gellner, David N. 2001. 'Studying Secularism, Practising Secularism. Anthropological Imperatives.' *Social Anthropology* 9: 337–340. https://doi.org/10.1111/j.1469-8676.2001.tb00160.x

Gellner, David N. 2003. 'Introduction: Transformation of the Nepali state.' In *Resistance and the State: Nepalese Experiences*, 1–30. New Delhi: Social Science Press.

Gellner, David N. 2010. 'Initiation as a Site of Cultural Conflict among the Newars.' In A. Zotter and C. Zotter eds. *Hindu and Buddhist Initiations in India and Nepal*, 167–181. Wiesbaden: Harrassowitz Verlag.

Gellner, David N. 2016. 'Scholar, Reformer and Activist. Dharma Ratna.' In Samuels, J. McDaniel J. T., and M. M. Rowe eds. *Figures of Buddhist Modernity in Asia*, 50–53. Honolulu: University of Hawaii Press.

Gellner, David N. 2018. 'Politics of Buddhism in Nepal.' *Economic and Political Weekly* LIII/ 3:17–20.

Gellner, David N. 2019. 'Masters of Hybridity: How Activists Reshaped Nepali Society.' JRAI 25/2: 265–282. Open access at: https://onlinelibrary.wiley.com/doi/full/10.1111/1467-9655.13025. https://doi.org/10.1111/1467-9655.13025

Gellner, D. N. and M. B. Karki 2008. 'Democracy and Ethnic Organizations in Nepal.' In Gellner D. N. and K. Hachhethu eds. *Local democracy in South Asia: microprocesses of democratization in Nepal and its neighbours*, 105–27. New Delhi: Sage Publications.

Gellner, D. N., S. L. Hausner, and C. Letizia eds. 2016. *Religion, Secularism, and Ethnicity in Contemporary Nepal*. New Delhi: OUP.

Gellner, D. N., and C. Letizia 2016. 'Introduction: Religion and Identities in Post-Panchayat Nepal.' In Gellner, D. N., S. L. Hausner, and C. Letizia eds. *Religion, Secularism, and Ethnicity in Contemporary Nepal*, 1–32. New Delhi: OUP.

Gellner, D. N. and C. Letizia 2019. 'Hinduism in the Secular Republic of Nepal.' In Brekke T. ed. *The Oxford History of Hinduism: Modern Hinduism*, 275–304. New Delhi: OUP.

Gombrich, Richard 1988. *Theravāda Buddhism: A Social History from Ancient Benares to Modern Colombo*. London: Routledge.

Gombrich, R. and G. Obeyesekere 1988. *Buddhism Transformed: Religious Change in Sri Lanka*. Princeton: Princeton University Press.

Guneratne, Arjun 1998. 'Modernization, the State, and the Construction of a Tharu Identity in Nepal.' *Journal of Asian Studies* 57/3: 749–773. https://doi.org/10.2307/2658740

Guneratne, Arjun 2003. *Many Tongues, One People: The Making of Tharu Identity in Nepal*. Ithaca-London: Cornell University Press.

Hachhethu, Krishna 2003. 'Democracy and Nationalism: Interface Between State and Ethnicity in Nepal.' *Contribution to Nepalese Studies* 30.2:217–252.

Hangen, Susan I. 2005. 'Race and the Politics of Identity in Nepal'. *Ethnology* 44/1:49–64. https://doi.org/10.2307/3773959

Hangen, Susan I. 2007. *Creating a 'New Nepal': The Ethnic Dimension*. Washington, D.C.: East-West Center Washington.

Hangen, Susan I. 2010. *The Rise of Ethnic Politics in Nepal: Democracy in the Margins*. Abingdon: Routledge.

Hartmann, Jens-Uwe 1996. 'Cultural Change Through Substitution: Ordination Versus Initiation in Newar Buddhism'. In Lienhard S. ed., *Change and Continuity: Studies in the Nepalese Culture of the Kathmandu Valley*, 355–365. Torino: Edizioni Dell'Orso.

HBEF Newsletter. 1996. *The Newsletter of Himalayan Buddhist Education Foundation* 1. Chakupat-Lalitpur-Kathmandu: M.B. Shakya.

Jondhale, Surendra and Johannes Beltz, eds. 2004. *Reconstructing the World: B. R. Ambedkar and Buddhism in India*. New Delhi: Oxford University Press.

Kloppenborg, Ria 1977. 'Theravāda Buddhism in Nepal.' *Kailash* 5.4: 301–322.

Krauskopff, Gisèle 2003. 'An "Indigenous Minority" in a Border Area: Tharu Ethnic Associations, NGOs, and the Nepali State.' In Gellner D. N. ed., *Resistance and the State*: *Nepalese Experiences*, 199–243. New Delhi: Social Science Press.

Krauskopff, Gisèle 2009a. 'Intellectuals and Ethnic Activism: Writings on the Tharu Past.' In Gellner D. N. ed. *Ethnic Activism and Civil Society in South Asia*, 241–268. New Delhi: Sage Publications.

Krauskopff, Gisèle 2009b. 'Descendants du Bouddha. La Construction d'un passé bouddhiste par des Intellectuelstharu (Népal)'. In Krauskopff G. ed. *Les faiseursd'histoires. Politique de l'origine et écrits sur le passé*, 247–274. Nanterre: Société d'Ethnologie.

Kunreuther, Laura 1994. 'Newar Traditions in a Changing Culture: An Analysis of Two Pre-pubescent Rituals for Girls.' In Allen M. ed. *Anthropology of Nepal: Peoples, Problems and Processes*, 339–48. Kathmandu: Mandala Book Point.

Lecomte-Tilouine, Marie 2002. 'La désanskritisation des Magar; ethno-histoire d'un groupe sans histoire.' In Carrin M., and C. Jaffrelot ed. *Tribus et basses castes. Résistance et autonomie dans la sociétéindienne* (Purusartha 23), 297–327. Paris: Éditions de l'EHESS.

Lecomte-Tilouine, Marie 2009. 'Ruling Social Groups—From Species to Nations: Reflections on Changing Conceptualizations of Caste and Ethnicity in Nepal.' In Gellner D. N. ed. *Ethnic Activism and Civil Society in South Asia*, 291–336. New Delhi: Sage Publications.

Lecomte-Tilouine, Marie 2010. 'To be More Natural than Others. Indigenous Self-determination and Hinduism in the Himalayas.' In Lecomte-Tilouine M. ed. *An Exploration of the Categories of Nature and Culture in Asia and the Himalayas* 118–155. New Delhi: Social Science Press.

Lecomte-Tilouine M. and P. Dollfus eds. 2003. *Ethnic Revival and Religious Turmoil in the Himalayas*. New Delhi: Oxford University Press.

Letizia, Chiara 2000. 'Le Rite d'Initiation Monastique (bare chuyegu) chez les Hautes Castes Bouddhistes Néwar dans la Vallée de Katmandou.' *Studi e Materiali di Storia delle Religioni* 66.2: 317–362.

Letizia, Chiara 2005. 'Retournerau Bouddhisme Moderne Desorigines: Remarques sur la Diffusion du bouddhisme Theravada chez les Tharu et les Magar du Népal.' *Annales de la Fondation Fyssen* 20: 69–78.

Letizia, Chiara 2007. 'La Costruzione di un'Identità Buddhista in Nepal: l'Esempio dei Tharu e dei Magar.' In Malighetti R. ed. *Politiche dell'identità*, 45–73. Roma: Meltemi Editore.

Letizia, Chiara 2011. 'Shaping Secularism in Nepal.' *European Bulletin of Himalayan Research* 39: 66–104.

Letizia, Chiara 2014. 'Buddhist Activism, New Sanghas, and the Politics of Belonging among Some Tharu and Magar Communities of Southern Nepal.' In Toffin, G.

and J. Pfaff-Czarnecka eds., *Facing Globalization in the Himalayas: Belonging and the Politics of the Self*, 289–325. New Delhi: Sage.

Letizia, Chiara 2016a. 'Ideas of Secularism in Contemporary Nepal.' In Gellner, D. N., S. L. Hausner and C. Letizia eds. *Religion, Secularism, and Ethnicity in Contemporary Nepal*, 35–76. New Delhi: OUP.

Letizia, Chiara 2016b. 'Buddha was Tharu?' In Samuels, J., M. Rowe, and J. McDaniel eds. *Figures of Buddhist Modernity in Asia*, 88–91. Honolulu: University of Hawaii Press.

Leve, Lauren 2002. 'Subjects, Selves and the Politics of Personhood in Theravada Buddhism in Nepal.' *The Journal of Asian Studies* 61.3: 833–860. https://doi.org/10.2307/3096348

Leve, Lauren 2007a. '"Secularism is a Human Right!" Double-Binds of Buddhism, Democracy, and Identity in Nepal'. In Goodale, M. and S. E. Merry eds. *The Practice of Human Rights: Tracking Law Between the Global and the Local*, 78–113. Cambridge: CUP.

Leve, Lauren 2007b. '"Failed Development" and Rural Revolution in Nepal: Rethinking Subaltern Consciousness and Women's Empowerment.' *Anthropological Quarterly* 80.1: 127–172. https://doi.org/10.1353/anq.2007.0012

Leve, Lauren 2017. *The Buddhist Art of Living in Nepal: Ethical Practice and Religious Reform*. London: Routledge.

LeVine, Sarah 2005. 'The Theravada Domestic Mission in Twentieth-Century Nepal.' In Learman, Linda ed. *Buddhist Missionaries in the Era of Globalization*, 51–76. Honolulu: University of Hawaii Press.

LeVine, Sarah and David N. Gellner 2005. *Rebuilding Buddhism: The Theravada Movement in Twentieth-Century Nepal*. Cambridge MA: Harvard University Press.

McMahan, David L. 2008. *The Making of Buddhist Modernism*. Oxford: Oxford University Press.

Pfaff-Czarnecka, Joanna 1999. 'Debating the State of the Nation: Ethnicisation of Politics in Nepal-A position paper.' In J. Pfaff-Czarnecka et al. eds. *Ethnic Futures*, 41–98. New Delhi: Sage.

Pfaff-Czarnecka, Joanna 2008 1997. 'Vestiges and Visions: Cultural Change in the Process of Nation-Building in Nepal.' In Gellner, D. N., J. Pfaff-Czarnecka, and J. Whelpton (eds.) *Nationalism and Ethnicity in Nepal*, 419–70. Kathmandu: Vajra [First ed. Harwood, 1997].

Pigg, Stacy Leigh 1992. 'Inventing Social Categories Through Place: Social Representations and Development in Nepal.' *Comparative Studies of Society and History* 34.3: 491–513. https://doi.org/10.1017/S0010417500017928

Pigg, Stacy 1996. 'The Credible and the Credulous: The Question of 'Villagers' Beliefs' in Nepal.' *Cultural Anthropology* 11.2: 160–201. https://doi.org/10.1525/can.1996.11.2.02a00020

Schlemmer, Grégoire 2004. 'New Past for the Sake of a Better Future: Re-inventing the History of the Kirant in East Nepal.' *European Bulletin of Himalayan Research* 25–26: 119–144.

Shakya, Dharma Ratna 'Trisuli.' 2003 (2060 BS). *Bauddha samskar paddhati* (Handbook of Buddhist rituals). Butwal: Nepal Magar Bauddha Seva Samaj.

Shakya, K. M. 2006 (2063 B.S.). 'Yuba Bauddha Samuhara Dharma nirapeksa-koabhyana (The Youth Buddhist Group and the campaign for secularization)'. Smarika, Kathmandu: Dev Ranjit.

Shakya, K. M. 2008. 'Foreign Aid, Democracy, and Development: Personal Experiences.' In Gellner D. N. and K. Hachhethu eds. *Local democracy in South Asia: microprocesses of democratization in Nepal and its neighbours*, 258–275. Delhi: Sage.

Shneiderman, Sara 2018. 'Temple Building in Secularising Nepal: Materializing Religion and Ethnicity in a State of Transformation.' In Iqtidar, H. and T. Sarkar eds. *Tolerance, Secularization and Democratic Politics in South Asia*, 75–107. Cambridge: Cambridge University Press.

Singh, Ramanand Prasad 1988. *The Real Story of the Tharus*. Kathmandu-Lalitpur: Tharu Samskriti.

Singh Subodh K. 2006. *The Great Sons of the Tharus*: *Sakyamuni Buddha and Asoka the Great*. Kathmandu: Babita Singh.

Singh Subodh K. 2010. *Community that Changed Asia*. Lalitpur: Babita Singh.

Smarika (Souvenir). 2006 (2063 B.S. 1127 N.S.). *Special issue* published on the 25 years anniversary of Yuba Bauddha Samuha, Kathmandu: Dev Ranjit.

Thapa Magar, M. S. 2002 (2059 B.S.). *Prachinmagarraakkhalipi* (Ancient Magars and the *akkha* script). Lalitpur: Briji Prakasan. (1st ed. 1992, 2049 BS).

Toffin, Gérard 2009. 'The *Janajati/Adivasi* Movement in Nepal: Myths and Realities of Indigeneity.' *Sociological Bulletin* 58.1: 25–42. https://doi.org/10.1177/0038022920090103

Von Rospatt, Alexander 2005. 'The Transformation of the Monastic Ordination (*pravrajyā*) into a Rite of Passage in Newar Buddhism.' In Gengnagel, J., U. Hüsken and S. Raman eds. *Words and Deeds*: *Hindu and Buddhist Rituals in South Asia*, 199–234. Wiesbaden: Harassowitz.

Whelpton, John 2008 (1997). 'Political Identity in Nepal: State, Nation, and Community.' In Gellner, D. N., J. Pfaff-Czarnecka, and J. Whelpton, eds. *Nationalism and Ethnicity in Nepal*. Kathmandu: Vajra. [First ed. Harwood, 1997].

Zelliott, Eleanor 1992. *From Untouchable to Dalit*: *Essays on the Ambedkar Movement*. New Delhi: Manohar.

Author biography

Chiara Letizia is Professor of South Asian Religions at the Université du Québec à Montréal (UQAM). She has been conducting fieldwork on religion and society in contemporary Nepal since 1997, focusing on religion and politics, ethno-religious activism, the meaning and implementation of secularism, and the role of the courts in reforming religious practices. She is the author of *La dea bambina: Il culto della Kumari e la regalità in Nepal* (FrancoAngeli, 2003) and the co-editor of *Religion, Secularism and Ethnicity in Contemporary Nepal* (Oxford University Press, 2016) and of *Wind Horses: Tibetan, Himalayan, and Mongolian Studies* (Università degli Studi di Napoli 'L'Orientale', 2019).

Chapter 4

An Unshakeable Awareness: *Siddhas* and *Jīvanmukti* According to the *Mokṣopāya*[1]

Bruno Lo Turco

This study aims to return to the topic of the 'liberation while living' (*jīvanmukti*) in the *Mokṣopāya* ('The way to liberation'), a huge philosophical work in verse composed around the 9th–10th century in Kashmir (Lo Turco 2002b; Slaje 2005), and to add some details that may have been previously neglected. In particular, the chapter (*sarga*) 6.259 (≈ *Yogavāsiṣṭha* [YV/ed.] 7.102) along with Bhāskarakaṇṭha's commentary (*Ṭīkā*)[2] are edited and translated here for the first time.[3] The *Mokṣopāya* (MU) revolves around the idea of *cidākāśa* (literally 'consciousness-space'), the all-pervasive principle that is absolute, inasmuch as it is consciousness (*cit*), and at the same time empty, inasmuch as it is space (*ākāśa*) (Lo Turco 2015: 25–28). This vision shows obvious contact points with both the non-dualist Śaiva tradition of Kashmir and the Buddhist schools of the Śūnyavāda and the Vijñānavāda, although, in actual fact, the work does not declare an affiliation with either of them, nor can its doctrine be simply assimilated to them (Hanneder 2006: 136–156). The teaching method of the MU consists in alternating doctrinal exposition with tales (*upākhyāna*) intended to illustrate that exposition (Lo Turco 2005a: 207–210). The MU was roughly revised in order to bring it into line with the Brahmanic-Vedāntic orthodoxy (Hanneder 1998; Slaje 2001). Such a revision has turned it into the *vulgata* or YV, well-known especially through Śāstrī Paṇśīkar's edition (YV/ed.), which dates back a century. Thus, two traditions of transmission of the text are known to us: the first, known as MU and relatively free of Brahmanic-Vedāntic amendments, made use prevalently of the Śāradā script and is connected to the commentary *Mokṣopāyaṭīkā* of Bhāskarakaṇṭha (17th century); the second, known as YV, is characterized by the predominant use of the Devanāgarī script and is connected to the commentary *Vāsiṣṭhamahārāmāyaṇatātparyaprakāśa* of Ānandabodhendra Sarasvatī (17th–18th century) (Slaje 1994, 1996).

A propensity to incorporate typical Buddhist teachings was recognised in the work at an early stage of research (Divanji 1935: 29). In fact, the philosophy attributed to Vasiṣṭha in the work does not come from the orthodox tradition on Vasiṣṭha or any other *ṛṣi* (Bhattacharya 1925: 546). There is no specific attack on teachings that are unorthodox from the Brahmanic point of view; the Buddha is held in high regard[4]. After all, the most frequently mentioned *vāda* is the Buddhist one (Slaje 1992: 310). The work seems to involve, moreover, the ineffability (*anākhyeyatā* or *anirdeśyatā*) typically associated with Buddhism (YV/ed. 3.10.39 ≈ MU[III]10.39; YV/ed. 7.104.41 ≈ MṬ[VIb]263.41; cf. Bhattacharya 1948: 204). Typical Buddhist terms, such as *śūnya* (see below, v. 4), *tṛṣṇā* (below, v. 7), *karuṇā* (below, v. 23), are often found in the work. Mainkar (1955: 99, 134–138, 146, 161) also claims that the YV, initially inspired by an Upaniṣadic context, was reworked by a Kashmiri Buddhist author, and took the name of MU at this stage. This author is allegedly influenced, above all, by the *Laṅkāvatārasūtra* (LS), even if he shows a good knowledge of most of the Buddhist schools. The LS (2.35.157, 2.42.166) teaches that only the mind (*citta*) is real, denying the existence of an external world, which is therefore similar to a mirage. The non-existence of the world is explained through a series of analogies, like the iridescent net seen by pressing the eye with the finger (*keśoṇḍuka, keśoṇḍraka*) (LS 2.148) or the child of a barren woman (*vandhyāputra*) (LS 2.164), which are in the repertoire of the YV as well (see e.g., MṬ[VIa]200.18; MṬ[VIa]196.7). Furthermore, the YV (ed. III.5.6 = MU[III]5.6; MṬ[VIa]195.4) often mentions a specific Buddhist school, the Vijñānavāda, with which it seems to be well-acquainted, as long noted (Atreya 1932: 17).

The most substantial Buddhist influence, in fact, derives from the Vijñānavāda, to such an extent that Dasgupta (1932: 231) claims that the doctrine of the work may be taken as a 'Brahmanical modification of the Buddhist idealism.' In particular, Atreya (1936: 298) observes that Vasiṣṭha's Brahmā arises out of the *brahman* spontaneously, similarly to how the *ālayavijñāna*, the function of which is similar to that of Brahmā, derives from the *tathatā* (YV/ed. IV.44.14–15 ≈ MU[IV]26.16bc–18ab). According to Dasgupta (1932: 272), the YV undeniably borrows from the Vijñānavāda, even if it shows a special relationship with Kashmir Śaivism. In reality, it is probably in the wake of the Vijñānavāda and Gauḍapāda, insofar as the latter appropriates Buddhist doctrines (cf. Hanneder 2006: 36), that the YV affirms a complete non-existence (*atyantābhāva*) of the world (MṬ[VIa]212.15)—a doctrine that Kashmir Śaivism would actually judge harshly. Finally, in the YV the echoes of Buddhist thought are so intense that it was even argued that the work was to be considered Buddhist in its origin and essence (Bhattacharya 1925: 546).

Nevertheless, according to Dasgupta (1932: 272), the YV, although influenced by various philosophical schools, displays a special connection with Kashmir Śaivism, which is supposedly evidenced by its doctrine of *spanda*, understood as 'immanent activity' (but cf. Lo Turco 2002a). Atreya (1936: 312) claims that the YV outlines the relationship between absolute consciousness and *śakti* in the same way as Kashmir Śaivism. Bhattacharya (1951a; 1951b: 91) maintains that the core of the text adheres to Śaivite non-dualism and has nothing to do with Śaṅkarian nondualism, which some scholars superficially considered an essential component of the text.[5] Mainkar (1955: 145–146) speculates that the YV originated within an Upaniṣadic school and later on underwent two revisions: the first under the influence of Buddhism, the second under the influence of Śaivism. Divanji (1959–1960: 49, 52–53, 57) is also convinced that the YV is characterised by a non-dualism closely related to that of Śaivite masters such as Vasugupta, Kallaṭa, Somānanda, more than to that of Gauḍapāda. While Gauḍapāda explains only briefly how the emergence of phenomena is possible within the only reality of the *brahman*, the YV seems to clarify it in detail by resorting to Kashmir Śaivism. It is not without reason that terms such as *cit* (e.g. MṬ[VIa]217.23), *cicchakti* (e.g. MṬ[VIa]227.18), *cetyonmukhatva* (e.g. MṬ[VIa]206.21), *kalanā* (e.g. MṬ[VIa]195.42), *ābhāsa* (e.g. MṬ[VIb]229.16), *unmeṣa*, and *nimeṣa* (e.g. MṬ[VIb]257.47), appear in the text. Thus, the YV mediates, allegedly, between the absolute idealism of Gauḍapāda and the teachings of Kashmir Śaivism or, more specifically, the Trika school.

The abovementioned studies on the work, which pinpoint a relationship between YV and Buddhism on the one hand, and a relationship between YV and non-dualistic Śaivism on the other, were mostly based on a text, the *vulgata*, that had already suffered a Brahmanic-Vedāntic revision, which is all the more reason to regard them as solid in relation to the recension that is relatively exempt from reworking, the MU, which exposes the futility of Brahmanical ritualism, along with *śruti* and *smṛti* (Slaje 1994: 57). Therefore, the co-existence of these two strands, Buddhism and Śaivism,[6] in the MU has been sufficiently proved. This concurrence is consistent with the teaching of a *siddha* (literally 'perfect one'), since the ambit of the *siddhas* is typically syncretic (White 1996: 80). Moreover, the *siddhas* typically display an anti-ritualist stance (Dowman 1985: 202). The chapter of the MU edited and translated here shows that the figure of the *jīvanmukta*, 'liberated while living', in the MU (e.g. YV/ed. 5.18.1–12; see Slaje 2000: 177; cf. Slaje 1998), also known as *puruṣottama*, 'superior man' (below, v. 1), or *jña*, 'knower' (below, vv. 17, 36), is perfectly comparable to the figure of the *siddha*, who never abandons a supreme kind of awareness and who, at the same time, lives an ordinary life; he can even belong to a low social class—being thus affected by severe impurity from a Brahmanic perspective—without flaunting his achievement (Dowman 1985: 2, 5–6). In the words of the chapter translated here (below, v. 15), although on the outside the *siddha* plays a role on the stage of the world, he never forgets, inside himself, his true nature (*svabhāva*). And what is this true nature? The last verse (62) answers the question: it is pure consciousness (*cinmātra*), which never vanishes, similar to space, and is still, eternal, welcoming. Indeed, the *jīvanmukta*, who clearly represents the highest model for the MU, is, precisely, a *siddha*—even if in the chapter below the word *siddha* itself appears only in passing (v. 57). After all, the MU/YV (e.g. 6.13) is familiar with *haṭhayoga* (Timalsina 2012: 304–305; cf. Divanji 1959–1960: 53), one of the main features of the *siddha* practice (White 1996: 5). Furthermore, the chapter below (v. 57) clarifies how the 'knower' can be, among other things, an expert on another cornerstone of the *siddha* practice: taking tablets (*gulikās*), which make it possible for the unbreakable subtle body to emerge from the material one (White 1996: 287), or which confer invisibility, one of the eight 'common powers' (*sādhāraṇasiddhi*). In the same verse, two other typical powers are mentioned (while the remaining ones are implied by *-ādi*, 'et cetera'): 'sword' (*khaḍga*), namely the power to overcome any enemy; 'eye ointment' (*añjana*), which confers remote viewing (Bhattacharyya 1932: 88).

Bhattacharya (1948: 203) was the first to put forth the hypothesis of a connection between the *siddhas* and the origin of the YV/MU. His observations were initially based mainly on the epitome generally known as *Laghuyogavāsiṣṭha* (which he called *Yogavāsiṣṭhasāra*). He subsequently confirmed this view, providing a more stringent analysis (Bhattacharya 1951b). He completely overlooked the chapter of the YV/MU presented here, which in any case would have corroborated his assumptions.[7] This chapter only serves to support the supposition that the MU originated from the preaching of a *siddha*-like figure.

Kalhaṇa (13th century), in his RT (5.66), the celebrated poem on the history of Kashmir, stated that for the sake of the people, at the time of the king Avantivarman (9th century), the *siddha*s, beginning with Kallaṭa, descended to the earth.[8] This is approximately the time when the MU, the origin of which is indeed situated in Kashmir, was composed (Divanji 1935; Lo Turco 2002b; Slaje 2005). Broadly speaking, the *siddha*s were semi-legendary figures of travelling ascetics and magicians who expressed themselves especially in *apabhraṃśa* (Dowman 1985: xv). The figure of the *siddha* arose as an innovative type of Buddhist model, heavily influenced by Tantric Śaivism, around the 5th century. From Kṣemarāja we learn that at the time of Vasugupta (8th–9th century) both Buddhist *siddha*s, like Nāgabodhi, and Śaivite *siddha*s, like Vasugupta, lived in Kashmir (ŚSV, p. 2).

In the chapter of the MU presented below, the reference to Buddhism is transparent. For example, the ultimate goal is defined as 'the other shore' (v. 50), which is the most typical Buddhist metaphor for *nibbāna* already in the Pāli Canon (see e.g. the *Alagaddūpamasutta*, MN n. 22, or the *Mahāmāluṅkyaputtasutta*, MN n. 64). The *siddha* represented an alternative ideal as against the monk or the devout layman. He was a Tantric adept who had reached his goal, namely *siddhi*, 'perfection': this can be understood in terms of either magical power or, most importantly, liberation while living, namely *jīvanmukti* (Dowman 1985: 4; White 1996: 2).

In this regard, it is essential to note that the MU retains traces of oral preaching. It presents itself as a *śāstra* that openly admits its human origin (Bhattacharya 1925: 548; Slaje 1994: 57 ff.). Several stanzas convey a homiletic discourse, directly addressed to an audience consisting of ordinary people, called *yūyam* (you), *janāḥ* (people), and then *mūḍhāḥ* (fools), *mahāmūḍhāḥ* (idiots) (Slaje 2001). This is also an argument in favour of a strong initial influence from a *siddha*, since 'siddha ... scriptures arose as preeminently social events" and originated from "performers, players, street preachers' (Davidson 2002: 238). Just as in the teaching of a *siddha*, in the MU the practical side, namely the method—not without reason the word 'method', *upāya*, is mentioned in the title itself—is pivotal. The value of the MU lies in its practical component, in the same way as the *siddha*s' teaching was predominantly practical. The teaching of the *siddha*s was not a vector of refined culture (Gnoli 1994: 51). On the contrary, sometimes it openly despised literary and philosophic culture. The *siddha*s made fun of the technical language of philosophy. Instead, their teaching was dense with images and symbols, and this constituted its fascination to many (Dowman 1985: 2, 9; Gnoli 1994: 51). In the context of its anti-intellectualism, the MU also overtly criticises all philosophical schools, or equates them all with each other (MU[III]96.42-51; Slaje 1992: 309 ff.). Its teaching is exceedingly rich in images and metaphors, which represent its most original ingredient (Lo Turco 2005b). Its method consists in constantly harbouring the awareness that the whole world is but space (MU[III]15.1). The notion of separateness of the object (*bhedadhī*) must be appeased through a constant exercise of meditation (*abhyāsayoga*) (MU[III]21.37), which should not be understood as "contemplation to be carried out sitting in a traditional yogic posture" (Slaje 2000: 178). Instead, the adept should at all times and in all situations cultivate the awareness that any object that arises in his consciousness can have no claim to objectivity, since, tautologically, it cannot but show itself within his consciousness (MU[VIa] 195.4). Thus, the knowledge of an object is the object (see below, v. 30): where, then, is the world? The world is empty (*śūnya*), since it is projected by imagination (*kalpanā*) (MU[III] 17.11-12). It is remarkable that the method does no more than anticipate the goal. The *jīvanmukta* is precisely the one who definitively knows—a 'knower' (*jña*)—that there is no world: liberation (*mokṣa*) means forgetting absolutely the object (*dṛśya*) as such (MU[III] 21.11).

The narrative structure of the MU appears to be comparable to that of the legends of the *siddha*s: Rāma's dissatisfaction with worldly matters is similar to the discontent of the typical protagonist of the legends; as in the legends a *guru* provides a cure, namely a *sādhana* (Dowman 1985: 13), so Vasiṣṭha instructs Rāma; in both cases the disciple achieves liberation in the end.

The MU refers to *siddha*s, understood mainly as a class of celestial beings (cf. Davidson 2002: 174), at every turn—apparently, the human *siddha*s shaped themselves after this semi-divine model (White 1996: 335). It would be impossible here to examine all occurrences of the term in the MU (e.g., [III]16.25; 18.33; 22.16; 24.5). This high incidence alone may be intended as an allusion. But then the *siddha*s are overtly celebrated (as in the story of Lavaṇa, YV/ed. 5.8, analysed in Bhattacarya 1951b: 99–100 and Stephan 2008; also, YV/ed. 6.161.38). What is even more striking is that sometimes a *siddha* appears in circumstances that are so strange that they must be a wink to the audience. For instance, in MU 6.250–251 (see MṬ[VIb]250-251) Vasiṣṭha, the narrator, after leaving his hut (*kuṭī*) in the sky (*ambara*), created through his volition, in order to travel with his subtle body, goes back to it, but he cannot see his own material body anymore. Instead, he sees a *siddha*, sitting in the lotus position, absorbed in *samādhi*, who has occupied the place. So Vasiṣṭha decides to leave. While he is leaving, the hut disappears unexpectedly, because of the dissolution of the volition that created it.

The *siddha*, now being supportless, falls down, still absorbed in *samādhi*. Vasiṣṭha wakes him by creating clouds that generate rain and thunder. So, the *siddha* flies back to Vasiṣṭha, who asks him who he is. He answers that he had been long wandering in the regions of the divine gardens. But then he had thought that he was overwhelmed by the waves of the sea of the *saṃsāra*. So, after much time, he achieved indifference towards heaven and deliverance. Then he came to that spot in the space, where he saw the hut. He thought that Vasiṣṭha's body had belonged to a *siddha* who had abandoned it in order to go to *nirvāṇa*. Vasiṣṭha admits that both of them, the *siddha* and he, did not reflect appropriately on the situation, otherwise even he would not have let the hut disappear. Vasiṣṭha urges the *siddha* to rise: they will dwell in the worlds of the *siddha*s (*siddhaloka*), the most appropriate abode for them. So, after making their obeisance, they fly away from each other. This incident is included in the Story of the Stone (Pāṣāṇopākhyāna), towards the end, but it is not justified in any way by the requirements of the narrative itself. If there had not been a *siddha* in Vasiṣṭha's hut, the point of the story would have been the same. Additionally, this character remains, unusually, nameless. When Vasiṣṭha asks him who he is (v. 250.27c), the *siddha* avoids saying his name. Perhaps, the original audience would have inferred a reference to a real person—the founder of the tradition? the author himself?—and guessed his name. Here Vasiṣṭha does not shrink from using the word *sādhana*, "means of accomplishment" (v. 251.5d), a term that explicitly relates to the context of the *siddha*s (Dowman 1985: 5).

As we have seen, the above episode takes place in the sky. According to the chapter of the MU shown below, a *jīvanmukta* can decide to go and live in the sky (v. 57), and one of the hallmarks of the *siddha*s is indeed their ability to fly to the sky and reside in it (Dowman 1985: 5; Davidson 2002: 195; White: 1996: 3). In the MU, the imagery of the sky or space or ether (*ākāśa*, *kha*, *ambara*, *nabhas*, *gagana*, *vyoman*) is amazingly abundant; it far exceeds imagery devoted to any other typical subject of poetic description. The sky is depicted as a realm of infinite possibility (Lo Turco 2001: 31–34; 2005a: 216).

As already mentioned, the family background and social status of the *siddha*s could vary widely. There were *siddha*s among 'kings and ministers, priests and *yogin*s, poets and musicians, craftsmen and farmers, housewives and whores' (Dowman 1985: 2). Thus, they transcended the world and at the same time lived in it. This is the same scenario described by the MU (below, vv. 54–58): the 'knower' can be a householder, a monk, a hermit, a learned man, a commentator or a hearer of the revelation or of the tradition, a prince, a Brahmin, an alchemist, an artisan, a lower-class man, a leader of Brahmins expert in the Veda, or the member of a mendicant order. Moreover, the *siddhas* challenged rules, rituals, and caste borders. Among them some 'were dissenters and anti-establishment rebels' (Dowman 1985: 2). Again, the knower of the MU can 'live as if he were ignorant', 'abandon the proper conduct', or 'perform foolish deeds' (vv. 56, 58). Dowman (1985: 6) reminds us that while the *siddhi* understood as liberation necessarily implies the *siddhis*, namely the eight supernatural powers, the possession of supernatural powers does not prove the attainment of liberation. The same idea is expressed in the chapter of the MU presented here (v. 32–35, 53): *mantras* and herbs give the adept the power to fly (cf. Rastelli 2000: 338, 343, 347, 349, 355), but that does not prove that he is a *jīvanmukta*. Moreover, compassion permeates the *siddha* (Dowman 1985: 10), and the *jīvanmukta* of the MU is caring (*vatsala*) and extremely compassionate (*karuṇākula*; below, vv. 7, 17).

According to Dowman (1985: 6) a *siddha*, through his powers, aims at demonstrating 'the nature of reality as a dream, an illusion, an hallucination'. This illusory nature of the ordinary world is also the central tenet of the MU, repeated countless times (Lo Turco 2001: 30–31), as well as in the chapter below (vv. 24, 36): the object of perception (*dṛśya*) is unreal (*asat*); this world (*idam*) is nothing.

The chapter of the MU presented here, after a couple of introductory stanzas, sets out the theme of paradox (vv. 3–8). For example, to the *jīvanmukta*, the worldly life (*vyavahāra*) is asceticism (*mauna*); the ordinary absence of concentration (*asamādhi*) is contemplation (*samādhāna*). All of these instances of *coincidentia oppositorum* are dependent, in the final analysis, upon the archetypal, paradoxical *coincidentia* between universal consciousness (*mahācit*) and world (*jagat*, *sarga*): the world is inseparable from consciousness as fluidity is from water (MṬ[VIa] 6.199.6). At the same time, the only reality is consciousness; the world as such is mere illusion (*bhrama*) (MṬ[VIa] 6.199.50; cf. Lo Turco 2001: 29–31). But then why, as asked on numerous occasions by the commentator playing devil's advocate, does the world keep manifesting itself (MṬ[VIa] *ad* v. 6.196.6)? A similar paradox is an integral part of the Buddhist *siddha* legends: emptiness is form and form is emptiness (Dowman 1985: 9–10).

In conclusion, I believe that serious consideration must be given to the possibility that the MU intends to propose the figure of the *siddha* as an ultimate ideal since it is itself the product of a *siddha*'s predication. Unfortunately, due to limited space it is not possible to consider all the implications of this possibility. Nonetheless, I am confident that the arguments that have briefly been put forward here allow for a reconsideration of the issue of the MU origin.

Text[9]

oṃ | śrīrāmaḥ pṛcchati
    parijñāte[10] pare vastuny anādinidhanātmani |
    sampadyate vada brahman kīdṛśaḥ puruṣottamaḥ ||1||
anādinidhana ādyantarahitaḥ | *ātmā* yasya | tādṛśe ||1||
śrīvasiṣṭha uttaraṃ kathayati
    śṛṇu sampadyate kīdṛg jñātajñeyo narottamaḥ |
    yāvajjīvaṃ kathaṃ caiṣa kimācāro 'vatiṣṭhate ||2||
spaṣṭam ||2||
    upalā asya mitrāṇi bandhavo vanapādapāḥ |
    janamadhye sthitasyāpi[11] svajanā mṛgapotakāḥ ||3||
svajanā bāndhavajanāḥ | etena mitrādiṣv asyopalādivad upekṣayā darśanam uktam ||3||
    ākīrṇaṃ śūnyam evāsya vipadaś cātisampadaḥ |
    sthitasyāpi mahāraṇye vyasanāny eva sūtsavaḥ ||4||
ākīrṇaṃ janabharitaṃ deśam | *sūtsavaḥ* praśasta utsavaḥ ||4||
    asamādhiḥ samādhānaṃ duḥkham eva mahat sukham |
    vyavahāro 'pi sanmaunaṃ karmāṇy evātyakarmatā ||5||
atiśayenākarmat*ātyakarmatā* ||5||
    jāgrad eva suṣuptastho jīvann eva mṛtopamaḥ |
    karoti sarvam ācāraṃ na karoti ca kiṃcana ||6||
akaraṇaṃ cātra leparāhityamātreṇa jñeyam ||6||
    rasiko 'tyantaviraso nirghṛṇo bandhuvatsalaḥ
    nirdayo 'tyantakaruṇo vitṛṣṇas tṛṣṇayānvitaḥ ||7||
spaṣṭam[12] ||7||
    sarvābhinanditācāraḥ sarvācārabahiṣkṛtaḥ |
    vītaśokabhayāyāsaḥ saśoka iva lakṣyate ||8||
*saśoka*tvaṃ ca pravāhāgate saṅkaṭe jñeyam ||8||
    tasmān nodvijate loko lokān nodvijate ca saḥ |
    param udvegam āpannaḥ saṃsṛtau rasiko 'pi san ||9||
spaṣṭam ||9||
    nābhinandati samprāptaṃ nāprāptam abhivāñchati |
    āste 'nubhūyamāne 'rthe na ca harṣaviṣādayoḥ ||10||
spaṣṭam ||10||
    anācāro 'sya cācāraḥ[13] sukhite sukhasaṅkathaḥ |
    āste sarvāsv avasthāsu hṛdayenāparājitaḥ ||11||
aparājito 'dīnaḥ ||11||
    karmaṇaḥ prakṛtād anyad asmai kiṃcin na rocate |
    svabhāva eṣa mahatāṃ na tu yatnaviceṣṭitam ||12||

eṣaḥ prakṛtarocanam | *yatnaviceṣṭitaṃ* yatnena ceṣṭākaraṇam ||12||

na lambhante rasikatāṃ na ca nīrasatāṃ kvacit |
artheṣu vicaranty arthād vītarāgāḥ sarāgavat ||13||

artheṣu kāryeṣu | *arthāt* paramārthena ||13||

yathāśāstraṃ vyavahṛtaiḥ sukhaduḥkhaiḥ kramāgataiḥ |
anāgatair ivāyānti na harṣaṃ na viṣāditām ||14||

spaṣṭam ||14||

samprahṛṣṭāś ca lakṣyante lakṣyante duḥkhitās tathā |
na svabhāvaṃ tyajanty antaḥ saṃsṛtyārabhaṭīnaṭāḥ ||15||

saṃsṛtir e*vārabhaṭī* | tasyāṃ *naṭāḥ* ||15||

ātmīyeṣv arthajāteṣu mithyātmasu sutādiṣu |
budbudeṣv iva toyānāṃ na snehas tattvadarśinām ||16||

arthajāteṣv arthasamūheṣu ||16||

asneha eva sughanasnehārdrahṛdayo yathā |
vatsalāṃ darśayan vṛttiṃ jñas tiṣṭhati yathāsukham ||17||

vatsalāṃ snehamayīm ||17||

vāyūn iva pravāhasthāḥ spṛśanti viṣayān budhāḥ |
dehasattāvaśān mūḍhā līyante viṣayodare ||18||

spaṣṭam ||18||

bahiḥ sarvasamācāram antaḥ sarvārthaśītalam |
nityam antar anāviṣṭa āviṣṭa iva tiṣṭhati ||19||

anāviṣṭo viṣayair āveśaviṣayatām anītaḥ ||19||

śrīrāmaḥ pṛcchati

svarūpam īdṛśaṃ tasya ko vetti munināyaka |
vada satyam asatyaṃ vā bhavaty ajño 'pi hīdṛśaḥ ||20||

svarūpaṃ svabhāvam | nanv īdṛśasvarūpāsatyatvam ayuktam eveti | atrāha *bhavatī*ti ||20||

aśvavad brahmacaryeṇa caranto 'cārucetasaḥ |
mithyā tapasvino dārḍhyād bhavanty evaṃvidhā api ||21||

brahmacaryeṇa brahmacāribhāvena | *caranto* 'dantaḥ | *acārucetaso*[14] 'śuddhamanasaḥ ||21||

śrīvasiṣṭha uttaraṃ kathayati

asatyam astu satyaṃ vā svarūpaṃ varam īdṛśam |
viddhi vedyavidāṃ tv eṣa svabhāvo 'nubhave sthitaḥ ||22||

varaṃ śreṣṭham | nanu katham etad iti | atrāha *vedyavidām* iti | *vedyavidāṃ* jñātajñeyānām | *tu* yataḥ | *anubhave sthito* 'nubhavaviṣayatāṃ gataḥ ||22||

anāviṣṭā viceṣṭante vītarāgāḥ sarāgavat |
gatahāsaṃ hasanty ajñān sahāsān karuṇākulāḥ ||23||

anāviṣṭā rāgādibhir āveśaviṣayatām anītāḥ | *gatahāsam* iti paramārthābhiprāyeṇoktam ||23||

cittādarśagataṃ dṛśyaṃ sarvaṃ kapaṭakuṭṭimam |
paśyanty asat parijñāte svapne hemeva hastagam ||24||

kapaṭakuṭṭimam asatyam | *asat parijñāte* 'satyam anubhūte ||24||

antaḥśītalatā teṣāṃ tāṃ na jānanti kecana |
dūrāc candanadārūṇām āmodam iva jantavaḥ ||25||

spaṣṭam ||25||

ye tu vijñātavijñeyās tādṛśāḥ pāvanāśayāḥ |
jānanti ca ta evāntar[15] aheḥ pādān ivāhayaḥ ||26||

tān iti śeṣaḥ | tāñ jñātajñeyān | *ta eva* jñātajñeyā eva ||26||

nanu te pareṣāṃ tām ātmanaḥ śītalatāṃ kiṃ na kathayantīti | atrāha

bhāvaṃ nigūhayanty eva te tam uttamam uttamāḥ |
grāmye 'rghati kilānarghaḥ kva cintāmaṇir āpaṇe ||27||

bhāvaṃ tattvam | *taṃ* śītalatārūpam | nanu kimarthaṃ nigūhantīti | atrāha *grāmya* iti | *grāmya* āpaṇe grāmasambandhinyāṃ niṣadyāyām[16] | *arghaty* arghayukto bhavati | kathyamānasyāpi bhāvasya ta ādaraṃ na kurvantīti bhāvaḥ ||27||

tasmin nigūhane bhāve yatnas teṣāṃ na darśane |
nirvāsanā gatadvaitā gatamānāḥ kilāṅga te ||28||

tasmin bhāve nigūhane tadbhāvaviṣaye gopane | nanu kimarthaṃ teṣām atra yatno 'stīti | atrāha *nirvāsanā* iti | *kila* yataḥ ||28||

ekāntamānadaurgatyajanāvajñaptayas tu tān |
sukhayanti yathā rāma na tathaitā maharddhayaḥ ||29||

mānadaurgatyaṃ mānarāhityam ||29||

tasya bhāvasya parān prati prakaṭīkaraṇe śaktatvam apy asya kathayati

svasaṃvedanasaṃvedyasārā viditavedyatā |
naiṣā darśayituṃ śakyā darśyate na ca tadvidā ||30||

svasaṃvedanena | yat *saṃvedyaṃ* bhāvapradhāno nirdeśaḥ saṃvedyatvam | tad eva *sāro* yasyāḥ[17] | tādṛśī | *viditavedyatā* lakṣaṇayā viditavedyatāvyabhicāriṇy antaḥśītalatā | *tadvidā* viditavedyena ||30||

guṇaṃ prakāśayāmy eṣa janaḥ pūjāṃ karotu me |
ity ahaṅkāriṇām īhā na tu tanmuktacetasām ||31||

īhā ceṣṭā | *tanmuktacetasām* ahaṅkārān muktamanasām ||31||

nanu tarhy ākāśagamanādinātiśayena te jñāyanta iti | atrāha

kriyāphalāni digvyomagamanādīni rāghava |
ajñānām api sidhyanti mantrauṣadhivaśād iha ||32||

spaṣṭam ||32||

yo yādṛk kleśam ādhātuṃ samarthas tādṛg eva saḥ |
avaśyaṃ phalam āpnoti prabuddho 'stv ajña eva vā ||33||

spaṣṭam ||33||

āmodaś candanasyeva spandanasya phalaṃ hṛdi |
sarvasyaivāsti tan nūnaṃ tadvatā samavāpyate ||34||

spandanasya kriyāyāḥ | *tat* spandanam | *tadvatā* spandanavatā ||34||

ahantāvāsanādvaitaṃ vastutā dṛśyavastuṣu |
yasyāsty asau sādhayati khagamādikriyāphalam ||35||

vastutety atra caśabdo 'dhyāhāryaḥ ||35||

idaṃ na kiṃcid bhrāntir vā khaṃ veti jñas tu vetti yaḥ |

so 'vāsanaḥ kām iva tāṃ kathaṃ sādhayati kriyām ||36||
spaṣṭam ||36||
naiva tasya kṛtenārtho nākṛteneha kaścana |
na cāsya sarvabhūteṣu kaścid arthavyapāśrayaḥ ||37||
arthavyapāśrayaḥ svaprayojanasiddhisthānam ||37||
na tad asti pṛthivyāṃ vā divi deveṣu vā kvacit |
yad udāramanovṛtter lobhāya viditātmanaḥ ||38||
udāramanovṛtter bhogākṛpaṇacittavṛtteḥ ||38||
jagad eva tṛṇaṃ yasya na kiṃcid raja eva vā |
kiṃ nāma tasya bhavatu nanūpādeyatāṃ gatam ||39||
spaṣṭam ||39||
nirvāhitajagadyātraḥ paripūrṇamanā muniḥ |
yathāsthitam asāv āste samprayāti yathāsthitam ||40||
nirvāhitā kṛtakṛtyatvena samāptiṃ nītā | *jagadyātrā* yena | tādṛśaḥ ||40||
nityāntaḥśītalo maunī sattvībhūtamanovaniḥ |
paripūrṇārṇavākāro gambhīraḥ prakaṭāśayaḥ ||41||
rasāyanaparāpūrṇahradavad dhlādam[18] ātmani |
dhatte karoti cānyasya sakalendur ivāmalaḥ ||42||
sattvībhūtaḥ sattvabhāvaṃ gatā | *manovaniś* cittabhūmir yasya | tādṛśaḥ | *parāpūrṇo* 'tipūrṇaḥ | *sakalenduḥ* pūrṇacandraḥ ||41-42||
mandāramañjarīpuñjapiñjarād eva bhūmayaḥ |
tathā nāhlādayanty[19] etā yathā paṇḍitabuddhayaḥ[20] ||43||
spaṣṭam ||43||
candrabimbair vasantaiś ca mahatām ahatāśayaiḥ |
sāraṃ saubhāgyasaundaryaṃ manye śikṣitam antikāt ||44||
sāraṃ śreṣṭham ||44||
bhrāntimātram idaṃ viśvam indrajālam asanmayam |
tyajatīti viniścitya dinānudinam eṣaṇāḥ ||45||
iti | kim *iti* | *bhrāntimātram* ityādi | *eṣaṇā* icchāḥ ||45||
śītātapādiduḥkhāni nijadehagatāny api |
anyadehagatānīva jñaḥ paśyaty avahelayā ||46||
*avahelayo*pekṣayā ||46||
karaṇodārayā vṛttyā dhṛtyā dhuryādridhīrayā |
nīraso nīrasārābhrasarasaṃ śirasi sthitam[21] ||47||
vyavahāraṃ yathāprāptaṃ lokasāmānyam ācaran |
carācarāṇāṃ bhūtānām upary evāvatiṣṭhate ||48||
dhuryaḥ śreṣṭhaḥ | yo '*driḥ* | tadvad *dhīrayā* dṛḍhayā | yugalakam ||47-48||
prajñāprasādam ārūḍhas tv aśocyaḥ śocato janān |
bhūmiṣṭhān iva śailasthaḥ sarvān prājño 'nupaśyati ||49||
śocataḥ svaviṣayaṃ śocanaṃ kurvataḥ ||49||
ciraṃ kallolavalitaḥ saṃsārajaladhau bhraman |
paraṃ pāram upāgatya parāṃ viśrāntim eti saḥ ||50||

kallolai rāgādirūpair mahātaraṅgaiḥ | *valita* āvṛtaḥ ||50||
hasan saṃśāntayā vṛttyā prāktanīr jāgatīr gatīḥ |
smayamāna ivāste 'ntar janatājaghanabhramāḥ ||51||
jāgatīr gatīḥ kathambhūtāḥ | *janatāsu* | *jaghano* 'varaḥ | *bhramo* yāsu | tādṛśīḥ ||51||
vatāvāntaranirmagnam[22] imāḥ saṃsāradṛṣṭayaḥ |
asatyo hṛtavatyo mām ity antar yāti vismayam ||52||
vate 'tikaṣṭe | *avāntare* bhogarūpe 'vāntaraviśrāntisthāne | *nirmagnam* ||52||
diṣṭyāṣṭaguṇam aiśvaryam[23] aniṣṭaṃ me tṛṇāyate |
ity upaity upaśāntatvāt smayamāno 'pi na smayam ||53||
spaṣṭam ||53||
kaścid giriguhāgehaḥ kaścit puṇyāśramāśrayaḥ |
kaścid gṛhasthāśramavān kaścit paṭuraṭan[24] sthitaḥ ||54||
spaṣṭam ||54||
kaścid bhikṣācarācāraḥ kaścid ekāntatāpasaḥ |
kaścin maunavratadharaḥ kaścid dhyānaparāyaṇaḥ ||55||
spaṣṭam ||55||
kaścid vipaścid vyākhyātā kaścic chrotā śruteḥ smṛteḥ |
kaścid rājā dvijaḥ kaścit kaścid ajña iva sthitaḥ ||56||
vyākhyātā vyākhyākārī ||56||
gulikāñjanakhaḍgādisiddhaḥ kaścin nabhogataḥ |
kaścic[25] chilpakalājīvī kaścit pāmararūpabhṛt ||57||
spaṣṭam ||57||
kaścit tyaktasamācāraḥ kaścic chrotriyanāyakaḥ |
kaścid unmattacaritaḥ pravrajyāṃ[26] kaścid āśritaḥ ||58||
spaṣṭam ||58||
puruṣo na śarīrādi na ca cittādi kiṃcana |
puruṣaś cetanaṃ nāma na sa naśyati karhicit ||59||
acchedyo 'sāv adāhyo 'sāv akledyo 'śoṣya eva ca |
nityaḥ sarvagataḥ sthāṇur acalo 'sau sanātanaḥ ||60||
iti samyak prabuddho yaḥ sa yathā tatra tiṣṭhati |
tathā tiṣṭhatu tatrātra sthānāsthāniyamena kim ||61||
spaṣṭam | tilakam ||61||
sargāntaślokena cinmātrākhyasya puruṣasya nāśarāhityaṃ kathayati
pātālam āviśatu yātu nabho vilaṅghya
diṅmaṇḍalaṃ bhramatu peṣaṇam etv agena |
cinmātram etad ajaraṃ na tu yāti nāśam
ākāśakośa iva śāntam ajaṃ śivaṃ tat ||62||
spaṣṭam | iti śivam ||62||

Translation[27]

Rāma asked:
1. Having entirely known the supreme reality, the essence of which has no beginning or end, say, O Brahmin, what the excellent man proves to be like!
Such that its 'essence' 'has no beginning or end', is free from beginning or end.
Vasiṣṭha replied:
2. Hear what the excellent man, who has known what had to be known, proves to be like, how he exists during his whole life, what his conduct is like!
Clear.
3. His friends are stones, his relatives are forest trees, his own people are young gazelles, even if he lives among people.
'His own people', kinsmen. By that it is stated that, by virtue of equanimity, it is as if in his friends etc. he saw stones etc.
4. Crowded is empty, adversities are prodigious blessings, even calamities are a good festival to him, who stays in the great forest.
'Crowded', a place filled with people. 'Good festival', propitious festival.
5. Agitation is meditative absorption, pain itself is great joy, even ordinary life is pious silence, actions themselves are extreme inaction.
'Extreme inaction', inaction par excellence.
6. Awake, he is immersed in deep slumber; living, he is like dead; doing all his duty, he does nothing.
And here the absence of action should be understood just as freedom from impurity.
7. Utterly tasteless, he is full of taste; ruthless, he is devoted to friends; pitiless, he is extremely compassionate; free from longing, he is endowed with desire.
Clear.
8. Endowed with all the approved conducts, he is stranger to all conducts; free from sorrow, fear, effort, he appears as sorrowful.
And the being 'sorrowful' should be understood in relation to a strait that has come from the flow.
9. The world is not agitated because of him and he is not agitated because of the world; even if fallen in a supreme agitation, he is delighting in the world.
Clear.
10. He is not pleased with what he has obtained, he does not long for what he has not obtained; he dwells in the object that he is experiencing and not in excitation or depression.
Clear.
11. His conduct does not follow the rules; he speaks nicely about nice things; he remains unconquered under all circumstances thanks to his heart.
'Unconquered', joyful.
12. He does not like anything apart from the action he has undertaken; such is the natural condition of the great, and not laborious action.
'Such', the act of loving what is being done. 'Laborious action', acting with effort.

13. They relish no circumstance and feel disgust for no circumstance; they live among things as if they were passionate, in fact devoid of passion.

'Among things', among worldly matters. 'In fact', in reality.

14. According to scriptures they do not get excited or sad because of the sequence of mundane joys and sorrows, as if these did not happen.

Clear.

15. They look excited and likewise they look sorrowful; actors of the dramatic representation of the world, inwardly they do not abandon their own nature.

'Actors' in that, the 'dramatic representation' that is the 'world'.

16. Those who see the reality have no affection for all their own things, sons etc., which are illusory, as if they were bubbles of water.

'All things', the totality of things.

17. The knower, totally without affection, lives comfortably showing a gentle disposition, as if he had a deeply affectionate tender heart.

'Gentle', full of love.

18. The wise, who stay in the course of action, touch the object as the winds; the stupid adhere to the interior of the objects on account of the [alleged] reality of the body.

Clear.

19. Inwardly always undedicated, he lives as if he were dedicated outwardly to every good conduct, inwardly to coldness towards all objects.

'Undedicated', who is not led, by objects, to the condition of object of the condition of being dedicated.

Rāma asked:

20. O leader of the sages, explain who can know if such nature of his is real or unreal! Since even the ignorant is such.

'Nature of his', his own condition. It might be objected that the unreality of such nature of his is unreasonable. With regard to this he says: 'Since even…'.

21. The evil-minded ascetics who graze, like horses, practicing the pious life, are falsely such, thanks to their perseverance.

'The pious life', the condition of one who observes the religious precepts. 'Who graze', 'who eat'. 'Evil-minded', impure-minded.

Vasiṣṭha replied:

22. Be it real or unreal, such intrinsic nature is superior. And know that this condition of his lies in the experience of those who have known what has to be known.

'Superior', the most excellent. It might be objected: how is that? With regard to this he says: 'And know that…'. 'Of those who have known what has to be known', of those for whom what has to be known is known. 'And', since. 'Lies in the experience', has entered the condition of object of experience.

23. Those who are not possessed, free from desire, act as if they had desires;[28] without laughing, they, full of compassion, laugh at the laughing ignorant.

'Those who are not possessed', not led to the condition of object of possession by attachment etc. 'Without laughing' is stated in terms of ultimate truth.

24. All the perceivable, which lies in the mirror of the mind, is a fake surface. They see the unreal in what is known, as a piece a gold held in hand in a dream.
'A fake surface', untrue. 'The unreal in what is known', the untrue in what is experienced.
25. No one knows their inward coldness, as people do not perceive the fragrance of sandal sticks from a distance.[29]
Clear.
26. But those who are such, who have known what has to be known, whose minds are pure, only they know inwardly, as serpents know a serpent's feet.
Supply 'them'. Them, who have known what has to be known. 'Only they', only those who have known what has to be known.
It might be objected: why do they not describe that coldness of the self to others?
27. Those excellent ones hide that excellent condition; the priceless gem that grants wishes is hardly priced in the village market.
'Condition', reality. 'That', the nature of which is coldness. It might be objected: what is the point of hiding? With regard to this he says: 'the priceless gem…'. 'In the village market', in the bazaar belonging to the village. 'Priced', provided with price. The implication is that they do not care about the condition that, however, is being discussed.
28. Their effort in respect of that condition is in hiding, not in showing; indeed, they are without inclinations,[30] free from duality, free from self-conceit.
'In hiding, in respect of that condition', in concealing, the object of which is that condition. It might be objected: what is the point of their effort to do that? With regard to this he says: 'they are without inclinations…'. 'Indeed', since.
29. As the lonely places, the poverty of self-conceit, the being ignored by people, Rāma, so not even these great powers cheer them up.
'The poverty of self-conceit', the absence of self-conceit.
He discusses also the capacity of that one to clarify that condition to other people.
30. This state of having known what has to be known, the essence of which is that the perceivable exists through one's own perception, cannot be shown and is not shown by the knower of that.
'State of having known what has to be known', in a broad sense the state of being inwardly cold, which does not deviate from the state of having known what has to be known; such that its 'essence' is that, 'the perceivable', the condition of being perceivable (the actual statement is based mainly on the activity expressed by the verbal root) that 'exists through one's own perception'. 'By the knower of that', by one for whom what has to be known is known.
31. Those who have the sense of 'I' strive to show their merit, and to be revered by people, while those whose thought is free from that do not.[31]
'Strive', struggle. 'Those whose thought is free from that', those whose minds are free from the sense of I.
It might be objected: then they are mainly recognized from their ability to go through the space. With regard to this he says:
32. O Rāma, even the ignorant achieve the fruits of action such as travelling in all direction of the space etc. by virtue of *mantra*s and herbs.
Clear.

33. One who is capable of laying a certain defilement obtains inevitably a corresponding fruit, be he completely awakened or totally ignorant.
Clear.
34. As the fragrance of sandal, the fruit of movement exists for everyone, in the heart; it is certainly achieved by one who has that.
'Of movement', of action. 'That', movement. 'By one who has that', by one who is provided with movement.
35. He for whom there is the duality of the inclination of egoity, objectivity in knowable objects, accomplishes the fruit of action such as wandering in space etc.
Supply the word 'and' before this: 'objectivity'.
36. But how could the knower who, being without inclination, knows that this world is nothing—or delusion or space—accomplish an action? What possible action?
Clear.
37. He has no aim at all with his action, not even with his inaction. And for him in all entities there is no place for an aim.
'Place for an aim', site for the achievement of his purpose.
38. For one who has known the self, whose state of mind is the highest, there is nothing anywhere that is object of greed, on earth, on heaven, or among the gods.
'Whose state of mind is the highest', whose mental state is free from the misery of enjoyments.
39. What could he, for whom the world is not even straw or dust, prefer then?
Clear.
40. The sage, whose mind is content, who has carried out his worldly affairs, abides when it is appropriate, moves when it is appropriate.
Such that by him 'worldly affairs' 'have been carried out', have been led to completion, since he has done what had to be done.
41–42. The sage, who is always internally cold, whose forest of the mind has become pure essence,[32] who has the form of a whole ocean, profound, whose mind is manifest, possesses in himself a delight, similar to a lake utterly filled with an elixir, and creates it for another, like the moon with all its digits.
Such that his 'forest of the mind', mental level, 'has become pure essence', has gone to the condition of pure essence. 'Utterly filled', overflowing. 'The moon with all its digits', the full moon.
43. The lands do not cause delight with the golden colour of the heaps of the coral tree flowers as much as these whose intellects are clever.
Clear.
44. I consider the teaching one achieves by the unsullied minds of the great, thanks to their proximity, as the precious beauty and happiness one achieves by moon-discs and springs.
'Precious', most excellent.
45. The whole Indra's net is mere illusion, made of non-existence. Having ascertained thus, he abandons his longings day after day.

'Thus'. 'Thus' what? 'The whole Indra's net' etc. 'Longings', desires.

46. The knower sees the pains of cold and heat etc. inside his body without any preoccupations, as if they were inside someone else's body.

'Without any preoccupations', with equanimity.

47–48. By virtue of a state of magnanimity, a firmness constant as that of a celebrated mountain, he, devoid of affections, above movable and immovable beings, continues to live normally the everyday life common to ordinary people, which, full of affections like a cloud full of water, hangs over the head.

'Constant', sound, in manner similar to that, a 'celebrated', most excellent, 'mountain'. Couple of stanzas.

49. Having reached the serenity of wisdom, the wise one, irreproachable, looks at all the people lamenting on the ground, as if he were on a peak.

'Lamenting', producing a lamentation the object of which is themselves.

50. Wandering for a long time in the ocean of the *saṃsāra* he, encircled by billows, approaches the other shore and goes to the supreme rest.

'Encircled', surrounded. 'By billows', by big waves consisting of attachment etc.

51. It is as if he continued to smile inwardly, laughing at the past worldly existences, with their vulgar people illusion, by virtue of his condition totally pacified.

'Worldly existences', being how? Such that in it there is a 'vulgar', low, 'illusion', among 'people'.

52. He is pleasantly surprised inwardly, thinking: 'these false visions of the *saṃsāra* overwhelmed me, sunk into a painful intermediate state.'

'Sunk' into a 'painful', terrible, 'intermediate state', condition of standstill in an intermediate state, which consists of enjoyments.

53. Whilst smiling thanks to his tranquility, he does not become arrogant thinking: 'Fortunately the eightfold superhuman power, undesirable, is like a straw to me'.[33]

Clear.

54. Someone has the mountain caves as his home; someone has the Puṇyāśrama as his shelter; someone is in the stage of life of a householder; someone continues to shout shrilly.[34]

Clear.

55. Someone follows the conduct of a monk; someone is a hermit; someone observes a vow of silence; someone is devoted to meditation.

Clear.

56. Someone is a learned man; someone is a commentator or a hearer of the revelation or of the tradition; someone is a prince; someone a Brahmin; someone lives as if he were ignorant.

'A commentator', an author of commentaries.

57. Someone is thoroughly versed in pills, ointments, swords etc.; someone has gone to the sky; someone is an artisan; someone has the figure of a lower-class man.

Clear.

58. Someone has abandoned the proper conduct; someone is a leader of Brahmins expert in the Veda; someone performs foolish deeds; someone entered a mendicant order.

Clear.

59–61. The subject is not the body etc. and not any mind etc.; indeed, the subject is conscious activity; he does not dissolve at any time; he is indivisible, he is just impermeable and undryable; he is constant, all-pervading, steady, immovable, eternal. Thus, in which manner the completely awakened one remains in his condition, in that manner he should remain in his condition; what does the restraint caused by the regard for a certain worldly position matter?

Clear. Group of three stanzas.

With the last stanza of the chapter, he explains that the subject, known as pure consciousness, is free from dissolution.

62. Let him fall into hell; having crossed it, let him go to the sky; let him wander around the compass; let him be crushed by a stone! Still, this undecaying pure consciousness does not dissolve; like the receptacle of space, it is quiescent, not born, benign.

Clear.

Notes

1 I owe my interest in Indian thought entirely to Prof. Corrado Pensa, whose classes I had the honour and pleasure to attend for several years, far longer than I, as a university student, was supposed to.

2 As recalled by Ganeri (2010: 3): 'A commentary whose function is only to elucidate obscure or otherwise tricky words in the text is styled a *ṭīkā.*' Bhāskarakaṇṭha's commentary sometimes takes on this role. Nevertheless, *ṭīkā* 'is also used in a more general sense, as a synonym then of *vṛtti* or *vivaraṇa*'. A *vṛtti* 'is the first support' of the *mūla*-text, 'a kind of simple and succinct commentary […], which paraphrases the text, filling the ellipses and bringing into focus the evolution of the reasoning in its general lines' (Torella 2008: 140). *Vivaraṇa* can be a synonym of *vṛtti*, but 'in a more technical sense, a *vivaraṇa* is a kind of grammatical-semantic analysis, combining structural paraphrase and lexical substitution' (Ganeri 2010: 2). Bhāskarakaṇṭha's commentary also assumes these roles, shifting from the explanation of a single word in a stanza to an extensive paraphrase of the whole stanza (or group of stanzas). There are also episodic digressions on subjects broached in the stanzas.

3 My edition is based on a *codex unicus* on paper in Kashmiri Nāgarī, whose condition is excellent, kept in the Bhandarkar Oriental Research Institute, call number Viśrāma I.623. For a description of the manuscript, see Lo Turco 2011: 17. In Slaje's (1994: 30–48; 1996: 217–219) and Hanneder's (2005: 139–140) catalogues this *codex unicus* is identified by the *siglum* N 26.

4 See e.g. YV/ed. 6.93.61; cf. Mainkar 1955: 137; Divanji 1959–1960: 52.

5 In fact, clear connections to Śaṅkara's Vedānta are only found in the later additions, namely in the frame stories appended to the YV (Hanneder 2006: 62–64).

6 However, in spite of all the similarities mentioned above, the Vijñānavāda is explicitly criticized and put on an equal footing with other philosophical schools (Slaje 1992: 312). Similarly, the Śaivite propensity of the MU/YV, which cannot be denied, remains, however, quite superficial overall (Lo Turco 2002a; Hanneder 2006: 136–149). In short, even if the MU is influenced in particular by Buddhism and Śaivism, it does not fully adhere to either of them.

7 The chapter was not taken into account even by Slaje 1995–1996 and 2000, and Fort 2015, who are explicitly dedicated to *jīvanmukti* in the MU/YV but never mention the *siddhas*.

8 *anugrahāya lokānāṃ bhaṭṭaśrīkallaṭādayaḥ* | *avantivarmaṇaḥ kāle siddhā bhuvam avātaran* ||

9 As regards the present edition, the scribe who first supplemented the commentary with the original stanzas might not have had in hand the same manuscript(s) of the MU as used by Bhāskarakaṇṭha. Accordingly, I have tried to trace the readings of the stanzas back to readings that were certainly or presumably known to Bhāskarakaṇṭha and commented on by him. I have made use of two Śāradā manuscripts of the MU: Ś1, reproduced in Chandra 1984, and Ś3 (*sigla* according to Slaje 1994: 30–48; 1996: 217–219 and Hanneder 2005: 139–140). The latter is kept in the Sri Pratap Singh Library of Śrīnagar, No. 8771 (microfilm: Bibliothek des Indologischen Seminars, Bonn Di804; F66). Symbols: < > deletion; [ ] addition; ( ) deletion marked by the scribe; * * interlinear or marginal addition made by the scribe. In the commentary the *explicanda* are in italics. Sandhi has been normalised. On punctuation see MṬ(VIa) p. 15.

10 Ś1,Ś3: par<e>[i]jñāte

11 Ś1,Ś3: sthit<o>[a]syāpi

12 *folio* 179^{r}

13 anācāro 'sya cācāraḥ; Ś1: anācāro 'pi sācāraḥ; Ś3: duḥkhite duḥkhitakathaḥ

14 f. 179^{v}

15 <jñā>[ca] ta evāntar, conj.; Ś1: tāṃ ta evāntar; Ś3: tāṃs ta evāntar

16 niṣ<i>[a]dyāyām

17 f. 180^{r}

18 Ś3: °vad <h>[dh]lādam; Ś1: °vad hlādam

19 f. 180^{v}

20 paṇḍita(bhūma)*buddha*yaḥ

21 nīraso nīrasārābhrasarasaṃ śirasi sthitam; Ś1: nīraso nīrase rāma sarasorasike sthitaḥ; Ś3: nīraso nīrase rāma sarasarasike sthitaḥ

22 Ś1,Ś3: v<ā>[a]tāvāntara°

23 aiśvarya(ṃ)*m*

24 kaści<d b>[t p]aṭuraṭan, conj.

25 f. 181^{r}

26 Ś1,Ś3: pr<ā>[a]vrajyāṃ

27 The translation of the commentary is in the smaller font size.

28 Cf. YV/ed. 7.125.62

29 The condition of *jīvanmukti*, described as internal coldness (*antaḥśitalatā*), namely profound detachment or equanimity, is not outwardly apparent. See Slaje 2000: 176–178.
30 On the 'inclinations' (*vāsanās*) see Slaje 2000: 178.
31 On the 'sense of I' (*ahaṅkāra*) see Slaje 2000: 178.
32 On the concept of 'pure essence' (*sattva*) as a fundamental feature of the *jīvanmukta*'s mind, see Slaje 2000: 178; Hanneder 2006: 158–159.
33 Cf. MṬ(VIa) 6.195.23
34 On shouting see Rastelli 2000: 335.

Bibliography

Texts

LS = [*Laṅkāvatārasūtra*] *Saddharmalaṅkāvatārasūtra*, ed. by P. L. Vaidya. Darbhanga: The Mithila Institute, 1963.

MN = *Majjhima-nikāya*, ed. by V. Trenckner, R. Chalmers. Oxford: Pali Text Society, 1888–1902.

MṬ(VIa) = *Mokṣopāya-Ṭīkā of Bhāskarakaṇṭha. The Fragments of the Nirvāṇaprakaraṇa. Part I. Critical Edition*, ed. by B. Lo Turco. Halle an der Saale: Universitätsverlag Halle-Wittenberg, 2011.

MṬ(VIb) = *Mokṣopāya-Ṭīkā of Bhāskarakaṇṭha. The Fragments of the Nirvāṇaprakaraṇa. Part II. Critical Edition*, ed. by B. Lo Turco. Halle an der Saale: Universitätsverlag Halle-Wittenberg, 2019.

MU(III) = *Mokṣopāya. Das dritte Buch. Utpattiprakaraṇa*, ed. by J. Hanneder, P. Stephan, S. Jager. Wiesbaden: Harrassowitz, 2011.

MU(IV) = *Mokṣopāya. Das vierte Buch. Sthitiprakaraṇa*, ed. by S. Krause-Stinner, P. Stephan. Wiesbaden: Harrassowitz, 2012.

RT = *The Rājataraṅgiṇī of Kalhaṇa*, ed. by Durgāprasāda. Bombay: Nirnaya-Sagar Press, 1892.

ŚSV = [Śivasūtravimarśinī of Kṣemarāja] *The Shiva Sūtra Vimarshinī Being the Sūtras of Vasu Gupta with the Commentary Called Vimarshinī by Kṣhemarāja*. Srinagar: Archaeological and Research Department, 1911.

YV/ed. = *The Yogavāsiṣṭha of Vālmīki. With the commentary Vāsiṣṭha-mahārāmāyaṇa-tātparyaprakāśa*, 2 vols., ed. by W. L. Śāstrī Paṇśīkar, 3rd ed., revised and re-edited by Nārāyaṇ Rām Āchārya 'Kāvyatīrtha' with the co-operation of Śāstrīmaṇḍal. Bombay: Pāṇḍurang Jāwajī, 1937 (reprint New Delhi 1984).

Studies

Atreya, Bhikhan Lal 1932. *The Yogavāsiṣṭha and Its Philosophy. Lectures Delivered under the Auspices of the Kashi Tattwa Sabha, Theosophical Society, Varanasi*. Varanasi: Theosophy in India (2nd ed. Benares, R. Pathak 1939. [3rd ed. revised and expanded: Moradabad: Darshana Printers, 1966]).

Atreya, Bhikhan Lal 1936. *The Philosophy of the Yogavāsiṣṭha: A Comparative, Critical and Synthetic Survey of the Philosophical Ideas of Vasiṣṭha as Presented in the Yoga-Vāsiṣṭha-Mahā-Rāmāyaṇa*. Madras: The Theosophical Publishing House, Adyar (reprint: Moradabad: Darshana, 1981).

Bhattacharya, Sivaprasad 1925. 'The Yogavāsiṣṭha Rāmāyaṇa, Its Probable Date and Place of Inception.' In *Proceedings and Transactions of the Third All-India Oriental Conference, Madras, 1924*, 545–554. Madras.

Bhattacharya, Sivaprasad 1948. 'The Emergence of an Ādhyātma-Śāstra or the Birth of the Yogavāsiṣṭha Rāmāyaṇa.' *The Indian Historical Quarterly* 24: 201–212.

Bhattacharya, Sivaprasad 1951a. 'The Cardinal Tenets of the Yoga-Vāsiṣṭha and Their Relation to the Trika System of Kaśmira.' *Annals of the Bhandarkar Oriental Research Institute* 32(1.4): 130–145.

Bhattacharya, Sivaprasad 1951b. 'The Siddhas in the Yogavasistha Ramayana and a Peep into Their Creed.' In *Indian Culture. Mahendra Jayanti Volume*, 91–112. Calcutta: Bharat-Sanskrit Parisat.

Bhattacharyya, Benoytosh 1932. *An Introduction to Buddhist Esoterism*. Humphrey Milford: Oxford University Press (first Indian reprint: Delhi, Motilal Banarsidass, 1980).

Chandra, Lokesh ed. 1984. *Sanskrit Texts from Kashmir. Volume 9. Yoga-Vāsiṣṭha*. New Delhi: Sharada Rani.

Dasgupta, Surendranath 1932. 'The Philosophy of the Yoga-Vāsiṣṭha.' In *A History of Indian Philosophy*, vol. II, 228–272. Cambridge: Cambridge University Press.

Davidson, Ronald M. 2002. *Indian Esoteric Buddhism*. New York: Columbia University Press.

Divanji, Prahalad C. 1935. 'The Date and Place of Origin of the Yogavāsiṣṭha.' In *Proceedings and Transactions of the Seventh All-India Oriental Conference, Baroda, 1933*, Baroda, 15–30 (also *The Calcutta Oriental Journal* 1 [1933–34] 153–170).

Divanji, Prahalad C. 1959–1960. 'Bhagavadgītā and Bhāgavata Purāṇa as Models for the Yogavāsiṣṭha.' *Journal of the Asiatic Society of Bombay* N.S. 34–35: 44–58.

Dowman, Keith ed. 1985. *Masters of Mahāmudrā: Songs and Histories of the Eighty-four Buddhist Siddhas*. Albany: State University of New York Press.

Fort, Andrew 2015. 'Embodied Liberation (Jīvanmukti) in the Yogavāsiṣṭha.' In Ch. K. Chapple, A. Chakrabarti eds. *Engaged Emancipation: Mind, Morals, and Make-Believe in the Mokṣopāya* (*Yogavāsiṣṭha*), 247–266. Albany: State University of New York.

Ganeri, Jonardon 2010. 'Sanskrit Philosophical Commentary.' *Journal of the Indian Council of Philosophical Research* 27: 187–207, PDF file, available at http://ftp.columbia.edu/itc/mealac/pollock/sks/papers/Ganeri(commentary).pdf, accessed 26/01/2016, 1–13.

Gnoli, Raniero 1994. 'Introduzione.' In Nāropā, *Iniziazione. Kālacakra*, ed. by R. Gnoli and G. Orofino, 12–103. Torino: Adelphi.

Hanneder, Jürgen 1998. 'Śaiva Tantric Material in the Yogavāsiṣṭha.' *Wiener Zeitschrift für die Kunde Südasiens* 42: 67–76.

Hanneder, Jürgen 2005. 'A List of Manuscript Sources for the Mokṣopāya.' In J. Hanneder ed. *The Mokṣopāya, Yogavāsiṣṭha and Related Texts*, 139–140. Shaker: Aachen.

Hanneder, Jürgen 2006. *Studies on the Mokṣopāya*. Wiesbaden: Harrassowitz.

Lo Turco, Bruno 2001. 'The Story of Līlā. A Paradigm of the World of the Shared Experience.' *Pandanus '01*, 27–43.

Lo Turco, Bruno 2002a. 'Il terzo Prakaraṇa dello *Yogavāsiṣṭha* (Utpatti) e la dottrina śivaita della vibrazione (*spanda*).' *Rivista degli Studi Orientali* 76: 87–118.

Lo Turco, Bruno 2002b. 'Towards a Chronology of the Yogavāsiṣṭha/Mokṣopāya.' *Annali dell'Istituto Orientale di Napoli* 62: 42–71.

Lo Turco, Bruno 2005a. 'Love and Nature in the Mokṣopāya.' In L. Sudyka ed. *Love and Nature in Kāvya Literature. Proceedings*, 207–221. Kraków: Księgarnia Akademicka.

Lo Turco, Bruno 2005b. 'The Metaphorical Logic of the Moksopaya.' In J. Hanneder ed. *The Mokṣopāya, Yogavāsiṣṭha and Related Texts*, 131–138. Aachen: Shaker.

Lo Turco, Bruno ed. 2015. 'Ākāśa and Jīva in the Story of Līlā.' In Ch. K. Chapple and A. Chakrabarti eds. *Engaged Emancipation. Mind, Morals, and Make-Believe in the Mokṣopāya* (*Yogavāsiṣṭha*), 23–52. Albany: State University of New York.

Mainkar, T. G. 1955. *The Yogavāsiṣṭha Rāmāyaṇa: A Study*. Sangli: Prabha Press (2nd ed.: New Delhi, Meharchand Lachhmandas, 1977).

Rastelli, Marion 2000. 'The Religious Practice of the Sādhaka According to the Jayākhyasaṃhitā.' *Indo-Iranian Journal* 43: 319–395. https://doi.org/10.1163/000000000124994128

Slaje, Walter 1992. 'Sarvasiddhāntasiddhānta. On "Tolerance" and "Syncretism" in the Yogavāsiṣṭha.' In G. Oberhammer and R. Mesquita eds. *Wiener Zeitschrift für die Kunde Südasiens* 36, Supplement: *Proceedings of the VIIIth World Sanskrit Conference, Vienna 1990*, 307–322. Vienna: ÖAW.

Slaje, Walter 1994. *Vom Mokṣopāya-Śāstra zum Yogavāsiṣṭha-Mahārāmāyaṇa. Philologische Untersuchungen zur Entwicklungs- und Überlieferungsgeschichte eines indischen Lehrwerks mit Anspruch auf Heilsrelevanz*. Wien: Verlag der Österreichischen Akademie der Wissenschaften.

Slaje, Walter 1995–1996. 'Zur Traditionsgeschichte der Vorstellung von einer "Erlösung noch im Leben" (*jīvanmukti*).' *Bulletin d'Études Indiennes*, 13–14: 387–413.

Slaje, Walter 1996. 'The Mokṣopāya Project.' *Annals of the Bhandarkar Oriental Research Institute* 77: 209–221.

Slaje, Walter 1998. 'On Changing Others' Ideas: The Case of Vidyāraṇya and the Yogavāsiṣṭha.' *Indo-Iranian Journal* 41: 103–124. https://doi.org/10.1163/000000098124992448

Slaje, Walter 2000. 'Liberation from Intentionality and Involvement. On the Concept of Jīvanmukti According to the Mokṣopāya.' *Journal of Indian Philosophy* 28.2: 171–194. https://doi.org/10.1023/A:1004742001659

Slaje, Walter 2001. 'Observations on the Making of the Yogavāsiṣṭha (caitta, nañartha and vaḥ).' In R. Torella ed., *Le parole e i marmi*, 771–796. Roma: IsMEO.

Slaje, Walter 2005. 'Locating the Mokṣopāya.' In Jürgen Hanneder ed. *The Mokṣopāya, Yogavāsiṣṭha and Related Texts*, 21–35. Shaker: Aachen.

Stephan, Peter 2008. *Die Lavaṇa-Episode im Mokṣopāya. Über den illusionären Charakter personaler Identität. Textkritische Edition, Erstübersetzung, Studie*, Dissertation, Martin-Luther-Universität, Halle (pdf available online, http://digital.bibliothek.uni-halle.de/hs/urn/urn:nbn:de:gbv:3:4-2891).

Timalsina, Sthaneshwar 2012. 'Liberation and Immortality. Bhuśuṇḍa's yoga of *prāṇa* in the *Yogavāsiṣṭha*.' In K. A. Jacobsen ed. *Yoga Powers: Extraordinary Capacities Attained Through Meditation and Concentration*, 303–325. Leiden: Brill.

Torella, Raffaele 2008. *Il pensiero dell'India. Un'introduzione*. Roma: Carocci.

White, David G. 1996. *The Alchemical Body: Siddha Traditions in Medieval India.* Chicago: The University of Chicago Press.

Author Biography

Bruno Lo Turco is Associate Professor at the Italian Institute of Oriental Studies (ISO), Sapienza University of Rome, Italy. He teaches Religions and Philosophies of India, and Sanskrit Language and Literature. Recently he completed the critical edition of all fragments of Bhāskarakaṇṭha's commentary on the sixth book of the *Mokṣopāya.* He also works on the relationship between modernity and Indian philosophic-religious thought, and on orality, aurality and literacy in India.

Chapter 5

Framing the Other: Mindfulness, Photography, and a Reflexive Approach to Comparative Religions

Filippo Marsili

Introduction: Healthier Ways to Feel Lost

I was barely twenty years old when I took my first class with Corrado Pensa, at the beginning of my academic adventure. In the early nineties, his lectures on 'Religioni e Filosofie dell'India e dell'Estremo Oriente' were undoubtedly among the most popular at Università 'La Sapienza.' Right after high school, having spent five formative years studying the civilizations of Greece and Rome, I had decided to take a "sabbatical" and enrol in courses that had nothing to do with the ancient Mediterranean world. I knew that I would eventually go back to my old passion, the Classics, but I thought that changing area for a while would help me acquire a more balanced perspective on my own identity, both from a cultural and social point of view.

Although I was born in Rome, I had grown up in a small town in the countryside north of it, in the region of Sabina, which, in addition to representing the 'province' in its proverbial opposition to 'the City,' in the Bronze Age—at least according to legend—had succumbed to Rome's soon-to-be-unstoppable military power, thus losing its supremacy over central Italy.[1] However, more than these sophomoric historical musings, the real challenge for me was represented by being the first one in my family to attend college. And since the Classics seldom constituted the first choice among working-class students, focusing on the "exotic Orient," albeit for a short while, I hoped, would provide me with valuable alternatives upon which I could build a new cultural identity, especially as I coped with a deep sense of insecurity and displacement.

Ironically enough, that familiar sense of insecurity and displacement only increased when I started to sit in Professor Pensa's classes. The large room on the first floor of the imposing building of the faculty of 'Lettere e Filosofia,' a typical example of 'Rationalist architecture,' was abuzz with the chatter of hundreds of students, who, after filling the available seats, would crouch on the floor or perch on the sills of the large windows. Although always early, I regularly opted for the end rows, where I hoped the screen of cigarette smoke (still allowed in those years) would make me even more inconspicuous.

The textbooks listed for the final exam of Professor Pensa's class were twice or thrice as many as those required in any other course in the Asian Studies curriculum. In addition to the basic manuals on the history of Indian and Chinese thought, Theravāda and Mahāyāna Buddhism, Tibetan traditions, and handbooks on various meditation techniques, they included several texts on the relationship between religious experiences and psychoanalysis. It definitely looked like an extremely challenging syllabus, but equipped with my notebook, I was ready to jot down those abstruse terms, confident that with hard work I would eventually begin to grasp the intellectual breadth of that reading list. To my surprise, almost none of those topics would systematically feature in Professor Pensa's lectures. Rather than exclusively concentrating on the historical or theoretical aspects of the development of Buddhism, Daoism, or Hinduism, our instructor more often focused on topics that I would have never thought could belong in an academic curriculum. From reconstructing the trains of thought that led us to make judgments about the other passengers while sitting on a bus, to the restlessness of our thinking processes while occupied in activities as trivial as washing dishes, those classes aimed at introducing us to mindfulness and the 'dependent origination' or *paṭiccasamuppāda*. I soon realized that those lectures were beginning to affect the ways in which I approached the assigned textbooks and topics of that course in 'Religions and Philosophies of India and East Asia.' Questioning the very processes whereby we acquire knowledge and construct an intellectual notion of ourselves was becoming my preferred learning strategy. Naturally, that experience impacted all other cultural endeavours I undertook in those formative months, including the classes I was taking on Chinese culture and language and on the visual arts of Eastern and Central Asia.

Bodies of White Marble: Rome's Classical Visual Heritage

When I was not busy studying, especially over the weekends, I would spend my time taking photos in Rome's museums—a hobby I had picked up during my last year of high school, and that, thanks to weddings and some advertising work, constituted an important extra source of income. Ever since childhood, I loved drawing. Compared to this act of freely weaving imaginary worlds on a white piece of paper, photography constituted a positive change from a personal point of view. Creating images through a camera and the mysterious effects of light on silver-halide gelatine emulsion was surely less natural for me than forgetting myself behind the evolutions of the black lines spun by a pencil. But since it compelled me to acknowledge the existence of something objective and real outside my mind, I sensed it must somehow constitute a healthier activity in which to indulge. Even though I could not be completely sure about the reasons why it was so, I felt it was healthier—and to some degree painful—in the same ways the mindfulness practices I was discovering in that period were.

My major photographic project at the time involved the Greco-Roman statues of the innumerable Roman collections. Growing up, and especially as an adolescent, all the insecurities concerning my appearance and identity as a young male were fuelled by the eternal paragons of strength and harmony embodied by those pieces of stone, whose incompleteness further enhanced their aura of unrepeatable perfection.[2] After long days spent shooting in the halls of the various museums, striving to concentrate among throngs of tourists, I would spend hours in the darkroom developing films and photographs. While the first part of my job consisted in establishing some kind of relationship with portraits of deities, heroes, and aristocrats to whom I was supposed to be related both culturally and genetically, in the dim light of the projector and under the red lamp I tried to reconstruct, frame by frame, the processes that led me to choose particular compositions, angles, or exposures. After a while, I realized that my images were becoming consistent and meaningful (at least to me) as long as instead of striving to achieve specific artistic goals, I simply stayed with the process of observation.[3] The most successful photographs were those in which my ambivalence towards those statues and what they were supposed to evoke became evident. Instead of aiming at the complete (albeit conceptual) reconstruction of some mythical figure, those images would emphasize the fragmentary nature of the relics, drawing attention to the fracture lines and placing at the centre of the composition the void left by the lost marble limb or head. In some cases, I would not bother to conceal the anachronistic context of the exhibition rooms and let tourists and custodians become an integral part of my images. In other cases, I would manifest my frustration with the centuries of celebratory readings of those antiquities by juxtaposing different points of view through the usage of double exposures, moving the camera while shooting, or simply by blurring what the viewer would have expected to be the focal centre of the composition (Figures I–IV). However, I became aware of what I was doing only a couple of years later, when I started to examine the black and white images of my Rome project alongside those taken during my first study trip in Southwest China.

Yunnan 1995: The Other's Other

My first study period in China was in the Southwest province of Yunnan. My choice was determined by a documentary I watched in which Yunnan was described as the 'land of the eternal spring' because of its year-around mild climate. It also attracted me because it seemed far removed from the usual destinations of students and tourists in those years. As an enthusiastic undergraduate, the essentialist conceit of a 'more authentic China' and the possibility of *truly* getting in touch with it were irresistible. Moreover, the fact that Yunnan is home to more than fifty officially designated minorities persuaded me that, as an aspiring photographer, it would be an ideal place to carry out my first ethnographic reportage. At the time, I was in touch with the owner of a newly opened photographic gallery in Rome, and I knew that if my images were good enough, I could have my own exhibit on the river Tiber, just across the Vatican, and my own press agent.

Going back to the kind of subjects I would have been able to portray once in Yunnan, it had been thanks to the black and white images of the Magnum Photos photographic cooperative that I had begun to appreciate ethnographic reportage. In the words of Henri Cartier-Bresson, one of the photographers who had founded the photographic cooperative, Magnum, it represented 'a community of thought, a shared human quality, a curiosity about what is going on in the world, a respect for what is going on and a desire to transcribe it visually.'[4] Although it expressed as many different visions as the photographers who were its members, Magnum has been associated with a form of dramatic realism at the service of a firm humanitarian stance.[5] Not surprisingly, as some critics have pointed out, such an explicit social commitment could easily lead to the creation of images that expressed the ideological views of their authors rather than representing an objective take on reality. As in the case of the most famous photograph by one of Magnum's founders, Robert Capa's 'Falling Soldier,' which allegedly portrays an anarchist militia fighter in the act of being killed during the Spanish Civil War, this kind of picture could be suspected of being staged.[6] Nonetheless, Magnum's post-World War II ethnological works had an enormous influence on the popular perception of photo-journalism as a way to both document and engage with reality. In keeping with the contemporary development of Euro-American social sciences of the fifties and sixties, which strove to reject the "colonial gaze" of the previous decades, the contemporary international public was generally receptive to the interest in and respect for the other captured in Magnum photographs.[7]

As for my arrival in Yunnan, in that particular phase of my development as an "analytical observer," I was just getting acquainted with the postmodern and postcolonial critique of the pretence of objectivity in western representations of Asia.[8] Armed with the ethical models provided by Magnum and a visual sensibility steeped in the antiquities of ancient Greece and Rome, I was ready to ride my projections wilfully and unapologetically, confident that my classical upbringing would infuse my images with a further distinctive element. Fortunately, my actual experience behind the camera proved to me that identitary concerns are all but an obstacle towards an honest cognitive goal, as they would prevent me from establishing an effective relationship with the subjects of my photographs.

In the mid-nineties, Kunming, the provincial capital of Yunnan where I had my first encounter with Asia, was just at the beginning of the process of urban modernization that would transform all the major cities of China within just a few years. Even though the local authorities were tearing down old neighbourhoods, the city's skyline was still clear of high-rises. Yunnan University, with the dorms where I lived, stood as the largest building complex in my neighbourhood. During the second Sino-Japanese War (1937–1945), the school had briefly experienced a period of intellectual prominence, as it gave shelter to several distinguished academics fleeing the Showa occupation armies in the East.[9] In 1995, however, decades after those tumultuous days, there were no signs that the university would soon be shaken by a wave of excitement and frantic innovation. The 'Chinese march towards a market economy and enrichment,' inaugurated by Deng Xiaoping almost twenty years earlier with the Four Modernizations, had not yet reached that area of Kunming.[10] Judging from the magazines sold around campus, it seemed that the city was still copying with the ideological implications of the Cold War.

The innumerable markets in the alleys and streets surrounding the university surely did not belong to the 'capitalist West' (Figure V). Yet it would have been difficult to define them as 'traditional,' as I would have expected them to look based on the movies of Zhang Yimou that were becoming popular in Europe in those years.[11]

Perhaps, I thought, that sense of suspension and indetermination in the architecture of the city was caused by the fact that the generation of adults now in charge had grown up during the Cultural Revolution (1966–1976). Even though they seemed eager to leave behind the hardship and violence that characterized that era, they could not partake yet of the enthusiasm surrounding the government's focus on modernization and the market economy. In addition, the memory of the Tiananmen tragedy of June 1989, which had halted a push towards democratic reforms, was still fresh, and in that particular moment, in the peripheral province of Yunnan, probably no one could be certain whether China was headed toward successful political and economic changes.

During my photographic expedition in Kunming, as one of the few foreigners in the city, I was naturally elicited curiosity. However, in the few conversations I had with the locals, I never asked questions about China's development rate and its likelihood of 'catching up with the West,' as I would regularly be in my future visits. People would exchange with me a few words about the glory of ancient Rome or more generally about European culture and traditions, as though our current realities were hardly relatable. Disappointed my failure to establish a real connection with my potential subjects or to single out through my images any distinctive or essential trait in the life I was observing around campus, I gradually started to shift my focus from the reticent and elusive adults to the groups of children playing in the streets or going to school. They seemed eager to engage me in a friendly way without seeming to be bothered by my presence or my camera. It did not take long before I grew frustrated with this new approach (Figures VII, VIII). After all, I was just photographing children in the ways in which children at play could have been photographed in any other part of the world. Even if I could admit that some of my pictures were aesthetically satisfying, I was aware that I was reacting to external expectations and well-established clichés of the genre. When I moved my operations to the numerous Buddhist temples of the city, my sense of disconnect positively increased. I was genuinely interested in the subject of a tradition that had begun to exert a fundamental role in my life, especially as its study had introduced me to a reflexive approach towards processes of observation, judgment, and identification.[12] Yet the act of separating myself from that context in order to create the organized view of a photographic image felt in stark contradiction with the very reason I was there. My thought processes in those days would only become clear after my trip, during the long sessions in the dark room spent analysing my images and thanks to the study of the psychological implications in the application of mindfulness to photography.

Among the Chinese Minorities, the Other's Other and the Self

My undergraduate training tended to focus on aspects that emphasized the uniformity and timelessness of Chinese civilization. While living in Kunming, I realized that the cultural expectations produced by this approach were preventing me from having a fulfilling experience. A further source of my disappointment, I suspected, was probably due to the simple fact that I was overwhelmed by the complexity of a universe about which my knowledge was still too superficial. Since my priority was still taking satisfying photographs, I thought that perhaps travelling in the areas mainly populated by ethnic minorities about which I knew very little or nothing would provide me with more creative freedom. I assumed that working on a new subject, without any specific expectation, could at least allow me to establish with it a more direct, sincere interaction. In addition, at the time the only ways to reach the periphery of Yunnan was by bus, and long hours spent on a bumpy road in the Chinese countryside seemed to me an ideal way to become immersed in a new reality.

The destinations I had chosen for my two trips were the autonomous region of Sipsong Panna (Xinshuangbanna in Mandarin), a sub-tropical plateau at the border with Myanmar and Laos, and the southwestern area of Yunnan with the Yulong Autonomous County bordering Tibet, famous as the land of the Naxi or Nakhi minority. The biggest minority group inhabiting Xinshuangbanna were the Dai. Its leading families had succeeded in maintaining a surprisingly high level of independence throughout the 1990s.[13] When I visited Xinshuangbanna, the language most commonly spoken in the area was a form of Thai. Its written version was still used in the local Theravāda temples, which local children attended until their adolescence instead of the state schools.[14] The fact that this form of independence from the Communist party was an integral part of Dai identity was clearly manifest in a series of paintings representing Buddha defeating the Red Guards that decorated the Octagonal Pavilion of the Jingzhen Village in the county of Menghai.

The Naxi, on the other hand, had since the imperial era entertained a relationship of cooperation with the Chinese government aimed at the legitimization of local hierarchies. Even though they maintained their customs and religious practices, the Dongpa tradition, which consists of elements of Tibetan Bön and a form of Kagyu Buddhism, Naxi society, despite Marxism's staunch materialist stance, seemed perfectly integrated with Communist lore and ideology.[15] Colorful posters depicting Red Guards riding white horses and brandishing swords often replaced the more traditional apotropaic deities on the doors of several village houses. Portraits of historic party cadres were sold together with Cultural Revolution memorabilia in most markets, while busts of Mao Zedong appeared among bodhisattvas and other deities on several temples and shrines.

Going back to my plans about experimenting with a more unfettered photographic approach, I understood that my background and concerns with identity could affect how I visualized and represented my subjects even in more insidious ways. Upon my expedition and before entering the darkroom in Italy, I could not help but inform myself about the Dai and the Naxi by reading about them. However, I soon realized that my projections were not only detectable in explicit cultural expectations and intellectual stances; the ways in which I was selecting, framing, composing, and freezing specific postures or moments through photography were also determined by my upbringing, training, and assumptions about identity and its unitary nature. Hence, I decided to address more systematically the criteria by which I selected and depicted subjects and scenes I deemed meaningful. As a historian of religions focusing on early China, it became vital for me to reconstruct the Mediterranean and European origins not only of the conceptual models and methodologies that determined my approach, but also of the very tendency to see religion as the crucial point of intersection of individual development and social integration. The most practical application of this insight consisted in maintaining a high level of vigilance towards my instinct to revert to systemic theoretical models to make sense of empirical experiences. It occurred to me that more than the answers I was determined to obtain, I needed to scrutinize the questions I was bound to ask, or, in other words, the seemingly natural ways in which my eyes were moving about.

Two Images

The sense of dissatisfaction I experienced in Kunming stayed with me while I was taking photographs in the more peripheral regions of Yunnan. What represented a turning point was my decision to *stay with* my frustration and observe, as much as possible in a detached way, the ways in which my eyes moved, waited, chose, and excluded in order to create images that were meaningful to me but above all to a future Roman public who would see and judge these photographs. This kind of analysis continued in the long hours spent in the darkroom after I returned from Yunnan, when by studying preparatory shots frame by frame I could reconstruct the reasoning that led me to specific compositions.

The two images I selected to illustrate these points represent in a way the beginning and starting points of my reflection.

The first image was taken in the county of Menghai, south of Qinghong, the administrative centre of Xinshuangbanna. In this large plain all the activities seem to revolve around the waters of the Mekong River. The Dai mainly live in houses on stilts, while the children, when they are not attending class at the temple, accompany their parents on the riverbank diving and splashing in their colourful sarongs (Figure VIII). Judging from the amount of film and preparatory shots devoted to this photograph, it must have been one of the most carefully planned. After spending more than an hour among young monks flying their kites after class, I had noticed in the distance a scene with fewer people that appeared much easier to handle from the compositional point of view. The final image depicts four individuals working between what might have been two rice paddies or fishing ponds (Figure IX).

The image is enclosed by bamboo groves at the horizon and a child in the bottom right corner who is a little out of focus. He is observing three men in the act of dragging a net across a body of water, two of whom are in front of him on the opposite side of the paddy, the other closer in the left bottom corner (Figure IX). Even though it was not clear to me what was actually going on in front of my eyes, I was intent on composing the scene by repeating triangular patterns and achieving geometrical balance (compare with Figure VII). However, the preparatory shots showed that I was especially interested in catching the shirtless man on the left portion of the picture in a specific posture. And in hindsight, I clearly waited until his body looked like that of the Greek statue, the Diskobolos of Myron (c. 480–440 BCE), which survives in innumerable Roman copies. This sculpture of a naked disc thrower embodies the ideals of balance, rhythm, and harmony, or in other words intellectual control over physical strength, which epitomize classical art. Indeed, I remember the initial satisfaction of capturing this image being replaced by a deep sense of disappointment upon realizing that I was not capable of overcoming a solipsistic involvement with the tradition that was supposed to constitute an important component of my own identity.[16] Were my photographs the result of a real interaction with a foreign reality or was I simply projecting what was familiar to me onto something with which I was not able to come to terms?

The second picture was taken in the village of Baisha, in the Yulong Naxi Autonomous County. In the morning I had left the hostel very early, as I wished to reach a famous Buddhist temple hidden in the gorgeous mountains of eastern Himalaya. Since there was no clear path and my tourist map was not sufficiently detailed, I eventually decided to hike back downhill before sunset and visit a small village in the valley instead. I had heard that in one the old buildings there was a Ming dynasty (1368–1644) fresco representing local deities and state dignitaries in the form of a cosmographic thangka. The artistic level of the drawing was much higher than I had expected, but unfortunately the eyes of all the human and divine figures had been carefully carved out. When I turned and asked for an explanation from the local shepherds who had led me there, '*Wenhua geming*,' 'Cultural Revolution,' was the laconic answer.

Worn out and disappointed, all I wanted at that point was to return to my room for a shower. In the meantime, a small crowd had gathered in the room with the paintings. Most of the people convened there were just interested in the foreign guidebooks I had brought with me, as they hoped they might contain images of the fourteenth Dalai Lama, which were forbidden in the territories administrated by the PRC. After I had finished tearing out and distributing the few pages portraying His Holiness that I could find in my copy of the *Lonely Planet*, I felt I was finally ready to go. But when the group left, an old man stayed behind waiting for me. He had noticed my camera hanging from my back and asked me if I could follow him home and take a picture of his grandson.

When we arrived, I discovered that the child had no wish to be photographed. I have never been fond of taking portraits of unwilling subjects, but it seemed extremely important to the grandfather. He kept nudging the boy, trying to make him turn his eyes in my direction so that I could take a proper portrait. It was before the era of digital images, and it was not clear how I would deliver the photograph after my departure. However, convinced that obliging was the fastest way out, I tried to do my best and swiftly get a sense of the circumstances for a satisfying shot.

The man was wearing the typical communist-cadre beret and the Sun Yat-sen jacket, which he had fastened around his waist with a traditional Naxi soft sash belt. By contrast, the uncooperative boy was clad in a western-style sailor uniform of the kind I knew mainly because of Donald Duck. I was too tired and confused to conceal my uneasiness as well as the awkwardness of the whole situation. But that single shot proved to be a success (Figure X). The curator of the gallery with whom I was in touch selected it for the posters and flyers advertising my exhibit and for the Roman press, and, before my decision to apply for graduate school, it held a preeminent position in my portfolio. It captured in a dynamic way the precariousness, uncertainty, and embarrassment of a rather problematic attempt at interacting. The artificiality of that moment is not concealed in the image. Yet the resistance of the child, the optimism of the old man, and the confusion of the observer are all, in a way, sincerely displayed.

Its tripartite structure was determined by the different textures of the wooden door, plaster, and brick wall, which, together with an illegible Chinese character drawn on a broken white festoon occupying the upper right corner, achieved the effect of a flat, unapologetically preposterous backdrop of a stage play. At the centre of the picture stood the boy, with his face hidden under the sleeve of his grandfather, who had not realized yet that the grandson was not turning his head towards me. He had maintained a stoic expression, probably in the hope that it would inspire calm and solemnity in the boy. When he realized that it was impossible to obtain the portrait for which he was hoping, he apologized for the time he had made me waste and let me go.

Conclusions

Even though I briefly acquired an agent at one point, photography never became my main profession. Throughout graduate school I continued practicing photography in an increasingly systematic way as a form of walking meditation in which the observation and the shooting sessions were separated. After a while, it became rather natural for me to transfer the reflexive processes whereby I was becoming aware of my projections, or the ways in which in researching ancient China I tended to frame questions and answers so that they could produce familiar results. As someone trained in Greco-Roman literature and Mediterranean civilizations, it became fundamental for me, even before delving into an emic reconstruction of the context I was studying, to be as much as possible aware of my own hermeneutical approach and intellectual expectations.

Sati, or mindfulness, applied to my field, became what the historian Reinhart Koselleck defines as 'consciously admitted positionality.'[17] In my case, it consists in maintaining high intellectual vigilance on the tendency to project identitary, systemic, and ethical expectations onto my research subjects. My approach entails a special attention to the ways in which the themes, concerns, and methodologies of academic disciplines created in the ancient Mediterranean and developed in Europe, such as history, archaeology, anthropology, and religious studies, as well as the very notion of Abrahamic creeds, condition our understanding of ancient China. At the same time, I consider this process of learning inevitably dialogic, in that the comprehension of the other is intertwined with that of the self. For example, my focus on the formalization of a Christian identity in the context of the Roman empire, the divine cult of the emperor and through the language of Roman law and Greek philosophy, helped me realize how the sacred in ancient China, especially before the introduction of Buddhism from roughly the first century BCE, could be studied beyond our tendency to formalize it in systemic or universalistic terms. Conversely, the local discrete and individual nature of Chinese ghosts and spirits (*gui* and *shen*) allowed me to re-evaluate the non-theoretical, more idiosyncratic component of Mediterranean experiences of the sacred.[18]

Going back to the analytical gains connected to the application of mindfulness to photography, in the study of specific cultural phenomena, I am now bound to pay attention to the 'framing' and 'freezing' of elements under observation. For example, in the usage of notions that are not native to early China such as 'religion,' which was introduced as a loan word at the end of the nineteenth century, it becomes fundamental to discuss what aspects of human behaviour should be analysed under such a category and which ones excluded.

Furthermore, as in the case of the composition of a photograph, the historian's establishment of a discrete spatial and hierarchical relationship among the elements included in a specific concept should also be the object of reflexive scrutiny. As for the 'freezing'—or the 'decisive moment,' as Henri Cartier-Bresson aptly described it—this refers to the fact that researchers, while observing a given phenomenon or process, should be as much as possible aware of the criteria whereby they single out a specific instant as the most meaningful or representative.[19] Therefore, from this point of view, every intellectual choice made by the historian—as well as every shot taken by the photographer—entails operations of exclusion and omission. Although these are inevitable, I consider it important to acknowledge them reflexively in the introduction of the heuristic criteria underlying every scholarly project.

The practices of mindfulness, photography, and cross-cultural history belong to different disciplinary realms. However, they all share a concern with the relationship between the self and the other. The move from the visual to the discursive, in my case, brought to light for me the resilience of more or less subconscious analytical biases. Even though the historian's craft cannot be likened to the art of the photographer as an 'unrestrained wanderer,' its creative component, represented by the acts of choice, exclusion, and composition, nonetheless needs openly to be acknowledged.[20] While the ethical commitment to the independent objectivity of the sources and the necessity to abide by the traditional standards of academic communication might limit the demiurgic freedom of historians, the systematic application of 'unrestricted awareness' should enable them to benefit from recognizing their 'getting lost,' or, in other words, to account for those experiences that defy the limitations intrinsic to every professional field, as well as one's upbringing, expectations, biases, and projections.

I. Rome, Musei Capitolini

II. Musei Capitolini

III. Musei Capitolini

IV. Musei Capitolini

V. Kunming, Yunnan

VI. Kunming, Yunnan

VII. Lijiang, Yunnan

VIII. Menghai, Yunnan

IX. Menghai county

X. Baisha, Yunnan

Notes

1 On the history and cultural implications of the narration of the origins of Rome, see Grandazzi 1997; see also Cornell, 1995: 81–118.
2 After World War II, the humanities in Italy were deeply influenced by dialectic materialism and historicism as studies of past civilizations were customarily carried out within a discourse on the social and political role of intellectuals; see Bianchi-Bandinelli 1950; 1969.
3 A text that accompanied me in those days was Corrado Pensa's 1994.
4 From 'Magnum Photos,' accessed June 15, 2020, https://pro.magnumphotos.com/C.aspx?VP3=CMS3&VF=MAX_2&FRM=Frame:MAX_3.
5 For a critical view on the humanitarian pretences of photography, see Sontag1989.
6 Larry Rother 'New Doubts Raised Over Famous War Photo.' *The New York Times*, August 18, 2009, https://www.nytimes.com/2009/08/18/arts/design/18capa.html.
7 For an efficacious synthesis on the history of the so-called 'human interest' attitude in photography, see Jeffrey 1981: 178–203.
8 My exposure to postcolonial literature was taking place indirectly in those years through older students who had international connections, as it was not part of our regular curriculum. For example, Said (1978) saw its first Italian translation more than ten years later: *Orientalismo* (1991) but became popular only after the Feltrinelli edition of 1999.
9 Li 1994: 84–87.
10 Hsü 2000.
11 Gao 1998: 47–48.
12 Epstein 1995.
13 Hansen 1999.
14 Hansen reports that despite the freedom of receiving a religious training, elementary education in Xishuangbanna aimed at conveying the idea that the region was notably 'backward and less civilized' with respect to the rest of China; see Hansen 1999: 134–142.
15 See Emily Chao 1996: 208–239.
16 See Jean Charbonneaux, Roland Martin and Francois Villard 1970: 138–141; Becatti 1965: 173–175.
17 Koselleck 2002: 1–19.
18 My methodological approach is explained in detail in Marsili 2018.
19 Henri Cartier-Bresson 1952.
20 P. L. Gross, S. I. Shapiro 1997: 33– 57.

Bibliography

Becatti, Giovanni 1965. *L'arte dell'età classica*. Firenze: Sansoni.
Bianchi-Bandinelli, Ranuccio 1969. *Roma: L'arte romana al centro del potere*. Roma: Feltrinelli.
Bianchi-Bandinelli, Ranuccio 1950. *Storicità dell'arte classica*. Firenze: Electa.

Cartier-Bresson, Henri 1952. *The Decisive Moment*. New York: Simon & Schuster.
Chao, Emily 1996. 'Hegemony, Agency, and Re-representing the Past: The Invention of Dongpa Culture among the Naxi of Southwest China.' In Melissa Brown ed. *Negotiating Ethnicities in China and Taiwan*, 208–239. Berkeley: Institute of East Asian Studies, University of California.
Charbonneaux, Jean, Roland Martin, and Francois Villard 1970. *La Grecia Classica*. Milano: Rizzoli.
Cornell, T. J. *The Beginnings of Rome: Italy and Rome from the Bronze Age to the Punic Wars (c.1000–264 BC)*. New York and London: Routledge, 1995.
Epstein, Mark 1995. *Thoughts Without a Thinker: Psychotherapy from a Buddhist Perspective*. New York: Basic Books.
Gao, Minglu 1998. *Inside/Out: New Chinese Art*. Los Angele, Berkeley: University of California Press.
Grandazzi, Alexandre 1997. *The Foundation of Rome: Myth and History*. Ithaca, NY: Cornell University Press.
Gross, Philippe L., S. I. Shapiro 1997. 'The Tao of Photography: The Chuang-Tzu, Unconstricted Awareness, and Conscious Camerawork.' *International Journal of Transpersonal Studies* 16.1: 33–57.
Hansen, Mette Halskov 1999. *Lessons in Being Chinese: Minority Education and Ethnic Identity in Southwest China*. Seattle: University of Washington Press.
Hsü, Immanuel C. Y. 2000. *The Rise of Modern China*. New York: Oxford University Press.
Jeffrey, Ian 1981. *Photography: A Concise History*. London: Thames and Hudson.
Koselleck, Reinhart 2002. 'The Need for Theory in History.' In *The Practice of Conceptual History: Timing History, Spacing Concepts*, 1–19. Stanford, CA: Stanford University Press.
Li, Lincoln 1994. *Student Nationalism in China, 1924–1949*. Albany, NY: SUNY Press.
Marsili, Filippo 2018. *Heaven is Empty: A Cross-Cultural Approach to "Religion" and Empire in Ancient China*. Albany: State University of New York Press (SUNY Press).
Pensa, Corrado 1994. *La tranquilla passione. Saggi sulla meditazione buddhistadi consapevolezza*. Roma: Ubaldini/Astrolabio.
Said, Edward W. 1978. *Orientalism*. New York: Pantheon.
Sontag, Susan 1989. *On Photography*. New York: Doubleday.

List of captions for the figures

I. Rome, Musei Capitolini.
II. Rome, Musei Capitolini.
III. Rome, Musei Capitolini.
IV. Rome, Musei Capitolini.

V. Kunming, Yunnan.
VI. Kunming, Yunnan.
VII. Lijiang, Yunnan.
VIII. Menghai, Yunnan.
IX. Menghai, Yunnan.
X. Baisha, Yunnan.

Author Biography

Filippo Marsili (PhD from UC Berkeley) is Associate Professor of History at Saint Louis University. His research focuses on cultural translation and the impact of Greco-Roman historiography and Abrahamic traditions on contemporary conceptualizations of early Chinese realities. His *Heaven is Empty: A Cross-Cultural Approach to "Religion" and Empire in Ancient China* (SUNY Press 2018) offers a reconceptualization of Chinese experiences of the sacred before the arrival of Buddhism. His current project rethinks European discourses on institutionalized violence in light of early Chinese mythological and historiographical narratives concerning the relationship between the state, individuals, and communities.

Chapter 6

The Teaching of Awareness in Corrado Pensa's Thought

Chiara Neri

Premise[1]

I first met Corrado Pensa in 1998 when I enrolled at the Faculty of Literature at La Sapienza University in Rome. I was undecided whether to study Art or what was known as 'Oriental Studies.' Thus, I began to follow courses belonging to both disciplines, including Professor Pensa's Religions and Philosophies of India.

When I walked in, I saw a very unusual scene for the Department of Oriental Studies: the classroom was full of people and no seat was available; even the window spaces were occupied. I had to stand, crammed against the wall at the back of the classroom. After a few minutes Professor Pensa came in carrying a bag full of books, coloured with post-it markers. He opened a window to ventilate the room, and then sat down and started reading some *sutta*s from the Pāli Canon. He was dressed distinctively, but with no affectation. What immediately struck me was his deep voice. He read, commented, and examined each passage, providing numerous references to other Pāli and Sanskrit sources. These thorough analyses were followed by long maieutic discussions where students were encouraged or even probed to interact with him.

Despite his having the outlook of a serious academic, he conducted those classes with humour, often making smart jokes. In retrospect, I'm not surprised at all at those students and even hangers-on not enrolled at the

University packing his lectures, because whoever participated 'was helped to overcome his suffering in life,' as a fellow student used to say.

The heart of Corrado Pensa's teaching was always the study of Early Buddhism and the Theravāda tradition, and especially the teaching of awareness (Pāli *sati*, Sanskrit *smṛti*). Corrado Pensa dedicated a lot of academic classes, writings and Dharma discourses to this topic. The invitation to awareness is also found in the name of the association of meditation he founded in 1987, the Association for the Meditation of Awareness (In Italian: Associazione per la Meditazione di Consapevolezza, A.Me.Co). *Sati* is also the name of the journal published by the association. For this reason, this essay will investigate Corrado Pensa's understanding of *sati* and discuss his position as a contemporary Dharma teacher.

1. A brief introduction on the meaning of *sati* in the *Suttapiṭaka*[2]

In Early Buddhism and in Theravāda Buddhism[3] *sati* is a pregnant and central practice in the teaching of the Buddha. The word is commonly translated with 'mindfulness' or 'awareness,'[4] and has been interpreted differently over the centuries.[5] Many studies have been dedicated to this topic, but here I will limit myself to describing briefly the general meaning of this term, in order to reconnect it with Corrado Pensa's interpretations.

The word *sati* is related to the Vedic root *smṛ* (from which the Sanskrit word *smṛti,* corresponding to Pāli *sati*, is derived) and has a double meaning: 'memory, recognition, calling to mind' and 'consciousness, wakefulness of mind, mindfulness.' Many scholars have debated the reason and function of this double meaning[6] and the standard definition they propose designates *sati* as the faculty through which it is possible to remember or recollect what was done and said.[7] In particular, Gethin (2001: 36) proposed two important textual passages as reference. The first one is in the *Saṃyuttanikāya*:

> *katamañ ca bhikkhave satindriyaṃ. idha bhikkhave ariyasāvako satimā hoti paramena satinepakkena samannāgato cirakataṃ pi cirabhāsitaṃ pi saritā anussaritā* (S V 198).

> And what, *bhikkhus,* is the faculty of *sati?* Here, *bhikkhus,* the noble disciple has *sati,* he is endowed with perfect *sati* and intellect, he is one who remembers, who recollects what was done and said long before.[8]

The second passage is in the *Milindapañha* (see Mil 37–38) in which it is said that *sati* has two main characteristics: 'calling to mind' (*apilāpana*) and 'taking hold' (*upagaṇhana*). Thus, Gethin (2001: 39) concludes:

> What the *Milindapañha* account is suggesting, I think, is that *sati* should be understood as what allows awareness of the full range and extent of *dhammas*; *sati* is an awareness of things in relation to things, and hence an awareness of their relative value. Applied to the *satipaṭṭhānas* presumably what this means is that *sati* is what causes the practitioner of yoga to 'remember' that any feeling he may experience exists in relation to a whole variety or world of feelings that may be skilful or unskilful, with faults or faultless, relatively inferior or refined, dark or pure.

In this way, he connects these two important meanings of *sati* and introduces its role in meditation practices.

In fact, in the Pāli Nikāyas *sati* is tightly linked to meditative practice, especially concerning the mindfulness of breathing (*ānāpānasati*), and it is practiced in preliminary and advanced meditative states. In the preliminary stages, called 'access concentration' (*upacārasamādhi*), there are six recollections (*anussati*);[9] in this context *sati* is fundamentally remembering these recollections. In advanced meditative states (*appanāsamādhi*), instead, *sati* is the mindfulness of the body and of breathing. In particular, two Suttapiṭaka discourses, the *Satipaṭṭhānasutta* and the *Mahāsatipaṭṭhānasutta*,[10] and in the *Vibhaṅga* of the Abhidhammapiṭaka,[11] describe four ways of 'establishing mindfulness' (*satipaṭṭhāna*).[12] This is based on the observation (*anupassanā*)[13] of the body (*kāya*), of feelings (*vedanā*), of the mind (*citta*), and of physical and mental processes (*dhamma*).

The standard formula is, e.g.:

> *ekāyano ayaṃ bhikkhave maggo sattānaṃ visuddhiyā sokaparidevānaṃ samatikkamāya dukkhadomanassānaṃ atthaṅgamāya ñāyassa adhigamāya nibbānassa sacchikiriyāya yad idaṃ cattāro satipaṭṭhānā. katame cattāro. idha bhikkhave bhikkhu kāye kāyānupassī viharati ātāpī sampajāno satimā vineyya loke abhijjhādomanassaṃ. vedanāsu vedanānupassī viharati ātāpī sampajāno satimā vineyya loke abhijjhādomanassaṃ. citte cittānupassī viharati ātāpī sampajāno satimā vineyya loke abhijjhādomanassaṃ. dhammesu dhammānupassī viharati ātāpī sampajāno satimā vineyya loke abhijjhādomanassaṃ.*[14]

> Bhikkhus, this is the direct path for the purification of beings, for the surmounting of sorrow and lamentation, for the disappearance of pain and

> grief, for the attainment of the true way, for the realisation of *Nibbāna*—namely, the four foundations of mindfulness. 'What are the four?' Here, bhikkhus, a bhikkhu abides contemplating the body as a body, ardent, fully aware, and mindful, having put away covetousness and grief for the world. He abides contemplating feelings as feelings, ardent, fully aware, and mindful, having put away covetousness and grief for the world. He abides contemplating mind as mind, ardent, fully aware, and mindful, having put away covetousness and grief for the world. He abides contemplating mind-objects as mind-objects, ardent, fully aware, and mindful, having put away covetousness and grief for the world (transl. Bodhi 1995: 145).

Once mindfulness is established, it leads to the extinction of suffering and allows the attainment of *nibbāna*. Hence, high value is given to the process.

The importance of *sati* in the Buddhist path, as outlined in early Buddhist texts, is also shown by the fact that it plays a key role in the most important Buddhist categories: it is a factor in the (Noble/Nobles') Eightfold Path, where it is called right-mindfulness (*sammāsati*).[15] Together with right-effort (*sammāvāyāma*) and right-concentration (*sammāsamādhi*), it is one of the more important elements of meditation;[16] it is the first awakening factor (*satisambojjhaṅga*)[17] and one of the faculties (*satindriya*).[18]

Furthermore, the practice of *sati* is the basis for the development of the subsequent meditative practices of the awareness of breathing, so-called 'insight, or deep meditation (*vipassanā*),'[19] frequently opposed to that of concentration (*samatha*) and the state of absorption (*jhāna*). There is no need here to go into the differences between these two meditative traditions nor into the thorny debate that has animated many scholars who try to determine which of these practices could be considered to be the original core practice of the Buddha's teaching.[20]

2. The meaning of *sati* for Corrado Pensa

Corrado Pensa combines the two meanings of *sati* in the following way:

> The Sanskrit word *smṛti* (in Pali *sati*) means 'memory,' 'remembering,' 'attention,' 'presence in the present,' and 'awareness.' Of course, remembering and 'being present' are two different meanings. Yet the moment we suddenly remember something we had forgotten, there is an awakening, not unlike a moment of lively attention in the present. In a certain sense, attention is like a continuous remembrance of the

> present, a continual awakening to the present. It is also interesting that, in addition to the word *smṛti* (*sati*), the word *smara*, which means love, is derived from the same root *smṛ*: another vector, so to speak, of fullness and presence. So, we have three meanings that, on early consideration are different, but yet are united by a value of awakening: the awakening of remembering, awareness as a profound awakening and the awakening of love.[21]

Pensa's idea is that awareness is remembering to pay attention to the present, because he defines *sati* as the ability to get in touch with things, with an attitude of non-attachment and non-identification.[22]

This idea is clear in the Italian word that Pensa uses to translate *sati*: 'consapevolezza.' This noun is formed by the preposition 'con,' 'with,' and by the verb 'sapere,' 'to know,' so it not only means 'to get to know something,' but also 'to come into contact with this knowledge.' In the Italian word, there is the nuance of the presence of something that is more than mere knowledge.

According to Pensa, all virtues are driven by *sati,*[23] a fundamental element in the cognitive and meditative process. In particular, relying on the Pāli texts, he distinguishes different levels in the cognitive process of reflection and interpretation. The first level concerns attention, called *manasikāra*, translated by Pensa as 'pure attention,' (attenzione pura e semplice), the faculty normally used to decode what you see and hear.[24] Then, there is *yonisomanasikāra,*[25] 'wise attention,' indicating not only our capacity for attention, but also for understanding. Its opposite is *ayonisomanasikāra*, 'unwise attention,' which nurtures the three poisons, or defilements (*kilesa*): greed, aversion, and ignorance.

Pensa (2002a: 35) makes reference to some passages from the *Sabbāsavasutta* (MN I 7–12), and in particular from p. 7, which emphasize that wise attention is the ability to know and see (and that unwise attention is the opposite):

> *jānato ahaṃ bhikkhave passato āsavānaṃ khayaṃ vadāmi no ajānato no apassato. kiñ ca bhikkhave jānato kiṃ passato āsavānaṃ khayaṃ hoti yoniso ca manasikāraṃ ayoniso ca manasikāraṃ. ayoniso bhikkhave manasikaroto anuppannā ceva āsavā uppajjanti uppannā ca āsavā pavaḍḍhanti yoniso ca bhikkhave manasikaroto anuppannā ceva āsavā na uppajjanti uppannā ca āsavā pahīyanti,*
>
> Bhikkhus, I say that the destruction of the taints is for one who knows and sees, not for one who does not know and see. Bhikkhus, who knows and sees what? Wise attention and unwise attention. Bhikkhus, when

> one attends unwisely, unrisen taints arise and arisen taints increase. Bhikkhus, when one attends wisely, unrisen taints do not arise and arisen taints are abandoned.[26]

Bodhi 2011: 30 also underlines the importance of making distinctions within the attention/awareness category when these terms are used in common language. He explains:

> My reservation regarding "attention" derives from the use of this word as the standard rendering for another technical term in the Buddhist analysis of mind, *manasikāra*, which designates a mental function whose role is quite different from that of mindfulness. The principal role of *manasikāra* is to turn the mind to an object. It is a spontaneous and automatic function exercised whenever an object impinges on a sense faculty or arises at the 'mind door'. It is translated 'attention' in the sense that it is the turning of attention to an object, the mind's 'advertence to the object'. This, however, is not the role of *sati*. By explaining *sati*, even in its rudimentary stage, as "bare attention", Nyanaponika merged its meaning with that of *manasikāra*. But whereas *manasikāra* generally predominates at the inception of a cognitive process, *sati* supervenes at a later stage, sustaining attention on the object and making it appear vividly to lucid cognition.

'Wise attention,' *yonisomanasikāra,* is considered a nourishment for the factors of awakening and shares with *sati* the function of directing attention in a contemplative way.[27]

Moreover, 'wise attention' is closely connected to another element of *sati*: *satisampajañña,* mindfulness and clear comprehension. In fact, in the *Aṅguttaranikāya* we read:

> *yonisomanasikāro paripūro satisampajaññaṃ paripūreti* (AN V 115)

> Wise attention being fulfilled brings awareness and clear comprehension to fulfillment.

Satisampajañña is a compound formed by *sati* and *sampajañña* (the noun derived from *sampajāna*), which means comprehension, so the whole compound is generally translated as 'mindfulness and clear knowledge or comprehension.'[28] The word *sampajāna* is also connected with *sati* in the above-mentioned *satipaṭṭhāna* formula. The two adjectives, 'he who comprehends clearly (*sampajāna*)' and 'he who possesses mindfulness (*satimā*)' are frequently part of the description of an 'ardent' (*ātāpī*) monk who practices the awareness of body, feeling, etc.[29]

Bodhi (2011: 22) explains the difference between *sati* and *sampajāna* in this way:

> The two terms, *sato* and *sampajāno*, often occur in proximity, implying a close affinity between their respective nouns, *sati* or mindfulness and *sampajañña* or clear comprehension. To distinguish the two, I would describe mindfulness as lucid awareness of the phenomenal field. This element of lucid awareness prevails in the initial stages of the practice. But with the strengthening of mindfulness, clear comprehension supervenes and adds the cognitive element. In the practice of insight meditation, the meditator clearly comprehends the nature and qualities of arisen phenomena and relates them to the framework defined by the parameters of the Dhamma, the teaching as an organic whole. The expression 'clearly comprehending' thus suggests that the meditator not only observes phenomena but interprets the presentational field in a way that sets arisen phenomena in a meaningful context. As the practice advances, clear comprehension takes on an increasingly more important role, eventually evolving into direct insight (*vipassanā*) and wisdom (*paññā*).

Pensa (1997: 20) gives particular importance to this compound and explains that awareness (*sati*), at some point, must develop a capacity for understanding in order to be effective and transformative. Seeing in depth, thanks to *sati*, makes it possible to begin to achieve comprehension (*sampajañña*). It is this understanding that can be considered to be the transformative element that produces real change. Pensa (2008: 16) believes this comprehension is the key to understanding non-self, *anattā*, and he quotes a famous passage of Ud p. 8:

> *tasmāt iha te Bāhiya evaṃ sikkhitabbaṃ diṭṭhe diṭṭhamattaṃ bhavissati sute sutamattaṃ bhavissati mute mutamattaṃ bhavissati viññāte viññātamattaṃ bhavissatī ti. evañ hi te Bāhiya sikkhitabbaṃ yato kho te Bāhiya diṭṭhe diṭṭhamattaṃ bhavissati* [...] *viññāte viññātamattaṃ bhavissati tato tvaṃ Bāhiya na tena, yato tvaṃ Bāhiya na tena tato tvaṃ Bāhiya na tattha, yato tvaṃ Bāhiya na tattha tato tvaṃ Bāhiya nev'idha na huraṃ na ubhayamantarena es'ev'anto dukkhassā ti.*[30]
>
> 'Therefore here, Bāhiya, you should train yourself thus: in the seen there should be only the seen, in the heard there should be only the heard, in the thought there should be only the thought, in the cognized there

> should be only the cognized. Thus indeed, Bāhiya, you should train yourself. When, Bāhiya, in the seen there is only the seen [...] in the cognized only the cognized, then, Bāhiya, you will not be be [identified] with that. When you, Bāhiya, will not be [identified] with that, then you will not be [identified] 'there-in.' When you, Bāhiya, will not be [identified] 'there-in,' then you, Bāhiya, will be neither here nor there, nor in between either. Only this is the end of suffering.'[31]

He thinks that if we have an awareness that does not add anything to the experience that we are living, we will no longer be identified with this experience, and the suffering connected to self-referential experience will fail. Pensa explains the crucial link between *sati* and *anattā* by saying that awareness is exactly the opposite of the common idea: 'this is mine, this I am, this is my self (*etaṃ mama, eso 'ham asmi, eso me attā*).'[32] By being aware, it is possible to abandon the compulsive tendency to self-reference with 'I, mine', to realize *anattā*, and as a consequence, achieve the greatest happiness.[33]

In other words, awareness (*sati*) is a means by which we are able not to identify with external objects and with our thoughts, and which leads us to a comprehension (*sampajañña*) that means we are able to see that we are not our thoughts; that we do not possess the things we think we possess. This sets us in a position to put an end to the sense of possession and to the notion that we have a self that possesses something. Awareness is the starting point and the engine of this whole process.

Another central element connected with *sati* and *sampajañña* is *paññā*, sometimes found in compound with *sati* as *satipaññā*. This word came from the Vedic *prajñā* (*pra+jñā*) and it is frequently translated as 'insight or wisdom' that enables us to understand the four noble truths. In fact, the Buddha said:

> AN I 220: *katamā ca Mahānāma sekhā paññā. idha Mahānāma bhikkhu idaṃ dukkhan ti yathābhūtaṃ pajānāti...pe... ayaṃ dukkhanirodhagāminī paṭipadā ti yathābhūtaṃ pajānāti. ayaṃ vuccati mahānāma sekhā paññā,*
>
> And what, [Mahānāma][34] is the wisdom of trainees? Here, [Mahānāma] a *bhikkhu* understands as it really is: "This is suffering... This is the way leading to the cessation of suffering'. This is called the wisdom of a trainee. (Transl. Bodhi 2012: 306–307).

Moreover, according to Anālayo 2003: 40 *sampajañña*, or 'clearly knowing', leads to develop wisdom (*paññā*) and he notes that, according to the Abhidhamma, the 'clearly knowing' represents the presence of wisdom.

To summarize the meaning that Pensa attributes to these awareness elements, *yonisomanasikāra* is linked to discernment and is the 'wise vision' while *sati* is 'contemplative attention' (Pensa 2002a: 35) and is described as the ability to have intimate contact with things (Pensa 2002b: 15). Moreover, according to Pensa 1997: 22, it is from this capacity to connect with what happens which he calls, at a first level, 'simple *sati*' (for example: I know that I am walking, or that I am sitting, I am aware of my breathing, etc.) that we can reach a second level, which is accompanied by comprehension (*satisampajañña*), in which we realize, not only that there is an element (e.g., breathing or a sensation), but that this element is impermanent. The understanding that the flux of all things is the true nature of existence flourishes. Thus, it is possible to reach 'wisdom' (*paññā*).[35]

Pensa 1997: 22 gives a very significant example for meditators' understanding of impermanence. We can all rationally agree with the idea that the reality is that all things are impermanent, that life changes continuously, that nothing is fixed and stable forever. But it is one thing to agree with this idea rationally, another to be able to truly see this flow, perceive it, and then develop real non-attachment. The ability to have this vision and understanding is *paññā,* and *sati* is the element that triggers the process.

The process is also accompanied by other elements, terms that are often synonymous with awareness, such as *appamāda*, which Pensa translates as 'solicitude, diligence' (in Italian: sollecitudine, diligenza) since, to be transformative, 'contemplative attention' must also include connotations of solicitude and readiness.[36]

To conclude, according to Pensa's interpretation of the Pāli canonical material, awareness, *sati*, is part of a cognitive process that has various phases and facets, and is the element that generates wisdom (*paññā*) that is capable of understanding reality.

2.1. *Sati* in the meditative process

As we have said, *sati* is also an essential part of the meditative process. Already in the description of the eightfold path in the *Dhammacakkappavattanasutta* (e.g., SN V 420), right-mindfulness (*sammāsati*) is listed between two elements related to meditation: *sammāvāyāma* (right effort), and *sammāsamādhi* (right concentration).

The main descriptions of the role of *sati* in meditative practices are found in the aforementioned practices of *satipaṭṭhāna*. Pensa 2002a: 23–24 interprets these famous instructions that describe the process of attention to the body, sensations, etc. in this way: when the Buddha speaks of direct awareness to the body, he intends to invite us to be aware without our physical sensations acting as intermediaries.[37]

In particular, he comments on the Pāli expression in MN I 55 *bhikkhu kāye kāyānupassī viharati* 'a monk dwelling aware of the body in the body'[38] as an invitation to exclude the mind as much as possible from this process. We must not think about the body, but try to get in touch with it.[39]

The word 'body' (*kāye*) is in the locative case, the same expression in the locative is repeated for the sensations (*vedanā*), and according to Pensa this sentence is intentionally constructed, because this direct contact is the real way to achieve the mental presence. More precisely, Pensa 2002b: 12 explains the Buddha's instruction to mean being aware of the body in the body, of the breath in the breath, and so on, as opposed to a mediated contact through thought and imagination. He interprets this invitation to awareness as an invitation to have contact unfiltered by thought about the element experienced.[40]

This teaching is a means of focusing our experience on the present, in a non-conceptual and therefore more authentic way. In particular, the sensations, *vedanā*, play a key role in this process and the secret to working with them is to replace the power of our identification with these sensations with *sati*. Moreover, Pensa 2002b: 13 adds that only if we have developed a good capacity for awareness of the body (*kāya*) and feelings (*vedanā*) is it possible to direct non-judgmental attention to the more complex field of emotions and thoughts (*citta* and *dhamma*). Often, to connect to emotions, we must start from the physical sensations that they produce. Direct contact with physical sensations allows us to abandon the filter of the mind and its mental proliferations (*papañca*)[41], that cause attachment, aversion and ignorance. Therefore, Pensa believes, the sequence proposed in the *sutta*, i.e., starting by observing the body and then the sensations, also indicates a precise methodological practice; it is not a random approach at all, since it is easier to work on tangible sensations of the body first, and then work on the observation of more exacting intangible elements, like the psychic and mental (*dharma*).

As far as so-called 'informal practice' is concerned, i.e., the daily meditation practice recommended to meditators, Pensa provides plentiful instruction in his courses, but the heart of his teaching consists of making moments of awareness as frequent as possible in many different ways.

A canonical passage Pensa uses frequently is found in the *Ambalaṭṭhikārāhulovādasutta* (MN I 414–420) which depicts the Buddha providing instructions to his son Rāhula:

> MN I 415: *evam eva kho, rāhula, paccavekkhitvā paccavekkhitvā kāyena kammaṃ kattabbaṃ paccavekkhitvā paccavekkhitvā vācāya kammaṃ kattabbaṃ paccavekkhitvā paccavekkhitvā manasā kammaṃ kattabbaṃ*
>
> So too, Rāhula, an action with the body should be done after repeated reflection; an action by speech should be done after repeated reflection; an action by mind should be done after repeated reflection. (Transl. Bodhi 1995: 524).

Later the Buddha recommends to Rāhula that he should reflect before he does something, while he is doing it, and when he has finished it. In Pensa and Papachristou (2018: 48), Pensa comments: 'By referring to the Buddha's teaching to his son Rāhula, we can usefully propose to appeal to awareness in three moments of time, namely: before an activity, during an activity, and after an activity.'[42] Pensa's invitation is to observe the effects of our actions throughout their progress, as they arise, endure and fade. By virtue of awareness, we can enter into authentic contact with our experience and observe it.[43] For example, Pensa held a one-year course at A.Me.Co on the role of *sati* in right-speech practice (see Pensa 1996). He underlined the need to pay attention to the usage of language, which does not lead to a censorial attitude (because this would be a form of control, not awareness), but that allows us to observe our actions before, during and after they happen, taking for the Buddha's instruction to Rāhula just referred to as a model.

All this work naturally must rest on an ethical basis (*sīla*), one of the fundamental virtues (*pāramī*). *Sīla*, in the division of the eightfold path, is linked to the right speech (*sammāvācā*), to the right action (*sammākammanta*) and the right livelihood (*sammāājīva*). Pensa considers *sīla* to be central, especially as regards meditation. Pensa 2002a: 46 describes how this virtuous circle occurs in the noble eightfold path: 'right understanding nourishes right intention, and both sustain the ethical, which in turn sustains meditation, which in turn sustains right understanding, and the virtuous circle starts over again'[44]. Thus, the ethical element nourishes meditation, because it is what leads us to abandon what is harmful (*akusala*) and lead a life directed towards simplification. Furthermore, Pensa and Papachristou (2018: 43) argue that the fundamentals of spiritual training are: daily meditation, residential retreats, the study of Dhamma, and the practice of *sīla*, the ethical sensitivity that is closely related to wisdom and compassion.

Corrado Pensa connects meditation directed at the observation of our sensations and our reactions to another cardinal teaching of Buddhism: *paṭiccasamuppāda* or 'dependent origination or dependent arising'[45]. He claims that in the chain of twelve links that constitute *paṭiccasamuppāda*, that aim to explain the conditionality of all physical and psychical phenomena, there is a weak link, which can break the cycle of suffering. According to Pensa 2002b: 51 it is the sequence *pahassa* (contact between the senses, which includes the mind, and their respective objects), *vedanā* (pleasant, unpleasant or neutral feelings) and *taṇhā* (attraction, repulsion, confusion or distraction respectively in front of the pleasant, the unpleasant or the neutral). Why is this the weak link? Because the area of *phassa-vedanā-taṇhā* is one in which it is possible to intervene with practice, applying a precise awareness of the whole sequence. This will result in a progressive weakening of attachment (*upādāna*, the factor immediately following *taṇhā*) and in this way the weakening of the fundamental cause, together with the ignorance, of suffering.[46]

Thus, Pensa stresses the importance of work in the area of contact-feelings-reaction. The practice of meditation thus becomes the observation of the moment of contact, i.e., of the perception we have, and of everything that follows. Because we pay attention to feelings (unpleasant, pleasant or neutral) and our reactions to them, probably experiencing attachment if the sensation is pleasure, dislike if it is displeasure or indifference, and distraction, if it is neutral, we can introduce awareness, which becomes an understanding of how things are and wisdom after repeated observations according to the process already described. This precious interpretative key of the canonical teachings put forward by Pensa makes the teachings in the texts accessible and offers a concrete reading of some of the passages aimed at accomplishment.

3. Corrado Pensa's thinking in the context of the contemporary landscape of the teaching of *vipassanā* and the applications of mindfulness.

At the beginning of the twentieth century, *vipassanā* meditation, or insight meditation, became widespread thanks to a branch of Burmese insight meditation led by Ledi Sayādaw (U Nyanadaza, 1846–1923) and Mingun Sayādaw (U Nārada, 1870–1955), and later by one of Mingun's disciples,

Mahāsī Sayādaw (1904–1982). Braun (2013) traces this lineage in his research focused particularly on Ledi Sayādaw, who simplified the meditation process and made the method more accessible, opening it to lay people, principally to protect Buddhism from British colonial influence. After him, Mahāsī developed a method called "pure insight" (*suddhavipassanā*) that does not require deep concentration, simply more meditation sessions. This type of approach spread in the West and in particular in the United States. In 1975, in Barre, Massachusetts, following this Burmese tradition and other similar approaches, such as the Thai forest tradition[47], J. Kornfield, J. Goldstein and S. Salzberg founded the Insight Meditation Society (IMS), an important point of reference for many Dhamma teachers and practitioners. It was here that Corrado Pensa received part of his training, becoming one of the centre's senior teachers.

The simplified Burmese approach, and particularly Mahāsī's idea of *sati*, as the ability to live 'moment-to-moment', with 'non-judgmental awareness' of whatever appears to the consciousness and the idea of 'bare awareness' coined by Nyanaponika Thera[48] (a famous monk and scholar, disciple of Mahāsī), has been very successful, particularly in psychology and more generally in well-being movements. A very famous and successful offshoot of this trend was the programme called Mindfulness-Based Stress Reduction (MBSR) elaborated by the biologist Jon Kabat Zinn, former student of Kornfield, Goldstein, Thich Nhat Hanh and U Ba Khin. This programme uses 'mindfulness' to reduce negative stress, paving the way to psychological well-being.

In this way, an idea of mindfulness was brought outside of its Buddhist context and the 'psychologizing of meditation' became very popular. However, it is something very different from *sati*, as described in the Pāli Canon. Scholars and non-scholars alike have highlighted the problems of this approach, examples being Cousins (1996) and Gethin (2011). In particular, Sharf (2014: 475) synthesized this criticism in three points:

> Critics object to (1) Mahāsī's devaluation of concentration techniques leading to absorption (Pāli *jhāna*); (2) claims that followers of the Mahāsī method are able to attain advanced stages of the path, including the four stages of enlightenment (Pāli *ariya-magga*) in remarkably short periods of time; and (3) the ethics of rendering *sati* as bare attention, which would seem to devalue or neglect the importance of ethical judgment.

It is possible that this drift that Sharf underlined has come as an unexpected and unwanted effect. Bodhi, for example, thinks that his teacher, Nyanaponika, was probably not in agreement with the idea of 'bare attention' such as is attributed to him by some neo-*vipassanā* meditative movements.[49]

However, it is my intention here to consider whether these criticisms can be directed at Corrado Pensa's teaching. In the scenario described above, he appears to be follower of this meditative approach because he followed the Burmese and Thai traditions and is a senior teacher of IMS. However, his teaching differs greatly from positions attributed to the Mahāsī by Sharf. In fact, an analysis of the three points mentioned above concerning the relationship between *samatha* and *vipassanā* reveals that even if Pensa does not teach *jhāna* meditation directly, he believes that these two meditative techniques are closely intertwined and must go hand in hand. He claims: *vipassanā* is a synthetic definition: we should always say *samatha-vipassanā*, because they are intertwined dimensions.[50] His teaching does not promise rapid progress. On the contrary, he emphasizes the importance of patience[51], the necessity to persevere and the gradualness of the path.[52]

Concerning Sharf's third point, Pensa uses the definition 'non-judgmental awareness', but he explains this definition (Pensa 2002b: 37–39; 2002a: 108) by distinguishing thought from what is 'pure attention, or awareness', which is a 'pure vision', not contaminated by thoughts, labels, judgment. What he calls 'non-judgmental awareness or bare attention' is a state of presence that comes before words and language. It is something non-conceptual and therefore not egoistical, something that does not belong to us in a personal way. The practice of awareness is aimed at bringing attention to our judgments, without exerting control, but letting their observation make them less interesting. The observation of the processes of our mind allows us to de-identify ourselves and to access another dimension, that Pensa (2018: 27) called our 'native land', borrowing a metaphorical image from the *Satipaṭṭhānasaṃyutta* (SN V 146–147). This impersonal awareness, linked to other elements, such as equanimity (*upekkhā*)[53], will lead us to a dimension that points to the unconditional.

It is certainly true that, as Dreyfus (2011: 43) points out, the concept of 'non-judgmental awareness' is not found in the Pāli Canon, and that often *sati* figures associated with remembering in these texts (see for example some definitions of *sati* already discussed earlier in this article § 1), but perhaps we should consider what type of awareness, based on the terminological distinction in the texts adopted by Pensa in reference to its role in the cognitive process, could be inferred from other textual passages (such as Ud

8 and D I 70[54] already quoted). Furthermore, Pensa is certainly not the only one to support this double meaning of the term *sati*. For example, Bodhi and Wallace (2006: 4) also argue that in *satipaṭṭhāna* the word *sati* does not refer to memory[55].

Moreover, Sharf (2014: 475) claims:

> Paul Griffiths suggests that the closest thing to a state of unconstructed or pure experience in early Indian Buddhist scholasticism is *nirodhasamāpatti*—a state in which both objects *and* conscious experience cease altogether (Griffiths 1986, 1990). In such a framework, it seems misleading to construe *any* mode of attention or perception as 'bare'.

In his research as a young scholar, Pensa examined the meditative stages in Buddhism and Yoga and dealt with the concept of *nirodha-samāpatti* (that he studied comparing it with *samprajñātasamādhi* or *cittavṛtti-nirodha*) and declared that *nirodha* 'cannot be regarded as altogether different from *nirvāṇa*, even though it is considered only conducive to the *nirvāṇa* state and not equivalent to it' (Pensa 1977: 338)[56]. Thus, although this subject certainly deserves more in-depth study, I think that 'bare awareness' corresponds to a state of mindfulness, comparable to the canonical passages mentioned above and not to a state of complete cessation of mental activity, as implied by *nirodhasamāpatti,* so it seems that the comparison is not entirely adequate in this case.

Pensa certainly disagrees with the idea that awareness is separated from *sīla*, morality. As we have seen in § 2.1, for him morality is the nourishment of *sati* and, in turn, morality is nourished by the practice of *sati*.

In conclusion, we note that the teaching of Pensa is characterized by an undoubted capacity for synthesis and balance. He translates the ancient teaching into a modern language while remaining faithful to the substance. Although Pensa teaches *vipassanā* within the framework of the recent Burmese and Thai meditative traditions which emphasizes the role of mindfulness as primary, and although he uses the terminology utilized by the IMS, his academic background ensures that his teaching on *sati* conforms to canonical texts. He has managed to distance himself from the dangers inherent in certain more superficial approaches related to mindfulness. Among these 'reductionist' approaches to the practice of mindfulness, we note only two in closing: the reduction of mindfulness to a psychotherapeutic practice and the reduction of mindfulness to a mere technique.

For many years the discipline of psychology has looked at some aspect of the Buddhism, such as meditation and attention to suffering, as useful tools to help people to resolve their personal problems, ignoring the religious function and context of meditation, only seeing meditation to be of therapeutic value. However, Pensa is very clear that awareness and meditation are not a form of psychotherapy (1997: 114):

> There is also the tendency, perhaps linked to cultural conditions, to relate unconsciously to the practice of Dharma as a sort of psychotherapy. But meditation does not work like psychotherapy, even though it may have therapeutic effects. Meditation, the practice of Dharma—quite differently from psychotherapy—is a lifetime's work.[57]

Pensa was trained as a Jungian psychotherapist and he understood the danger of confusing the two approaches, both during private talks for practitioners and in his attitude towards the practice of Dhamma. A spiritual path, unlike a path of analysis, must be nurtured by faith based on morality and an ontological and existential vision.

Recently, the mindfulness protocol (MBSR) developed by the aforementioned Jon Kabat-Zinn, who also trained at IMS, has used *sati* as a lay aid for the reduction of suffering and stress. Without detracting from the benefit of the uses of awareness in other disciplines, the problem and differences that arise in the use of *sati* in these fields, in contrast to the cultivation of *sati* within the Buddhist path, has already been highlighted by various scholars, such as Gethin (2011). In short, we can add that in the former instance, namely in psychotherapy, awareness is used as a functional tool for achieving well-being; while in Buddhism, the development of *sati* is a life path, the acquisition of a mental habitus as permanent as possible, characterized by the gradual decrease of suffering, and the development of equanimity and peace. In short, mindfulness understood as *sati* is a means of activating a process of cognitive transformation, the aim of which is not psychological well-being or stress reduction, but liberation.

Corrado Pensa avoided these reductionist approaches, and his teaching can be considered to be a model for teaching *vipassanā* meditation in the West and for teaching Buddhism to practitioners based on canonical texts.

Notes

1 I would like to express all my gratitude first of all to Corrado Pensa, who transmitted to me his love for Buddhist Studies and to all the others who have helped me with this work, *in primis*: Mark Allon and Francesco Sferra, who provide me with helpful advice and suggestions. I would also like thank Geoffrey Samuel, who supplied me with a rich bibliography on the subject of awareness and Robert Sharf who, even in a non-academic context, had the patience to discuss with me his interpretation on the teaching of contemporary *vipassanā*.

2 Besides the Nikāyas there are other Pāli sources for the study of *sati*, including the canonical Abhidhamma texts and later literature, such as the *Visuddhimagga*. For the function of *sati* in Pāli literature, see Giustarini 2020. Here I have tried to restrict the research mainly to *sutta*s, since they lend themselves better to a comparison with Corrado Pensa's teaching.

3 According to Anālayo 2018: 1047–1048 we must first remember that what is called 'Early Buddhism' is not identifiable with Theravāda Buddhism and therefore also the idea of *sati* presents some differences: 'Hence, when speaking of mindfulness in early Buddhism, for example, it needs to be borne in mind that this does not simply equate to Theravāda notions of this quality [...] An example that illustrates the need to differentiate between the Theravāda and early Buddhist perspectives is the basic ethical quality of mindfulness or *sati*. According to early Buddhist thought, mindfulness is a quality that could be right (*sammā*) or wrong (*micchā*). This implies that *sati* can manifest in wholesome or unwholesome ways. According to the Theravāda exegesis, however, mindfulness is invariably a wholesome quality.' Cf. also Anālayo 2003: 50 n. 31.

4 See Gethin (2011 and in particular pp. 263–264) for an overview of the etymology and the translations used for this word. Cf. also Bodhi 2011: 22–27 and, for a good synthesis, Ditrich 2016: 14–15.

5 As Anālayo 2017: 20 stated: 'The theoretical construct of mindfulness and the practices informed by this notion have gone through considerable development during nearly 2,500 years in the history of Buddhist thought, making it practically impossible to speak of "Buddhist mindfulness" as if this were a monolithic concept.'

6 An interesting discussion on the relation between these two important meanings of *sati* is found in Bodhi and Wallace (2006), cf. also Anālayo 2003: 45–46.

7 E.g. Anālayo 2017: 26–27: 'The standard definition of mindfulness in the early discourses describes someone who is mindful and able to recollect and remember what has been done and said long ago.'

8 Transl. Gethin 2001: 36. Unless explicitly stated otherwise, all translations are mine.

9 They are recollections of the Buddha, the Dharma, the Saṅgha, of good conduct, generosity and the gods (along with the mindfulness of death), cf. e.g., AN I 30, AN III 284, DN III 250, III 280.

10 See MN n. 10 at MN I 55–62 and DN no. 22 at DN II 290–315.

11 Vibh 193–202. For an interesting analysis of the more frequent formulas, see Gethin 2001: 47–59. Descriptions and instructions of this practice are present also in other Pāli texts, e.g., in the *Ānāpānasatisutta*, MN III 78–88 or the *Kāyagatasatisutta*, MN III 88–99. The *satipaṭṭhāna* are described also in non-Pāli sources, Kuan 2008 made a useful comparison of Sanskrit, Pāli and Chinese sources.

12 Concerning the meaning of the word *satipaṭṭhāna*, Anālayo 2006: 28–29 states: 'The term *satipaṭṭhāna* can be explained as a compound of *sati*, "mindfulness" or "awareness," and *upaṭṭhāna*, with the *u* of the latter term dropped by vowel elision. The Pāli term *upaṭṭhāna* literally means "placing near," and in the present context refers to a particular way of "being present" and "attending" to something with mindfulness. In the discourses, the corresponding verb *upaṭṭhāti* often denotes various nuances of "being present," or else "attending." Understood in this way, "*satipaṭṭhāna*" means that *sati* "stands by," in the sense of being present; *sati* is "ready at hand," in the sense of attending to the current situation. *Satipaṭṭhāna* can thus be translated as "presence of mindfulness" or as "attending with mindfulness."' See also Gethin 2001: 30–36 and Bodhi 2011: 25–27.

13 Bodhi 2011: 21 states: 'We usually translate *anupassanā* as "contemplation," but it might also be illuminating to understand it more literally as an act of "observation." The word is made up of the prefix *anu*, which suggests repetition or closeness, and the base *passanā*, which means "seeing." Thus, mindfulness is part of a process that involves a close, repetitive observation of the object.'

14 E.g., MN I 55–56 = DN II 290; cf. also SN V 141, Vism I 3. Sometimes this formula occurs without the initial part (*ekāyano* […] *satipaṭṭhānā*), e.g., DN II 216, III 58; SN V 167.

15 The standard formula used to define *sammāsati* is (similar to the *satipaṭṭhāna*, MN I 55) in e.g. DN II 313 = SN V 9–10: *katamā ca bhikkhave sammāsati. idha bhikkhave bhikkhu kāye kāyānupassī viharati ātāpī sampajāno satimā vineyya loke abhijjhādomanassaṃ vedanāsu vedanānupassī viharati* […] *ayaṃ vuccati bhikkave sammāsati*. 'And what, bhikkhus is right mindfulness? Here, bhikkhus, a bhikkhu dwells contemplating the body in the body, ardent, clearly comprehending, mindful, having removed covetousness and displeasure in regard to the world. He dwells contemplating feelings in feelings […] This is called right mindfulness'. Bodhi 2000: 1529.

16 *Sati* is also a requirement for the other path factors, cf. Anālayo 2006: 49.

17 E.g., SN V 90. The other *bojjhaṅga* are: investigation or investigation of *dhamma* (*dhammavicaya*); energy (*viriya*); joy (*pīti*); tranquility (*passaddhi*); concentration (*samādhi*) and equanimity (*upekkhā*). For more information see Gethin 2001: 146–189.

18 These faculties are twenty-two physical and mental phenomena; in this list *sati* is one of the five spiritual faculties (*bala*), the others are: confidence-faith (*saddhā*); energy (*viriya*), concentration (*samādhi*) and wisdom (*paññā*), e.g. AN II 149.

19 In Sanskrit *vipaśyanā*. This word is composed by the prefix *vi*- that means 'in, into, between' and the verbal root *paś*, 'to see'. This compound could be translated as 'to see into, see through or to see in a special way', but '*vi*' can function as an intensive, and Pāli *vipassanā* may mean 'seeing deeply'.

20 For example, on this topic King 1980 claims that the *jhanās* came from a Brahmanical-yogic spirituality and are not the heart of the Buddhist teaching on the meditation. Contrary to this, Vetter 1988 and Bronkhorst 1993 claim that *dhyāna*/*jhāna*s are the original practice of the Buddhist meditation; Gethin (2001) argues the same but for different reasons. According to Wynne 2007 the *jhāna*s was incorporated in the Brahmanical practices, but particular *samādhi* experiences present in them seem to be original Buddhist.

21 Throughout this paper my English translation is presented in the body of the text with Pensa's original Italian in the footnotes, see Pensa 2002b: 35: 'La parola sanscrita *smṛti* (in pāli *sati*) significa sia 'memoria', 'ricordarsi' sia 'attenzione', 'presenza nel presente', 'consapevolezza'. Certo ricordarsi e "essere presenti" rappresentano significati diversi. Eppure nel momento in cui ricordiamo improvvisamente qualcosa che avevamo dimenticato, c'è come un risveglio, non dissimile da un momento di attenzione viva nel presente. In un certo senso l'attenzione è come un continuo ricordarsi del presente, un continuo svegliarsi al presente. È anche interessante che dalla medesima radice *smṛ*, oltre alla parola *smṛti* (*sati*) venga la parola *smara*, che vuol dire amore: un altro vettore, per dir così, di pienezza e di presenza. Dunque tre significati che sono diversi da un lato e che tuttavia sono accomunati da una valenza di risveglio: il risveglio del ricordarsi, la consapevolezza come risveglio profondo, il risveglio dell'amore.'

22 Pensa 2002b: 42: 'Come possiamo definire la consapevolezza, la presenza mentale, *sati*? *Sati* è la capacità di entrare in intimità con le cose, ma secondo un atteggiamento di non attaccamento e di non identificazione [...] dal punto di vista dell'io è una contraddizione, è assolutamente incomprensibile, ma questa è per definizione la struttura stessa della consapevolezza'.

23 Pensa 1997: 62: 'Tutte le virtù fondamentali del cammino interiore sono—per dirla con i testi classici di questa tradizione—come "trainate" dalla consapevolezza'.

24 Cf. Pensa 1997: 81 and Pensa 2002a: 30, 33.

25 Pensa (2002a: 34) stresses that the term *yoniso* came from the female womb name (*yoni*), precisely because this understanding indicates something visceral and complete.

26 Quoted with slight changes from Bodhi 1995: 91.

27 They are described in this way by Anālayo 2003: 58: 'The resemblance in function between *sati* and attention is also reflected in the fact that wise attention (*yoniso-manasikāra*) parallels several aspects of *satipaṭṭhāna* contemplation, such as directing attention to antidotes for the hindrances, becoming aware of the impermanent nature of the aggregates or of the sense-spheres, establishing the awakening factors and contemplating the four noble truths.'

28 In particular Kuan 2008: 50 claims: 'The *sati-sampajañña* formula indicates that one is not just "fully aware" of what one is doing at the moment, but more importantly one is fully aware with the purpose of avoiding unwholesome mental states. In other words, while undertaking any activities, one reminds oneself to keep the evil unwholesome states away from one's mind. This is what is meant by "acting in full awareness" (*sampajānakārin*) in the *sati-sampajañña* formula. The *sati-sampajañña* formula is not just contemplation of the body, the first *satipaṭṭhāna*, but rather it serves as a general guideline for practice in daily life, probably including meditation as well.' For a more detailed analysis of this *dvandva* compound, see Kuan 2008: 45–51.

29 For other observations on the adjective *satimā*, see Wynne 2007: 51.

30 I adopt the Be reading of ... *tato tvaṃ Bāhiya na tena, yato tvaṃ Bāhiya na tena tato tvaṃ Bāhiya na tattha, yato tvaṃ Bāhiya na tattha tato tvaṃ Bāhiya nev' idha na huraṃ na ubhayamantarena*, which is the same as Ee of SN IV 73 rather than Ee edition which reads *tato tvam Bāhiya na tattha, yato tvaṃ Bāhiya nev' attha tato tvaṃ Bāhiya nev' idha na huraṃ na ubhayamantarena* ..., and translate accordingly.

31 For the difficult *na tena ... na tattha* I am guided by Bodhi's translation of the SN IV 73 passage (Bodhi 2000: 1176) and by his detailed note on it (note 75, pp. 1410–1411).

32 This formula is present very frequently in the Pāli Canon, e.g., MN I 135, III 19, III 264, SN III 18, SN IV 24.

33 This idea is present in Ud 10: *asmimānassa yo vinayo etaṃ ve paramaṃ sukhan ti*, 'That which is the driving out of the conceit "I am", this truly is the highest bliss.'

34 Bodhi here does not repeat the name Mahānāma.

35 Pensa 1997: 22: 'Noi possiamo pensare ad un primo livello di *sati* semplice, cioè sapere che sto camminando, o che sto seduto, seguire il respiro, ecc. Poi possiamo pensare ad un secondo livello, che è *sati* accompagnata da comprensione, in cui ci si accorge non soltanto che c'è il tale oggetto, ed esempio il respiro o una sensazione, ma che tale oggetto è impermanente: *sati* raggiunge un importante grado di maturazione allorché, in virtù appunto di sati, comincia a fiorire la comprensione del flusso cosante di tutte le cose.'

36 Pensa 2002a: 15: '*appamāda* è il contrario di *pamāda*, che è negligenza, disordine, incuria, distrazione. Dunque *appamāda* è diligenza, cura, sollecitudine. In realtà il termine è spesso usato come sinonimo di attenzione-consapevolezza. E, ovviamente, quando si sceglie di usare *appamāda*, si intende sottolineare l'aspetto della sollecitudine e della cura che debbono animare l'autentica consapevolezza.'

Pensa 1997: 119 uses a metaphor present in the Pāli canon to describe *appamadā*, which is compared to an elephant's footprint, in which all the other footprints fit, so this can include all the kinds of welfare (cf. SN I 86–87 = AN III 365).

37 Pensa 2002a: 23: 'Quando il Buddha parla di consapevolezza diretta al corpo (e la consapevolezza del respiro è una forma di consapevolezza o attenzione portata al corpo) usa l'espressione: "Stiamo attenti al respiro nel corpo".' Che cosa vuol dire questa espressione? Stare attenti in maniera assolutamente diretta, senza intermediari, alle sensazioni fisiche.

38 Another way to translate this sentence is 'contemplating the body as a body'; Kuan 2008: 114 provides a good account of the problem of translating this sentence.

39 Pensa 2002a: 23: 'Il 'corpo nel corpo' è diverso dal corpo nella mente. Quest'ultimo sarebbe un pensare al corpo, e non il volgere la consapevolezza al corpo. É un'enfasi, un'espressione che vuole sottolineare molto questa maniera diretta, questa immediatezza, questa intimità di contatto tra la consapevolezza e il suo oggetto.'

40 Pensa 2002b: 12: 'L'espressione peculiare (corpo nel corpo, eccetera) vuole proprio sottolineare con forza il carattere di immediatezza e intimità, ossia di connessione ferma e non superficiale che la consapevolezza meditativa (*sati*) deve sviluppare. Essere consapevole del corpo nel corpo, del respiro nel respiro, si contrappone a un contatto mediato attraverso il pensiero o l'immaginazione: si è consapevoli del respiro ma, anche, si nomina, si pensa, si immagina il respiro. Magari questa interferenza mentale è percentualmente modesta. Anche così, tuttavia, essa è sufficiente a impedire l'immediatezza totale, silenziosa, viva, ossia la pura consapevolezza, diretta, non verbale, non giudicante, non concettuale, in comunione partecipe, con il respiro o con un'altra espressione corporea.'

41 This word means 'obstacle or illusion, hindrance to spiritual progress', and the opposite term *nippapañca* is a synonym for *nibbāna*. In order to explain the mechanism of mental proliferation, Pensa and Papachristou (2012: 19) quote the

Madhupiṇḍikasutta, in particular MN I 109–112, and state: 'Thought born from perception. And from thinking is generated the mental proliferation (*papañca*). But when we come to the point that in the mental and emotional proliferation do not find anything to be happy, this is the end of the attachment and aversion. (…) the end of all negative mental states.' In the original Italian: 'Dalla percezione nasce il pensare. E dal pensare si origina la proliferazione mentale (*papañca*). Allorché però arriviamo al punto che nella proliferazione mentale ed emotiva non troviamo più nulla di cui rallegrarci, questa è la fine delle tendenze latente all'attaccamento, all'avversione. (…) la fine di tutti gli stati mentali negativi.'

42 'Riferendoci all'insegnamento del Buddha al figlio Rahula, ci possiamo utilmente riproporre di fare appello alla consapevolezza in tre momenti e cioè: prima della reattività, oppure durante la reattività, oppure dopo la reattività.'

43 Pensa and Papachristou 2018: 21: 'Grazie a *sati* possiamo illuminare le nostre esperienze, guardarle con gentilezza non giudicante, entrare in contatto con noi stessi con delicatezza, fiducia e pazienza. Solo ciò che la consapevolezza illumina, la saggezza comprende.'

44 In Italian: 'la retta comprensione, nutre la retta intenzione entrambe nutrono la parte etica, che nutre quella meditativa, che a sua volte nutre la comprensione e ricomincia questo circolo virtuoso'.

45 A long version of this teaching is in M I 49–54 and was considered so important by the Buddha that he said that one who is able to see dependent origination sees the Dhamma (cf. M I 190–191).

46 In the original Italian: 'É la sequenza *phassa* (contatto tra i sensi, che includono la mente e i loro rispettivi oggetti)—*vedanā* (sensazioni piacevoli, spiacevoli o neutra) conseguente a tale contatto e *taṇhā* (attrazione, repulsione, confusione o distrazione rispettivamente davanti al piacevole, allo spiacevole o al neutro). Questa sequenza è chiamata l'anello debole nella catena della produzione condizionata (*paṭicca-samuppāda*), che è il cuore dell'insegnamento del Buddha circa la sofferenza e le sue cause. Perché anello debole? Perché l'area di *phassa-vedanā-taṇhā* è quella in cui è possibile intervenire con la pratica, applicando una precisa consapevolezza su tutta la sequenza. Ciò avrà per effetto un progressivo indebolimento dell'attaccamento (*upādāna* il fattore immediatamente successivo a *taňhā*) e dunque della causa fondamentale, insieme con l'ignoranza, della sofferenza.

47 This center is largely orientated to follow the teaching of Ajahan Cha and U Ba Khin (see Braun 2013: 164)

48 This definition was coined by him in the famous book *The Heart of Buddhist Meditation* (first published in 1954) after a period studying under Mahāsī in Burma.

49 Bodhi and Wallace 2006: 8–9: 'I recall that when Ven. Nyanaponika would read statements about "bare attention" as interpreted by some of the neo-Vipassana teachers, he would sometimes shake his head and say, in effect, "But that's not what I meant at all!" I remember many years ago I meditated at the Insight Meditation Society in Barre. At the end of the corridor where I did walk meditation there was a sign that read, "Allow whatever arises." Whenever I walked towards the sign and it came into my field of vision, I would always think of the Buddha's saying, "Here, a monk does not tolerate an arisen thought of sensual desire … ill-will … cruelty … or any other arisen unwholesome state, but abandons it, eliminates it, and completely dispels it." I was tempted to replace the sign there with one that had this saying, but

fortunately I resisted the temptation. If I had been discovered, I might have been expelled'.

50 For a more complete explanation, see Pensa 1997: 8–9.

51 Pensa 2002b: 22: 'Vale forse la pena di ricordare che la pazienza, assai più della forza di volontà, è una struttura portante della pratica. Aggiungiamo inoltre, che è sempre la consapevolezza paziente quella che ci mette in grado di scorgere certi ingannevoli e frequenti 'doppi fondi' nel lavoro sulle emozioni.'

Pensa 2002b: 35: 'Perciò nella pratica della consapevolezza, noi abbiamo a che fare da una parte con una specie di paziente artigiano, con il lento e progressivo affinamento di uno strumento, dall'altro abbiamo a che fare con qualcosa di molto grande, che va oltre l'orizzonte della nostra comprensione immediata'.

52 Pensa and Papachristou 2018: 171: 'Ricordiamo poi che nelle Scritture la gradualità è descritta come una delle meraviglie del Dharma. Dunque alla felicità suprema della liberazione si perverrà per gradi.'

53 Pensa and Papachristou 2018: 212: 'Equanimità e consapevolezza sono l'una intrinseca all'altra. Due facce di una medesima medaglia. Quindi coltivare la capacità di essere presenti a ciò che è presente, ossia praticare la consapevolezza, ci rende equanimi, ed essere più equanimi ci rende più consapevoli'. The equanimity is strongly connected to *sati* also in the Canonical text, for example in the fourth *jhāna* there is the formula *upekkhāsatipārisuddhi* (e.g., DN I 37, DN II 186, MN I 22) 'purity of mindfulness (brought about) by means of equipoise'. For more information see Gethin 2001: 157 and Vetter 1988: XXVI, note 9.

54 Here, the mindfulness is defined 'gatekeeper', see Gethin 2011: 271.

55 Bodhi and Wallace (2006: 4): 'Then, in the next sutta the question is raised: "What is the faculty of mindfulness?" And the answer is given: "The mindfulness that one obtains on the basis of the four *satipaṭṭhāna*s." Here, mindfulness as memory doesn't seem appropriate at all'.

56 The topic is discussed by Griffiths 1986: 30–31.

57 In Italian: 'C'è inoltre la tendenza, forse legata a condizioni culturali, a rapportarsi inconsciamente alla pratica del Dharma come a una sorta di psicoterapia. Ma la meditazione non opera come una psicoterapia, anche se può avere effetti terapeutici. La meditazione, la pratica del Dharma—diversamente dalla psicoterapia—è l'opera di una vita'.

Bibliography

All references to Pāli texts are to the Pāli Text Society editions.

Anālayo, Bhikkhu 2003. *Satipaṭṭhāna. The Direct Path to Realization*. Selangor: Buddhist Wisdom Centre (Birmingham: Windhorse Publications, 1st edition 2006).

Anālayo, Bhikkhu 2017. *Early Buddhist Meditation studies*. Barre: Barre Centre for Buddhist Studies.

Anālayo, Bhikkhu 2018. 'Mindfulness Constructs in Early Buddhism and Theravāda: Another Contribution to the Memory Debate.' In *Mindfulness* 9: 1047–1051. Published on line: https://doi.org/10.1007/s12671-018-0967-3.

Bodhi, Bhikkhu transl. 1995. *The Middle Length Discourses of the Buddha: A Translation of the Majjhima Nikāya* (with Ñāṇamoli Bhikkhu). Boston: Wisdom Publications.

Bodhi, Bhikkhu transl. 2000. *The Connected Discourses of the Buddha: A New Translation of the Saṃyutta Nikāya*. Boston: Wisdom Publications.

Bodhi, Bhikkhu transl. 2012. *The Numerical Discourses of the Buddha: A Translation of the Aṅguttara Nikāya*. Boston: Wisdom Publications.

Bodhi, Bhikkhu and Alan Wallace 2006. 'The Nature of Mindfulness and Its Role in Buddhist Meditation. A Correspondence between B. Alan Wallace and the Venerable Bhikkhu Bodhi'. Not published.

Bodhi, Bhikkhu 2011. 'What Does Mindfulness Really Mean? A Canonical Perspective.' *Contemporary Buddhism* 12.1: 19–39. https://doi.org/10.1080/14639947.2011.564813

Braun, Erik 2013. *The Birth of Insight. Meditation, Modern Buddhism, and the Burmese Monk Ledi Sayadaw*. London: University of Chicago Press.

Bronkhorst, Johannes 1993. *The Two Traditions of Meditation in Ancient India*. Delhi: Motilal Banarsidass.

Cousins, L. S. 1996. 'The Origins of Insight Meditation.' In Skorupski, Tadeusz ed. *The Buddhist Forum IV, Seminar Papers 1994–1996*, 35–58. London: School of Oriental and African Studies.

Ditrich, Tamara 2016. 'Situating the Concept of Mindfulness in the Theravāda Tradition.' *Asian Studies IV* (XX), 2: 13–33. https://doi.org/10.4312/as.2016.4.2.13-33

Dreyfus, Georges 2011. 'Is Mindfulness Present-centred and Non-judgmental? A Discussion of the Cognitive Dimensions of Mindfulness.' *Contemporary Buddhism* 12.1: 41–54. https://doi.org/10.1080/14639947.2011.564815

Gethin, Rupert M. L. 2001. *The Buddhist Path to Awakening: A Study of the Bodhi-Pakkhiyā Dhammā*. Oxford: Oneworld Publications.

Gethin, Rupert M. L. 2011. 'On some Definitions of Mindfulness.' *Contemporary Buddhism* 12.1: 263–279. https://doi.org/10.1080/14639947.2011.564843

Giustarini, Giuliano 2000. *La Pratica della Consapevolezza: Sati nel Canone Buddhista Pali*. Monterotondo: Fuorilinea.

Griffiths, Paul 1986. *On Being Mindfulness: Buddhist Meditation and the Mind-body Problem*. La Salle: Open Court.

King, Winston 1980. *Theravāda Meditation: The Buddhist Transformation of Yoga*. University Park: Pennsylvania State University Press.

Kuan, Tse-fu 2008. *Mindfulness in Early Buddhism. New Approaches Through Psychology and Textual Analysis of Pali, Chinese and Sanskrit Sources*. London and New York: Routledge.

Nyanaponika Thera 1953. *The Heart of Buddhist Meditation*. Kandy: Buddhist Publication Society.

Pensa, Corrado 1977. 'Notes on Meditational States in Buddhism and Yoga.' *East and West*, Rome, 27, 1.4: 335–344.

Pensa, Corrado 1994. *La tranquilla passione. Saggi sulla meditazione buddhista di consapevolezza*. Roma: Ubaldini.

Pensa, Corrado 1996. *La consapevolezza e il suo uso. Corso del lunedì 1995–6.* Roma: A.Me.Co.

Pensa, Corrado 1997. *Consapevolezza, comprensione, lasciar andare. Corso del lunedì 1996–7*. Roma: A.Me.Co.

Pensa, Corrado 2002a. *Attenzione Saggia, Attenzione non Saggia*. Torino: Manganelli.

Pensa, Corrado 2002b. *L'intelligenza spirituale. Saggi sulla pratica del Dharma.* Roma: Ubaldini.

Pensa, Corrado 2008. *Il silenzio tra due onde. Il Buddha, la meditazione, la fiducia.* Milano: Mondadori.

Pensa, Corrado and Neva Papachristou 2012. *Dare il cuore a ciò che conta, il Buddha e la Meditazione di Consapevolezza*. Milano: Mondadori.

Pensa, Corrado and Neva Papachristou 2018. *Affrettati piano. Il cammino interiore e la meditazione di consapevolezza: una strada per la felicità*. Roma: Ubaldini.

Sharf, Robert 2014. 'Mindfulness and Mindlessness in Early Chan.' *Philosophy East & West* 64.4: 933– 964. https://doi.org/10.1353/pew.2014.0074

Sujato, Bhikkhu 2005. *A History of Mindfulness. How Insight Worsted Tranquillity in the Satipaṭṭhāna sutta*. Taipei: The corporate Body of the Buddha Educational Foundation.

Wynne, Alexander 2007. *The Origin of Buddhist Meditation*. London & New York: Routledge.

Vetter, Tilmann 1988. *The Ideas and the Meditative Practices of Early Buddhism*. Leiden: Brill.

Abbreviations

AN	*Aṅguttaranikāya.*
Be	Burmese edition(s)
DN	*Dīghanikāya.*
Dhs	*Dhammasaṅgaṇi.*
Ee	European (PTS) edition(s)
MN	*Majjhimanikāya.*
Mil	*Milindapañha.*
PTS	Pali Text Society
SN	*Saṃyuttanikāya.*
Ud	*Udāna.*
Vibh	*Vibhaṅga.*
Vism	*Visuddhimagga.*

Author Biography

Chiara Neri, PhD, is Honorary Associate in Sanskrit Language and Literature and Indology at the University of Cagliari, Italy. Her research predominantly focuses on the study of Pāli canonical and commentarial literature from a linguistic, historical and philosophical point of view and on tracing the conjunctive and disjunctive linguistic-cultural connections between Vedic and Pāli canonical literature (especially with T. Pontillo). She has published numerous research papers in conference proceedings and international journals and a monograph: *Compendio dell'essenza. Studio e traduzione di capitoli scelti del Sārasaṅgaha di Siddhattha Thera* (Dell'Orso, 2020).

Chapter 7
A Joyful Song Celebrating Buddhist Practice

Marta Sernesi

As a small token of gratitude for his guidance and kindness, I gladly offer to Corrado Pensa the translation of a Tibetan poem from the 13th century, which celebrates the benefits and joys of Buddhist practice. This is a merry composition, arising from a blissful mind, composed for a mountain retreat by the hermit Yang dgon pa rGyal mtshan dpal bzang po (1213–1258). He addresses it to his disciples, asking them: 'Are you happy?' It thus seems to me a fitting present for Corrado, who generously devoted so much of his time and energy to the welfare and happiness of his students.

Tibetan Religious Songs

Religious songs (*mgur*, sometimes also *glu* or *dbyangs*) are a genre of Tibetan literature that emerged in the early second millennium CE. They are versified compositions that incorporate stylistically some features of folk songs and epics, as well as borrowing themes and imaginary from the songs of the Indian *siddha*s, such as the *dohā* attributed to Saraha, Maitrīpā, or Kṛṣṇācārya.[1] They emerge in a Buddhist communicative context: they are intended to praise or thank masters and patrons on specific occasions, to narrate life episodes, to convey humoristic or critical viewpoints, and to express religious experiences and realizations. In particular, this versified format may be employed to convey teachings and answer pupils' questions, in what are known as 'songs of instruction' (*man ngag gi mgur*).

Songs were traditionally set to music, following widely known melodies, and performed. However, the majority of the literary witnesses lack musical notation, so that it is impossible to reconstruct the airs of the songs. This feature explains the very variable metres in which songs are written—both in terms of syllables per line and lines per verse.[2] Even though the recipient, theme, length and metre may differ greatly among different songs, often—as in the song translated here—it is possible to distinguish an introductory part, praising the master and setting the scene, a main body of the song, and a conclusion: 'Therefore, the beginning of the song is like the trunk of a lion, appearing lofty and majestic; the middle part is like a golden *vajra*, beautiful and firm; the end of the song is like the tail of a tiger, long and easy to lay it to rest.'[3]

These similes are from a 1503 treatise on the literary genre of songs, called *Opening the Eyes of Faith* (*Dad pa'i mig byed*) and composed by gTsang smyon Heruka (1452–1507), a master who left behind his own poetic compositions. This source specifies that the beginning of the songs should include praises and supplications composed in an elevated style, while the main body of the song—treating the subject matter—should be clear and straightforward, easy to understand; the end should be gentle, and include verses of auspiciousness (*bkra shis shog*).[4]

Songs are commonly found either within hagiographic narratives, or in compilations generally titled *Collected Songs* (*mGur 'bum*), which are corpora ascribed to a single master. Moreover, some examples of anthologies of songs by different masters exist, the best-known of which is the 16th century *Ocean of bKa' brgyud songs* (*bKa' brgyud mgur tsho*), which include compositions of masters of the bKa' brgyud tradition.[5] A short treatise that is found in conjunction with this anthology (as introduction or supplement depending on the editions of the work), interestingly gives instructions on the performance of the songs included therein:

> First, the introduction to the song are prayers, offerings, and praises.
> In between [the invocations and the song], the story of the origin [of the composition] provides the context of the song [i.e. where, when, to whom, it was first sung].
> The song is performed reciting the verses properly.
> The songs are combined according to the time and occasion.
> At the end, the liturgy must be concluded with a ritual feast, verses of auspiciousness, and aspirations.[6]

This suggests that the songs were written down not only to be preserved and handed over as literary compositions, but also to be ritually performed. They were introduced by invocations to the masters, and a narrative of varying length providing the context in which they were first sung: in the written collections this may often consist of a single line, but sometimes a full-fledged story which frames multiple songs is provided. The choice and combination of multiple songs should be adequate to the available time, and to the occasion for which they are sung. After the performance, a ritual feast (*tshogs 'khor, gaṇacakra*) is consumed and dedications and auspicious verses are offered.

According to the two mentioned treatises, songs of different content, complexity, and theme may be composed to be offered to audiences from all walks of life: they are not only to be exchanged among practitioners, intoned to inspire faithful pupils in retreat, or recited in pre-determined ritual contexts, but they are means to teach lay patrons and disciples, to delight common lay people of all extractions and ages, to present in exchange for alms, lodging, meals, and boat crossings, and even to dissuade brigands met travelling on the road.[7]

The most popular and well-known Tibetan religious songs are certainly those included in the *Collected Songs of Milarepa* or *Hundred Thousand Songs of Milarepa*, a work compiled from earlier sources in 1488 that has been translated in many languages and has enjoyed great popularity.[8] Indeed, the 11th–12th century master Milarepa (Mi la ras pa) has been celebrated as a "national poet" in the 20th century, both within the PRC and in exile. He has even been included in a sort of alternative canon of mystical poetics by the American beat poets such as Allen Ginsberg. The latter was influenced by Chögyam Trungpa (Chos rgyam drung pa, 1939–1987), who presented the Tibetan tradition of Buddhist songs to the American public, characterizing them as "spontaneous" compositions to express religious experiences (Gamble 2015; Ginsberg 1993).

However, Milarepa was by no means the only "composer" or "singer" of religious songs in Tibet, and in fact many teachers followed in his footsteps. In particular, there are song collections attributed to other early "cotton-clad" yogins (*ras pa*), that is to say masters who focused on meditative and yogic practices and chose mountain asceticism as their lifestyle: for example, both Gling ras pa Padma rdo rje (1128–1188) and gTsang pa rgya ras Ye shes rdo rje (1161–1211), considered forefathers of the 'Brug pa bKa' brgyud lineage, were prolific composers of *mgur*. Gling ras pa also composed a commentary to the collection of *dohā* verses attributed to Saraha, an indication that the

Indic compositions continued to represent a source of inspiration for Tibetan masters.[9] Songs of later teachers, practising different Buddhist traditions and often identified as reincarnations or emanations of Milarepa, have been translated into English, and provide a source to explore the great vitality of the genre.[10]

The Songs of Yang dgon pa

During the 13th century, in South-Western Tibet, in the region of La stod, the sacred mountain of [r]Tsib[s] ri hosted a small community of Buddhist practitioners. Many hermitages sprung up on the rough terrain, providing shelter to individuals who performed years long retreats.

One of these hermits was Yang dgon pa rGyal mtshan dpal bzang po (1213–1258), a native of the nearby village of lHa g[/m]dong. He is known especially for his teachings to mountain ascetics—the 'mountain teachings,' or 'mountain dharma' (*ri chos*)—that, besides meditation instructions, provide details on logistic and ritual aspects of mountain retreats related to pallets, food, clothing, etc. He transmitted teachings of the bKa' brgyud and Sa skya Buddhist traditions, such as instructions on the Great Seal (Phyag rgya chen po), the Six Teachings of Nāropa (Nā ro chos drug), the Path and Fruit (Lam 'Bras), and the subtle Vajra Body (Rdo rje lus). He had four main teachers, namely: rGod tshang pa mgon po rdo rje (1189–1258), Sa skya paṇḍita Kun dga' rgyal mtshan (1182–1251), 'Bri gung spyan snga Grags pa 'byung gnas (1175–1255), and Ko brag pa bSod nams rgyal mtshan (1170–1249).[11] While Sa skya paṇḍita is well known for his collection of versified "elegant sayings" (*legs bshad*), religious songs are attributed to the other three masters.[12] In particular, a song in the *Collected Sayings of Grags pa 'byung gnas* is said to have been sung to Yang dgon pa, and advises him on virtuous conduct and the continuation of his spiritual training.[13]

Ko brag pa, who was also a native of the Ding ri area in La stod, was Yang dgon pa's first important teacher. Even though he was a very influential master during his time, his affiliation remained elusive, and the memory and cult of this figure faded over the centuries. A volume of *Collected Songs of Ko brag pa*, edited and printed in the mid-sixteenth century, has been translated in full by Cyrus Stearns (2000): this poetical corpus is varied, including songs of experience, songs of instruction, as well as a "biographical" song.[14] One composition of the collection is devoted to the genre itself, and interestingly presents different kinds of songs (*glu*) as the tradition of different

Buddhist adepts. According to this source, to sing praises (*bstod pa*) as songs was the tradition of Śākyamuni, to sing visions (*mthong snang*) as songs was the tradition of *bodhisattvas*, to sing offerings (*mchod pa*) as songs was the tradition of the *śrāvakas*, to sing realizations (*rtogs pa*) as songs was the tradition of Saraha, and to sing experiences (*nyams myong*) as songs was the tradition of the former *siddhas*. Finally:

> The singing of understanding in song
> is the tradition upheld by me today,
> known by name as the experiential song of meditation.[15]

In this way, Ko brag pa represents himself as the heir of a long-standing Buddhist tradition, which stems from Śākyamuni himself and from the *Recitation of the Names of Mañjuśrī* (*Mañjuśrīnāmasaṃgīti*), and comes down to him via the *siddha* tradition of *dohās*.[16] He characterizes his own songs as an expression of his understanding (*go tshad*), and denotes them as songs of meditative experience (*sgom pa'i nyams dbyangs*). Indeed, many of the compositions in the collection are said to originate during a practice retreat, do not seem to have any specific audience, and celebrate the life style of the hermit. The song in question continues to recount his practice 'without distraction' that leads to the view of the Great Seal, that is to say to the understanding of the original emptiness of mind:[17]

> This living alone in solitude
> isn't a snub at secular life,
> it's the practice of birthless mind.[18]

Like his master, also Yang dgon pa is credited with composing spiritual songs of experience, many of which originated during his long retreats on rTsib ri mountain. And like his master, an anthology of *Collected Songs of the Venerable Master rGyal ba yang dgon* (*rGyal ba yang dgon chos rje'i mgur 'bum*) was collected and printed in the sixteenth century. In particular, it was printed in 1524 by the Bo dong master Chos dbang rgyal mtshan (1484–1549) at his hermitage of Kun gsal sgang po che in sKyid grong. He had received teachings of Yang dgon pa from his teacher bTsun pa chos legs (1473–1521), who was an important master, and royal chaplain, at the regional court of Mang yul Gung thang. bTsun pa chos legs was active in the codification and transmission of the teachings of his predecessors at the main Bo dong monastery in the kingdom, namely mNgon dga', and among the many works that he printed figure five volumes of Great Seal teachings in the tradition of Yang dgon pa.[19] By the mid-16th century, the latter's teachings had thus become part of the religious lore of the local Bo dong lineage, and Chos dbang rgyal mtshan continued the project of systematization of this received knowledge by printing the master's *Collected Songs*, together with a volume of *Collected Oral* [*Instructions*] *of Yang dgon pa* (*bKa' 'bum*).[20] According to the colophon, these two volumes were arranged and edited by Chos dbang rgyal mtshan on the basis of several manuscript copies (*phyi mo*) that he had previously collected for the purpose—analysing them, abandoning fabrications (*rang bzo*), and establishing a reliable (*yid brtan*) edition in accord with the sources—an indication that the literary legacy of Yang dgon pa was plentiful in Western Tibet at the time.[21]

The *Collected Songs* is a succession of songs with very little narrative context. They impart teachings, relate visions and prophetic dreams, and express meditative experiences. Apart from the initial songs, which are arranged chronologically (providing the age of the master when he sung them), for the remaining corpus there is no evident ordering principle. Often only a line introduces a song, and it merely mentions the place where it was sung: the locations include his birthplace (and later main residence) lHa gdong, the hermitage of Bu le (gangs) in northern La stod, and one of his principal retreat places on rTsib ri mountain, namely dPal gNam sdings.[22] According to the introduction to the collection, Yang dgon pa sung innumerable songs, which arose spontaneously from the blossoming of the subtle energies at the *cakra* of his throat: indeed, singing songs of realization is not considered an aesthetic accomplishment, but instead a sign of spiritual advancement. Ko brag pa's poetry, for example, is praised as 'free from mentally fabricated phrases, and dawned in a primordial, transcendent, self-arisen, unimpeded way' (*mgur 'bum snyan ngag blos byas tshig dang bral/ gnyung ma blo 'das rang 'byung 'gag med shar*).[23] However, according to the opening narrative, most of the songs sung by Yang dgon pa were not written down for lack of auspicious circumstances (*rten 'brel*). Still, his disciples wrote down a few songs and collected them in a volume, in order 'not to spill the nectar of [the master's] words' (*gsung gi bdud rtsi mi 'thor*). Hence, this is not written poetry, but instead the result of a process of remembrance and transmission of words held dear by the community of Yang dgon pa's followers. Indeed, these compositions, we are told, make the learned ones rejoice, and are able to awake positive karmic latencies in the individuals who rely on them, so that they bring much benefit by reading, hearing, or remembering them (*mthong ba dang thos pa dang dran pa*).[24]

A Song Reminder of Joyfulness

Among all the songs of the collection, I chose a composition that joyfully celebrates Buddhist practice.[25] The song is sung on the southern side of Mt. rTsib ri—called Glorious Mountain (Shrī ri or dPal gyi ri)—where most of the hermitages are located, including the main one, namely rGod tshang dgon. In this song, the mountain retreat is not depicted as a stern act of asceticism, characterized by deprivation of mind and body, but instead as a return to the essential clarity and bliss of one's mind and body, which arise spontaneously once the clouds of faulty thoughts are cleared. An overall feeling of sincere dedication to Buddhist practice, motivated by the joy and peace resulting from it, transpires from the song. The composition is called *Nyams dga' gsal 'debs ma*—that is, a song that brings to mind (or that prompts) the experience of joy—which I have rendered 'reminder of joyfulness.'

The composition is made of two longish introductory stanzas [1–2], nine main stanzas of four lines each [3–11], and one concluding stanza [12]. The first stanza is, as customary in Tibetan compositions of the genre, a homage to the master, who is not named (probably being Ko brag pa or rGod tshang pa). The next stanza presents the setting of the song: five disciples, being weary of transmigration, came together in order to engage in a practice retreat: the mountain, with its isolation, is considered as a propitious place in which to focus, to cultivate renunciation, and 'to protect the doors [i.e. the five sense organs and the mind] from unruly experiences [2].' Yang dgon pa intones the song wishing to inspire them by sharing the joys and the positive outcomes of practising in such an environment. In the last line of the stanza, he characterizes what follows as an 'uplifting (or joyous) talk in [the form of] a song of experience' (*dga' gtam nyams myong glu ru*).

In the remainder of the composition, the "unfixed"—that is to say the provisional, not institutionalized—mountain hermitage is described as the ideal setting to sustain the feeling of renunciation, which arises from contemplating the incertitude of the time of death [11]. In the main body of the song, Yang dgon pa employs common Tibetan images drawn from features of the natural landscape: the large bird of prey soaring in the sky and then perching on a boulder [3], the sun rising in the sky and piercing the morning clouds [4], the snow lion crouching on the glacier, majestically overpowering all the other wild animals [5], and the horse running on the grassland [6].[26] In particular, practice is compared to farming, that is to say, to plant the wholesome seeds of instruction in the fertile soil of faith and diligence [8]. The instructions are received from a qualified teacher (equated with an authentic jewel)[27] [7], and those explicitly mentioned in the song are Great Seal (Phyag chen) [4], Luminosity ('Od gsal) [5], and Great Bliss (bDe chen) [6].[28] Through such practice, one realizes the non-duality of *saṃsāra* and *nirvāṇa* [8], and therefore one is able to wield the sword of non-attachment (*zhen med kyi ral gri*), that severs attachment and aversion to whatever arises in the field of the senses [9].

The last stanza [12] of the composition recalls the setting of the song, that is the southern slopes of Mt. rTsib ri, and emphasizes how it arises from a feeling of joy and a sentiment of kindness, being offered as a gift to Yang dgon pa's students. And eight centuries later, this composition remains a sincere and inspiring testament of dedication to the *dharma*, a gift of uplifting words celebrating the fruits of spiritual practice.

Translation

Sung in front of the Glorious Mountain range, requested by five disciples.

Homage to the master!

Venerable, unequalled, precious master,
from the ocean of milk of the bKa' brgyud (teachings),
you churn the essential butter of the Aural Transmission,
and condense the nutrients of its experiences,
thus satiating the mental continuum of the fortunate disciple(s).
I bow to the feet of the father, king of the *dharma*,
May the son be blessed as equal to the father! [1]

This mountain has been given a name:
this mountain is the Glourios Mountain (Shrī ri dpal gyi ri)
the place of assembly of the joyful *ḍākinīs*:
at this marvellous great sacred abode,
gathered five men weary of transmigration,
protecting their own gates (of the senses) from unruly experiences.
Do you feel happy? [to] all (of you) disciples
I (your) father, (having) a blissful and joyful mind,
will give an uplifting talk, singing a song of experience. [2]

In the vast air of emptiness,
glides high the eagle of attaining realizations:
soaring (above) the pitfalls of the eight extremes
it rests on the rock of resolution. [3]

In the sky of the Great Seal teachings,
rises the sun of the co-emergent meaning:
cleared from the banks of clouds of faulty experiences,
the mind spreads in the state of *dharmatā.* [4]

The [snow-]lion of meditation, the great Luminosity,
adorned by the turquoise mane of the experiences of bliss, clearness and non-conceptuality,
overpowers [all] predators—the mind's faulty thoughts—
(majestically) crouching in the snow of the mind's genuine (nature). [5]

Riding the stallion of the qualities of one's body,
by means of the two paths of the generation and completion (stages),
governing [it] through the key points of the internal [subtle] winds and mind [energy],
[one] runs on the [grassland] plane of the experience of Great Bliss. [6]

By dedicating the virtues and the enjoyments of [one's] body
to that unequalled authentic jewel [who is the qualified teacher],
having tied faith and devotion to the top of the victory banner,
[one] receives the supreme and common attainments (*siddhi*s). [7]

The fertile soil of faith and diligence is the basis,
planted with a heap of seeds of [religious] instructions.
Having exerted oneself in practice, [which is] farming,
[one] reaps the harvest of experiences and realizations. [8]

The Buddha of the changeless *dharmakāya* resides
in the measureless celestial mansion of the non-duality of *saṃsāra* and *nirvāṇa*.
Offering the worship ritual (*pūja*) of bearing the vast phenomenal world,
[one] has a confident encounter with him.[29] [9]

A person whose five doors [i.e. whose sense organs] are self-liberated,
hits with the sword of non-attachment the five objects [of the senses]:
[thereby] directly severing the conditions of whatever arises,
he wards off the attack of aversion and attachment. [10]

In the *yoga* of the uncertainty of the time of death,
arises the attitude [regarding] everything as unnecessary.
In the unfixed mountain hermitage,
the experience of non-attachment is sustained. [11]

All those tunes were a reminder of joyfulness,
[sung] south of the rocky Glorious Mountain:
This local cotton-clad hermit
did not intone them from a feeling of grief, but of joy!
It has been offered as a gift! How kind! [12]

This is the '[song] reminder of joyfulness.'

Tibetan Text

The text below is a diplomatic edition of the song as found in the printed edition of 1524 (the pagination is marked A). Emendations are marked [= *xxx*]. Abbreviated spellings (*bsdud yig*) are marked supplying the missing letters within <>.

In the footnotes variants from two manuscript witnesses are supplied. Abbreviated spellings and variant punctuation are not recorded therein. Omissions are marked: om.

Witness B: A cursive (*dbu med*) manuscript in 219 folios titled *Collected Songs of rGyal ba yang dgon pa rgyal mtshan dpal* (Tianjin 1998). Its contents are very close to the printed edition, although it shows some minor variants.

Witness C: A manuscript (*dbu can*) copy of the collected songs, titled *rGyal ba yang dgon pa'i mgur 'bum*, included in a collection of works of Yang dgon pa reproduced from a copy preserved at Pha jo ldings monastery in Bhutan.

The variants are mostly minor differences in spelling and verb forms. However, in a few instances the readings of the manuscript(s) are preferable (*rlobs* for *brlobs* in verse 1; *sgo* for *rgo* in verse 2; and *bya rgyal* for *bya rgya* in verse 3; *kyis* for *kyi* in verse 6), and in one case the line differs in witness B (last line of verse 7). Also the introductory line in prose slightly differs in the three witnesses.

(A 46a.1; B 63b.1; C 222.4) *shrī ri ra* [=*rwa*] *sngon* [=*mngon*] *du sku 'khor lngas zhus dus bzhes so//*[30]

na mo gu ru /[31]
rje mnyam med kyi bla ma rin po che/
/⌊bka' brgyud⌉[32] *'o ma'i rgya mtsho nas/*
/snyan brgyud[33] *mar gyi snying po*[34] *bsrubs*[35]*/*
/de nyams myong gi bcud du bsdus nas kyang/
/bu skal ldan gyi shes rgyud tshim[36] *mdzad pa*[37]*/*
/pha chos kyi rgyal po'i zhabs la 'dud/
/bu pha dang mnyam par byin gyis brlobs [=*rlobs*][38]*/* [1]

/ri 'di la ming dang mtshan btags pa/
/ri 'di ni shrī ri[39] *dpal gyi ri/*
/nyams dga' mkha'<'>gro 'du pa'i[40] *sa/*
/⌊ngo mtshar⌉[41] *can gyi gnas chen*[42] *na/*
/'u[43] *'khor bas sun pa'i mi lnga 'tshogs*[44]*/*
/khrigs med nyaṃs kyi rang rgo[45] [=*sgo*] *skyong/*
/khyed dga' ru tshor ram bu slob kun/
/pha[46] *nga ni nyams* (C 223) *dga' shes pa bde/* (B 64a)
/dga' gtam nyams myong glu ru len/ [2]

/stong nyid kyi[47] *bar snang yangs mo la/*
/rtogs pa mngon gyur gyi bya rgya[48] [=*rgyal*] *lding/*
/mtha' brgyad kyi gol sa rlabs[49] *kyis bcad nas/*
/blo thag chod kyi brag la nyal ba lags so/ [3]

chos phyag rgya chen po'i nam<m>kha' la/ (A 46b)
don lhan cig skyes pa'i nyi ma shar/
/nyams skyon can gyi sprin tshogs mtha' nas sangs/
/blo chos nyid kyi ngang du 'byam[50] *pa lags so/* [4]

/sgom[51] *'od gsal chen po'i seng ge la/*
/nyams[52] *bde gsal mi rtog pa'i*[53] *g.yu ral rgyas/*
/blo 'khrul rtog gi sder chags zil⌊gyis mnan⌉[54]*/*
/sems gnyug ma'i gangs la 'gying ba lags so/ [5]

/rang lus yon tan gyi rta pho la/
/lam skyed[55] *rdzogs gnyis kyi* [=*kyis*] (B 64b) *skyen*[56] *bu zhon/*
/nang rlung sems gnad[57] *kyi*[58] [=*kyis*] *kha lo bsgyur nas/*
/nyams bde chen gyi thang la rgyug pa lags<s>o/ [6]

/⌊mtshan ldan mnyam med kyi⌉[59] *rin chen la/*
/lus longs spyod dge ba'i bsnyen⌊bkur bgyis⌉[60]*/*
/mos gus rgyal mtshan gyi[61] *rtse la btags nas/*
/mchog thun mong gi⌊dngos grub⌉[62] *zhu ba lags so*[63]*/* [7]

/gzhi dad brtson gyi zhing sa gshin pa[64] *la/*
/gdams[65] *ngag gi sa bon⌊lcogs* [=*lcog*] *mo btab⌉*[66]*/*
/nyams len gyi so nam 'grus par[67] *byas nas/*
/nyams rtogs kyi ston thog sdud[68] *pa lags so/* [8]

/'khor 'das gnyis med[69] *kyi gzhal yas na/*
/chos sku 'gyur med kyi sangs rgyas bzhugs/
/snang srid rgya⌊thegs kyi⌉[70] *mchod pa phul nas/* (A 47a)
/yid ches kyi zhal mjal byas pa lags so/ [9]

/sgo lnga (B 65a) *rang grol*[71] *gyi skyes bu la/*
/yul (C 224) *lnga zhen med kyi ral gri bskur/*
/gang byung gi[72] *rkyen snang thad kar bcad nas/*
/chags sdang[73] *gi g.yul ngo bzlog pa*[74] *lags<s>o/* [10]

/nam 'chi cha med kyi rnal 'byor la/
/cis kyang dgos med kyi blo sna shar nas[75]*/*
/phyogs ris med pa'i ri khrod du/
/zhen med kyi nyams myong skyong ba lags so/ [11]

/dbyangs de kun nyams dga' gsal 'debs ma/
/brag rgyal ⌊gyi shrī⌉[76] *ri'i lho phyogs<s>u/*
/rgyal khams kyi ri khrod ras pa yis/
/nyaṃs skyo nas ma blangs dga' nas blangs/
/mchod[77] *par 'bul lo bka' drin can/*
/nyams dga' gsal 'debs ma ithi// [12]

Notes

1 For a general introduction to the genre of *mgur*, see Jackson 1996. For a discussion of the sources of the genre, see Kapstein 2003: 769–773. For Tibetan folk songs, see Tucci 1966. For Tibetan epics, see Stein 1959. For the *dohā*s, see Guenther 1993; Jackson 2004; Kværne 1986; Schaeffer 2005.

2 For some examples of sources bearing a graphic representation of how chanting should be performed, see Helffer 1986: 71–78. Studies on Tibetan metrics are scarce; see Beyer 1992: 408–423; Stein 1959: 486–504; Sujata 2005: 112–161; Vekerdi 1952.

3 *Opening the Eyes of Faith* (*Dad pa'i mig byed*), fol.3b: *de yang dbyangs stod seng ge'i ro stod dang 'dra ste bzengs 'tho* [=*gzengs mtho*] *la 'gying chags pa/ bar skabs gser gyi rdo rje dang 'dra ste lhu jags* [=*chags*] *la grims cha ldan pa/ dbyangs zhabs stag gi 'jug* [=*mjug*] *ma dang 'dra ste ring la 'jogs bde ba'i sgo nas/*. Cf. Larsson and Quintman 2015: 116, 140.

4 *Ibid.* gTsang smyon Heruka (1452–1507) is known for compiling the best-known version of the life of Mar pa Chos kyi blo gros (11th c.) and of the life and songs of Mi la ras pa (11th–12th c.). For his life and legacy, see Sernesi 2021. For an edition, translation and study of *Opening the Eyes of Faith*, see Larsson and Quintman 2015. For the description of the printed edition, see Sernesi 2021: Handlist EP 4/1. I thank Prof. Franz-Karl Ehrhard and the students who read the treatise with me at LMU München in the Winter Semester of 2013.

5 This anthology is attributed to the 8th Karma pa Mi bskyod rdo rje (1507–1554); Chögyam Trungpa (Chos rgyam drung pa, 1939–1987) updated it with his own songs and supervised its translation by the Nālandā Translation Committee 1999.

6 *Comforting the Mind of the Fortunate Ones* (*sKal bzang yid kyi ngal so*), 332: *dang po gsol 'debs mchod bstod dang bcas nas mgur gyi sna 'dren/ bar du lo rgyus 'byung*

khung dang bcas nas mgur gyi khog dbubs/ tshig bcad 'bru snon dang bcas nas mgur gyi gsal btab/ dus tshod gnas skabs dang bstun nas mgur gyi mtsham sbyar/ mthar tshogs 'khor bkra shis smon lam dang bcas nas mgur gyi cho ga bsdu dgos/. Cf. Nālandā Translation Committee 1999: 11. Note that *Opening the Eyes of Faith* is organised in five very similar rubrics, as follows: 'First, the songs are introduced by supplications and praises. In between, the context of the song is the authenticating story. The arrangement of the songs should follow the index and introduction. The timing (of the performance) should accord with the (available) time and occasion. The conclusion of the songs is verses of auspiciousness.' (*dang po gsol 'debs bstod pa dang bcas te dbyangs kyi mgo 'dren/ bar du lo rgyus gtan tshigs dang bcas te dbyangs kyi khog 'bubs/ dkar chag ngo sprod dang bcas te dbyangs kyi 'tshams sbyar/ dus tshod gnas skabs dang bcas nas dbyangs kyi tshod 'dzin/ bkra shis smon lam dang bcas te dbyangs kyi 'jug bsdud pa lags shing/*). Cf. the different translation of both passages in Larsson and Quintman 2015: 116, 117, n. 81.

7 See Nālandā Translation Committee 1999: 9; *Opening the Eyes of Faith* 2b–3a, 8b–9a; cf. Larsson and Quintman 2015: 115, 127.

8 Among the many available translations of the collection, compare the English rendition by Chang 1962 with the recent Stagg 2017. For an Italian translation from the Tibetan, see Blancke and Pizzi 2002, of which only the first volume appeared. The compiler is gTsang smyon Heruka: for the master and the work, see Quintman 2014; Sernesi 2021.

9 See *Collected Songs of gTsang pa rgya ras 1*, *Collected Songs of gTsang pa rgya ras 2*; *Collected Songs of Gling ras pa*; these collections have not been translated. For these masters' life and works, and especially their role in the formation of the 'Brug pa bKa' brgyud school, see Martin 1979; Miller 2005; Miller 2006; Walther 2017. For Gling ras pa's commentary to Saraha's *dohā* collection, see Schaeffer 2005: 115–119. In *Ocean of bKa' brgyud Songs*, besides songs attributed to the lineage of the Karma bKa' brgyud pas, there are songs attributed, among others, to Mi la ras pa, his disciples sGam po pa bSod nams rin chen and Ras chung rDo rje grags pa, 'Jig rten mgon po Rin chen dpal (1143–1217), and Lo ras pa dBang phyug brston grus (1187–1250); see Nālandā Translation Committee 1999.

10 See e.g., Sujata 2005; 2011; 2015.

11 For the life story of Yang dgon pa, see Miller 2013: 18–41; Roerich 1976: 688–691. The main hagiography, titled *Great Mirror* (*Me long chen mo*) is translated in Guarisco 2015: 113–209. For the Ri chos and the community of rTsib ri practitioners, see Sernesi 2022 and forthcoming. For the sacred mountain of rTsib ri, see Buffetrille 2013. According to local lore, it flew from Bodhgayā with the *mahāsiddha*s on it, covered a poisonous lake, and was then tied to the ground (*ibid.*: 39–41).

12 For the famous *Sa skya legs bshad*, see Bosson 1969; Davenport 2000; Eimer 2014. For a collection of songs attributed to rGod tshang pa, see *Collected Songs of rGod tshang pa mgon po rdo rje*. gTsang smyon Heruka, in *Opening the Eyes of Faith* 6b–7a, lists Gling ras pa, gTsang pa rgya ras, rGod tshang pa, Yang dgon pa, and also the latter's disciple sPyan snga Rin [chen] ldan, and the latter's pupil Zur phug pa as eminent ancestors of the lineage who sung spiritual songs; see Larsson and Quintman 2015: 123.

13 *Slob dpon yang dgon pa la gdams pa*; in *Collected Sayings of Grags pa 'byung gnas*, pp. 350–356.

14 The collection was printed by lHa btsun Rin chen rnam rgyal (1473–1557) at Brag dkar rta so; the edition is undated. *Khams gsum 'dran bral grub thob ko rag* [=*brag*] *pa'i mgur 'buṃ*, 16 fols., witnesses known: NGMPP L 970/2; NGMPP E 2518/11; NGMPP L 456/8; *Early Xylographic Editions Collected by dPal brtsegs* no. 28. Illustrations: fol. 1b (centre) Ko brag pa. For the description of this printed edition, see Sernesi 2021: Handlist LT 22. The printing colophon is transcribed and translated in Stearns 2000: 174–175.

15 Trans. Stearns 2000: 61: *go tshad glu ru len pa de/ /bdag gis di ring bka' srol gzung/ /ming yang sgom pa'i nyams dbyangs zer/* (*ibid.*: 60).

16 Both these textual antecedents are mentioned in the song; see Stearns 2000: 58–59.

17 Indeed, the experience of meditation as described in the song entails that "looking at the internal intrinsic awareness of the mind, there was the groundless, rootless nature of mind that is forever empty" (*/nang rig pa sems la tshur ltas pas/ /gzhi rtsa bral gyi sems nyid ye nas stong/*); see Stearns 2000: 60–61.

18 Trans. Stearns 2000: 63: *cig pur dben par bsdod pa 'di/ /mi chos gyong pa ma lags te/ /sems skye med nyams su len pa lags/* (*ibid.*: 62).

19 For bTsun pa chos legs and Chos dbang rgyal mtshan, see Ehrhard 2000: 23–50; 2016. In particular, for the edition of Yang dgon pa's works, see Ehrhard 2000: 29–30, 71–72; for the Great Seal teaching collection, printed in 1514, see Ehrhard 2000b.

20 See NGMPP Reel L 66/2–3; IsIAO Tucci Collection no. 286/1–2. Xylographic edition. *rGyal ba yang dgon chos rje'i mgur 'bum*, 165 fols., volume number *Ka*. *rGyal ba yang dgon chos rje'i bka' 'bum*, 128 fols., volume number *Kha*. Cf. De Rossi Filibeck 2003: 2, s.v. The volumes are enriched by the portraits of Yang dgon pa and bTsun pa Chos legs (fols. 1b and 165a of the *mGur 'bum*), and of the four masters of Yang dgon pa (fols. 1b and 128a of the *bKa' 'bum*). For the Tibetan text of the printing colophon, see Ehrhard 2000: 88–93.

21 *Collected Songs of Yang dgon pa* A, fol. 160a–b: *rgyal ba yang dgon pa rgyal mtshan dpal bzang po'i gsung ngag/ mgur 'bum yid bzhin gyi nor bu phan bde'i dga' ston 'bad med du rtsol ba 'dis/ bkra shis dang dge legs chen pos phyogs thams cad khyab par gyur cig/ mgur yongs su grags pa brgya dang nyeg ma brgyad bzhugs so/ /bka' 'bum dang mgur 'bum 'di rnams rgyas bsdus go rims mi 'dra ba mang du snang yang/ phyi mo yid brtan thub pa du ma bsogs nas/ rang bzo spangs te gang legs brtag pa zhus pa'i nang ltar bsgrigs pa yin pas gzur gnas rnams kyis yid brtan bya zhing/ rnam dpyad dang ldan pa rnams kyis slar yang dag byed kyi chu bo bstsal du gsol cig/*.

22 For lHa gdong and gNam sdings (the latter not extant anymore), see *Guidebook to rTsib ri* (*rTsib ri gnas bshad*), 79–88, 106–110 respectively; Sernesi forthcoming.

23 This is from the printing colophon by lHa btsun rin chen rnam rgyal; trans. Stearns 2000: 175. The note about the throat *cakra* is found in *Collected Songs of Yang dgon pa* A, 2b: *mgrin pa'i rtsa kha bye bas tshig don gyi rgya ral nas gsung gi mdzod rdol* [=*brdol*]. Compare with the expression employed by gTsang smyon Heruka, in *Opening the Eyes of Faith* (fol. 5b), with reference to Mi la ras pa: *mgrin pa longs spyod kyi rtsa kha bye bas rdo rje glu yi mtsho brdol.*

24 *Collected Songs of Yang dgon pa* A, fols. 1b–3b.

25 *Collected Songs of Yang dgon pa* A, fols. 46a.1–47a.4.

26 These are very widespread metaphors in early Tibetan spiritual songs; see e.g. "The Song of the Dream of Four Great Pillars" attributed to Milarepa (in Nālandā Translation Committee 1982: 182–184), and songs no. 5 and no. 10 in the collection of Ko brag pa's songs (in Stearns 2000: 52–57, 76–79).

27 Teachers are often equated to wish-fulfilling jewels; see e.g. Ko brag pa's song no. 44 in Stearns 2000: 170–173.

28 These are core teachings transmitted within the bKa' brgyud lineage; see e.g. Guenther 1963; Lhalungpa 2006; Roberts 2011.

29 Emending the genitive *kyi* with the instrumental *kyis*, the last line can mean 'one encounters him faithfully,' or 'by this act of devotion, one encounters him.'

30 This line reads in B: *'di tsibs ri ra* [=*rwa*] *sngon* [=*mngon*] *du sku 'khor lnga'i dus su gsungs so//*: 'This was sung in front of the rTsib ri mountain range at the time of the five attendants.' This line reads in C: *shrī ri ra* [=*rwa*] *mngon du sku 'khor lnga tsam bcas bzhugs dus/ nyin cig yul dro ba shig la thams cad tshogs nas chos cig kyang gsungs/ nyams dga' dgu'i mgur 'di bzhes so/*: 'When [Yang dgon pa] was staying in front of the rTsib ri mountain range together with about five attendants, one day they all assembled in a warm place and [they requested:] "give us a teaching," [so] he sung this *Song of the Nine Joys*.'

31 B, C: line om.

32 C: *dkar rgyud*

33 B, C: *rgyud*

34 B: *khu*

35 B: *srubs*

36 C: *tshims*

37 B, C: *pa'i*

38 C: *rlobs*

39 C: om.

40 B, C: *ba'i*

41 B: *grags pa*

42 C: *mchog*

43 C: *bu*

44 C: *tsho*

45 B, C: *sgo*

46 C: om.

47 B: om.

48 B, C: *rgyal*

49 B: *brlabs*

50 B, C: *'byams*

51 B: *bsgom*

52 B: *nyam*

53 B, C: *gi*

54 B: *gyi mnan*; C: *mnan nas*

55 B, C: *bskyed*

56 B, C: *skyes*

57 C: *gnyis*

58 C: *kyis*

59 C: *mnyam med kyi mtshan ldan*

60 B: *bskur bgyid*
61 B: *gi*
62 C: *dgos 'dod*
63 The line reads in B: *mchog thun 'dod gnyis dgos 'dod zhu ba lags so/*
64 C: *po*
65 B, C: *gdam*
66 C: *bzang po btab nas*
67 C: *mor*
68 B: *bsdud*
69 B: om.
70 B: *theg gi*
71 B: *'grol*
72 C: om.
73 C: *snang*
74 B: inserts *pa*
75 B: om.
76 B: *tsibs*
77 C: *dbyangs mchod*

Bibliography

Tibetan Sources:

Collected Sayings of Grags pa 'byung gnas: *The collected works (gsuṅ 'bum) of Grags pa 'byuṅ gnas, a chief disciple of the Skyob-pa-'jig-rten-gsum-mgon, 1175–1255*, ed. by Konchog Tenzin Kunzang Thinley Lhundub. Delhi: Drikung kagyu publications, 2002 (TBRC W23785).

Collected Songs of Gling ras pa: *gSung mgur gyi rim pa*. In *The Collected Works (bKa' 'bum) of Gliṅ-chen ras-pa Padma-rdo-rje. Reproduced from a collection of rare manuscripts from Go-'jo Nub Dgon*. Tashijong: Khampa Gar Nyamso Gyunphel Parkhang, 1985, vol. 1, pp. 39–216 (TBRC W23778).

Collected Songs of gTsang pa rgya ras 1: *'Gro mgon rin po che'i gsung mgur gyi rim pa*. In *'Gro-ba'i mgon-po chos-rjer tsaṅ-pa rgya-ras ye-shes rdo-rje mchog-gi gsuṅ-'bum rin-po-che*, ed. by Khenpo Shedup Tenzin and Lama Thinley Namgyal. Kathmandu: Shri Gautama Buddha Vihara, 1998, pp. 1–186 (TBRC W23782).

Collected Songs of gTsang pa rgya ras 2: *Chos rje rin po che gtsaṅ pa rgya ras pa'i rnam thar mgur 'bum daṅ bcas śin tu rgyas pa. The collected songs (mgur) of gTsaṅ-pa rgya-ras ye-ses-rdo-rje. Reproduced from a rare manuscript from rTa-mgo Chos-dbyiṅs pho-braṅ by Kunsang Tobgay*. Thimpu, 1975.

Collected Songs of Ko brag pa: Xylographic edition, 16 fols. Edition and translation in Stearns 2000.

Collected Songs of rGod tshang pa mgon po rdo rje: *dPal mnyam med rgyal ba rgod tshang pa'i mgur 'bum chen mo*. Thimphu: Tango monastic community, 1981 (TBRC W23661).

Collected Songs of Yang dgon pa (*Yang dgon pa'i mgur 'bum*): A = *rGyal ba yang dgon chos rje'i mgur 'bum*. Xylographic edition, 165 fols. NGMPP Reel no. L 66/2; IsIAO Tucci Collection no. 286/1. B = *rGyal ba yang dgon pa rgyal mtshan dpal gyi gsung 'bum*. In *dPyad gzhi'i yig cha phyogs bsgrigs*. [Tianjin]: Tianjin guji chubanshe, [1998], vol. 3, pp. 165–270. C = *rGyal ba yang dgon pa'i mgur 'bum*. In *The Collected Works (gsuṅ 'bum) of Yaṅ-dgon-pa rgyal-mtshan-dpal. Reproduced from the manuscript set preserved at Pha-jo-ldiṅs Monastery*. Thimphu: Kunsang Topgey, 1976, vol. 3, pp. 165–376 (TBRC W1KG17449).

Comforting the Mind of the Fortunate Ones (*sKal bzang yid kyi ngal so*): *bKa' brgyud mgur mtsho'i go don khog dbubs spyi chings rnam par bshad pa skal bzang yid kyi ngal gso*. In: *bKa' brgyud mgur tsho*, vol. *pa*, [new pagination] pp. 321–333.

Early Xylographic Editions Collected by dPal brtsegs (*dPal brtsegs spar rnying*): *Bod kyi shing par lag rtsal gyi byung rim mdor bsdus*, ed. by dPal brtsegs bod yig dpe rnying zhib 'jug khang, 2013. A printed Book and two DVDs (numbers 1 to 50 as in the publication).

Great Mirror (*Me long chen mo*): *rGyal ba yang dgon pa'i rnam thar bstod pa ma'am me long chen mo*. Kathmandu: Shree Gautam Buddha Vihara, 2002.

Guidebook to rTsib ri (*rTsib ri gnas bshad*): *rGyal gyi shrī'am rtsibs ri'i gnas bshad dad gsum 'dren pa'i zhing sa*, by dGe ming grub thob shes rab. [Kathmandu], 2004 (TBRC W30067).

Ocean of bKa' brgyud Songs (*bKa' brgyud mgur tsho*): *mChog gi dngos grub mngon du byed pa'i myur lam bka' brgyud bla ma rnams kyi rdo rje'i mgur dbyangs ye shes char 'bebs rang grol lhun grub bde chen rab 'bar nges don rgya mtsho snying po*. Rumtek: Karma Chos sgar, 1972 (TBRC W21962).

Opening the Eyes of Faith (*Dad pa'i mig byed*): *mGur gyi dkar chags ma rig mun sel dad pa'i mig 'byed*. Xylographic edition, 9 fols. Staatsbibliothek zu Berlin, Sammlung Waddell no. 120h (part 1).

Secondary Sources:

Beyer, Stephan V. 1992. *The Classical Tibetan Language*. Delhi: Sri Satguru Publications.

Blancke, Kristin and Franco Pizzi trans. 2002. *I centomila canti di Milarepa*. Milano: Adelphi.

Bosson, James E. trans. 1969. *A Treasury of Aphoristic Jewels: the Subhāṣitaratnanidhi of Sa Skya Paṇḍita in Tibetan and Mongolian*. Bloomington: Indiana University [New ed. London: Routledge Curzon, 2017].

Buffetrille, Katia 2013. 'The rTsib ri Pilgrimage: Merit as Collective Duty?' In Franz-Karl Ehrhard and Petra Maurer eds. *Nepalica-Tibetica: Festgabe for Christoph Cüppers*. Andiast: International Institute for Tibetan and Buddhist Studies GmbH, 1: 37–64.

Chang, Garma C. C. trans. 1962. *The Hundred Thousand Songs of Milarepa*. New York: University Books [New ed. Boston: Shambhala, 1977].

Davenport, John T. trans. 2000. *Ordinary Wisdom: Sakya Pandita's Treasury of Good Advice*. Boston: Wisdom Publications.

De Rossi Filibeck, Elena 2003. *Catalogue of the Tucci Tibetan Fund in the Library of IsIAO*. Roma: Istituto Italiano per l'Africa e l'Oriente.

Ehrhard, Franz-Karl trans. 1990. *„Flugelschläge des Garuḍa." Literar- und ideengeschichtliche Bemerkungen zu einer Liedersammlung des rDzogs-chen*. Stuttgart: Franz Steiner Verlag.

Ehrhard, Franz-Karl 2000. *Early Buddhist Block Prints from Mang-yul Gung-thang*. Lumbini: Lumbini International Research Institute.

Ehrhard, Franz-Karl 2000b. *Four Unknown Mahāmudrā Works of the Bo-dong-pa School*. Lumbini: Lumbini International Research Institute.

Ehrhard, Franz-Karl 2016. 'Collected Writings as Xylographs: Two Sets from the Bo dong pa School.' In Hildegard Diemberger, Franz-Karl Ehrhard, and Peter Kornicki eds. *Tibetan Printing: Comparisons, Continuities and Change*. Leiden: Brill, 212–236.

Eimer, Helmut trans. 2014. *Sa skya Legs bshad. Die Strophen zur Lebensklugheit von Sa skya Paṇḍita Kun dga' rgyal mtshan (1182–1251)*. Wien: Arbeitskreis für Tibetische und Buddhistische Studien Universität Wien.

Gamble, Ruth 2015. '"Cosmic Onomatopoeia" or the Source of *The Waterfall of Youth*: Chögyam Trungpa and Döndrup Gyal's Parallel Histories of Tibetan *mGur*.' In Jim Rheingans ed. *Tibetan Literary Genres, Texts and Text Types*. Leiden: Brill, 110–135.

Ginsberg, Allen 1993. 'Buddhism and the Beats.' 'The Allen Ginsberg Project.' July 15, 2017. http://allenginsberg.org/2017/07/s-j-15/.

Guarisco, Elio trans. 2015. *Secret Map of the Body: Visions of the Human Energy Structure*. Arcidosso: Shang Shung Publications.

Guenther, Herbert V. trans. 1963. *The Life and Teaching of Nāropa*. Oxford: Oxford University Press.

Guenther, Herbert V. trans. 1993. *Ecstatic Spontaneity: Saraha's Three Cycles of Dohā*. Berkeley: Asian Humanities Press.

Helffer, Mireille 1986. 'Preliminary remarks concerning the use of musical notation in Tibet.' In Norbu Jamyang ed. *Zlos-gar: Performing Traditions of Tibet*. Dharamsala: Library of Tibetan Works and Archives, 69–90.

Jackson, Roger R. 1996. '"Poetry" in Tibet: *Glu, mGur, sNyan ngag* and "Songs of Experience."' In José I. Cabezón and Roger R. Jackson eds. *Tibetan Literature: Studies in Genre*. Boston: Wisdom Publications, 368–392.

Jackson, Roger R. trans. 2004. *Tantric Treasures: Three Collections of Mystical Verses from Buddhist India*. Oxford & New York: Oxford University Press.

Kapstein, Matthew T. 2003. 'The Indian Literary Identity in Tibet.' In Sheldon Pollock ed. *Literary Cultures in History*. Berkeley: University of California Press, 747–802.

Kværne, Per trans. 1986. *An Anthology of Buddhist Tantric Songs. A Study of the Caryāgīti*. Bangkok: White Orchid Press.

Larsson, Stefan and Andrew Quintman, 2015. 'Opening the Eyes of Faith: Constructing Tradition in a Sixteenth-Century Catalogue of Tibetan Religious Poetry.' *Revue d'Études Tibétaines* 32: 87–151.

Lhalungpa, Lobsang trans. 2006. *Mahamudra: The Quintessence of Mind and Meditation*. Boston: Wisdom Publications.

Martin, Dan 1979. 'Gling-ras-pa and the Founding of the 'Brug-pa School.' *The Tibet Society Bulletin* 13: 56–69.

Miller, Willa Blythe 2005. 'The Vagrant Poet and the Reluctant Scholar: A Study of the Balance of Iconoclasm and Civility in the Biographical Accounts of Two Founders of the 'Brug pa Bka' brgyud Lineages.' *Journal of the International Association of Buddhist Studies* 28/2: 369–410.

Miller, Willa Blythe 2006. ' *'Brug pa'i lo rgyus zur tsam*: An Analysis of a Thirteenth Century Tibetan Buddhist Lineage History.' *Tibet Journal* 31/3: 17–42.

Miller, Willa Blythe 2013. 'Secrets of the Vajra Body: *Dngos po'i gnas lugs* and the Apotheosis of the Body in the work of Rgyal ba Yang dgon pa'. PhD diss., Harvard University.

Nālandā Translation Committee trans. 1982. *The Life of Marpa the Translator: Seeing Accomplishes All*. Boulder: Prajna Press [New ed. Boston & London: Shambhala, 1999].

Nālandā Translation Committee trans. 1999. *The Rain of Wisdom*. Boston & London: Shambala.

Quintman, Andrew 2014. *The Yogin and the Madman: Reading the Biographical Corpus of Tibet's Great Saint Milarepa*. New York: Columbia University Press.

Roberts, Peter A. trans. 2011. *Mahāmudrā and Related Instructions: Core Teachings of the Kagyü Schools*. Boston: Wisdom Publications.

Roerich, George N. trans. 1976 [[1]1949]. *The Blue Annals*. Delhi: Motilal Banarsidass.

Schaeffer, Kurtis 2005. *Dreaming the Great Brahmin: Tibetan Traditions of the Buddhist Poet-Saint Saraha*. Oxford & New York: Oxford University Press.

Sernesi, Marta 2021. *Re-enacting the Past: A Cultural History of the School of gTsang smyon Heruka*. Wiesbaden: Dr. Reichert Verlag.

Sernesi, Marta 2022. 'The *History of the Mountain Teachings*: 13th century Practice Lineages at rTsib ri.' *Revue d'Etudes Tibétaines* 64: 479–515.

Sernesi, Marta forthcoming. 'rTsib ri Hermits and Hermitages: Historical Religious Landscape in South-western Tibet.'

Stagg, Christopher trans. 2017. *The Hundred Thousand Songs of Milarepa*. Boulder: Shambhala.

Stearns, Cyrus trans. 2000. *Hermit of Go Cliffs: Timeless Instructions From a Tibetan Mystic*. Boston: Wisdom Publications.

Stein, Rolf A. 1959. *Recherches sur l'épopée et le barde au Tibet*. Paris: Presses Universitaires de France.

Sujata, Victoria trans. 2005. *Tibetan Songs of Realization*. Leiden: Brill.

Sujata, Victoria trans. 2011. *Songs of Shabkar*. Berkeley: Dharma Publishing.

Sujata, Victoria 2015. '*Nyams mgur* of Pha bong kha pa bDe chen snying po (1878–1941): An Analysis of His Poetic Techniques.' In Jim Rheingans ed. *Tibetan Literary Genres, Texts and Text Types*. Leiden: Brill, 197–228.
Tucci, Giuseppe 1966. 'Tibetan Folk Songs from Gyantse and Western Tibet.' *Artibus Asiae. Supplementum* 22. https://doi.org/10.2307/1522600
Vekerdi, Jozsėf 1952. 'Some Remarks on Tibetan Prosody.' *Acta Orientalia: Academiae Scientarum Hungaricae* 2/2–3: 221–233.
Walther, Marco 2017. 'Gling-ras-pa Padma rdo-rje (1128–1188): Leben und Werk unter besonderer Berücksichtigung des Werkes *Eine Fackel, die das Wesentliche bündelt*.' PhD Dissertation, Ludwig-Maximilians-Universität Munich.

Author Biography

Marta Sernesi is Professor of Tibetan Religions at the École Pratique des Hautes Études (EPHE–PSL) in Paris. Her work focuses on the cultural and religious history of Tibet and the Himalayas, on early contemplative traditions and instructional literature, and on Tibetan book culture. Her recent monograph is titled *Re-enacting the Past: A Cultural History of the School of gTsang smyon Heruka* (Dr. Reichert Verlag, 2021).

Chapter 8
Evil According to Buddhism[1]

Francesco Sferra

The force of evil is well exhibited in stanza 121 of the *Dhammapada*, one of the first Buddhist works to have been translated in the West, and which is quite famous even among non-specialists. As is well known, the text is not at all speculative in character and has only sporadic references to specific Buddhist doctrines. It can be seen as an intersectarian, and perhaps even interreligious work. With the exception of a very few, clearly Buddhist-inspired stanzas, theoretically speaking, it could easily be integrated even into non-Buddhist contexts. Many stanzas recur in an identical form, or with variants that still allow them to be recognizable, in other fundamental works of ancient Indian literature as well and, in particular, in Brāhmaṇical works, such as the *Mahābhārata* and the *Manusmṛti*.[2] The stanza with which I will begin this essay, indeed, betrays nothing typically or exclusively Buddhist:

> Do not underestimate evil by thinking:
> 'It will not touch me!'
> With the falling drops of water
> even a jug is filled.
> The fool fills himself with evil,
> amassing it, little by little.[3]

Here, the focus is on evil and on the fact that, like a drop of water, it gradually infiltrates and permeates everything. In a sneaky and insidious way, it inevitably prevails and corrupts everything in the end.

In line with a fairly frequent narrative strategy found in the Pāli Canon, and in classical Indian literature more generally, this stanza is followed by another whose meaning is exactly the opposite. The first piece of information, which reflects a common experience, is followed by something less obvious and more significant from a soteriological point of view. The second verse is almost identical to the first; only the key term changes:

> Do not underestimate good by thinking:
> 'It will not touch me!'
> With the falling drops of water
> even a jug is filled.
> The wise man fills himself with good,
> amassing it, little by little.[4]

There are numerous examples of this kind of literary technique, in which the psychological effect on the listener is also taken into account. Indeed, if the two pieces of information had been reversed—that is, if the positive were followed by the negative—it would not have the same effect; it would have introduced a 'depressing' flavour: 'We fill ourselves up with good little by little ... evil does the same thing, too.' But there is more to it than that. There is also an unspoken element that needs to be explained, as it is a prominent strategy used in Indian literature: namely, postponing what is considered to be more valuable to give it greater importance and emphasis. In this case, it is as if we were saying that—as we all know—evil may creep in slowly, but good does the same thing, and it is more important, more intense. It uses the same mechanism, but goes deeper. The greater power of good over evil is not overtly expressed; it is only the relative position of the two stanzas that suggests it.

To sum up, we have a double message: one of common sense and one of optimism. The first is the possibility of a gradual cultivation of good, which is almost a mirror image, one might say, of the gradualness by which evil flourishes; the second, the prevalence of good over evil.

Graduality inevitably involves small doses of something, just like drops of water. It is not only evil that slowly seeps in, corrupting everything, nor is it the only thing that tenaciously imposes itself and prevails; good can also be cultivated and is stronger than evil.

The prevalence of good, the importance and preciousness of even small doses of good, and the graduality with which it can be cultivated is a starting point that must be kept in mind, and which will be analysed from various points of view.

Two main terms are used to identify or refer to evil in classical Buddhist texts.

The first is *māra,* which is connected to an Indo-European root from which, for example, Italian *morte* and Spanish *muerte* derive, as does the English adjective 'mortal' and French *mortel,* etc., the meaning of which is primarily 'death.' More precisely, the term derives from the causative of the root *mṛ-*; thus, it literally means 'that which causes death.' According to Buddhist tradition, there are at least four (sometimes five, or in some cases only three) specific aspects of *māra*, which in a general sense indicates something negative, hurtful, and unhealthy. Here, I shall limit myself to briefly illustrating the four most common ones.

The first three aspects of *māra* represent anything inherently linked to death, to the incessant flow of transmigration (*saṃsāra*), both at the physical and psychic level, and that of the karmic forces that perpetuate the cycle of birth, conservation, and dissolution: the forces of 'defilement' (*kleśa*) that influence a spiritually immature person's motivation to act. The classic list includes six or ten defilements, depending on the tradition, but the main ones are greed (*lobha*), aversion (*doṣa*), and delusion (*moha*).[5] Thus, we have: 1) *kleśamāra,* evil as the collection of defilements; 2) *mṛtyumāra,* the 'death *māra*' or '*māra* of death' (*mṛtyu* also derives from the root *mṛ-*, 'to die'), which here basically alludes to the uninterrupted succession of births and deaths; and 3) *skandhamāra,* the '*māra* of psychophysical constituents,' which metaphorically represents the entirety of conditioned existence.

In Buddhist cosmology, these first three aspects of *māra* are embodied in the form of a harmful divinity, which represents the fourth aspect of *māra.* The term 'Māra' is never translated when it has this fourth meaning: it is reported as a proper name, simply using a capital letter. In classical texts, it occurs simply as 'Māra' or, at times, more precisely as 'Devaputramāra,' that is, 'Māra, son of a god (*deva*)'; it is essentially a dynamic, active force, which, as we shall see, tends to perpetuate the suffering (*duḥkha*) inherent in the very nature of things. It takes on the appearance of a specific individual, often with human features; lives in our sphere of existence; and is not a purely metaphorical personification. Devaputramāra actually appears in different forms, in both the Pāli Canon and other Buddhist scriptures, and interacts with the Buddha, his monks, and so on.

The second term used to refer to evil is *pāpa*, often translated as 'sin,' 'vice,' or 'guilt.' This is relevant in our case because Māra himself is sometimes referred to as a 'sinner,' i.e. *pāpin* or *pāpimant,* literally 'one who possesses *pāpa.*' Yet 'sin,' 'vice,' and 'guilt' are not adequate translations for *pāpa*, which among other things means 'sterile' and 'unfertile,' as this term expresses something more dynamic: it is rather the negative energy that is released from unhealthy actions and coagulates in a negative karmic accumulation. A more appropriate translation could be 'bad energy' or 'demerit,' a sort of burden that derives from and increases by doing negative things; and *pāpa* is actually opposed to *puṇya,* 'merit,' 'positive energy,' which is also dynamic and springs from wholesome actions.[6] 'Guilt' and 'sin' are translations influenced by Judeo-Christian culture, which is based on these primary categories. We should bear in mind that the concept of *pāpa* was elaborated in the Indian ritual context, which bears the idea that the non-observance of sacrifices or their incorrect execution leads to demerit from which we must free ourselves—which is nothing like the Christian idea of original sin.[7]

Traditionally, Māra has three sons—Vibhrama ('error,' but also 'violence'), Harṣa ('excitement'), and Darpa ('arrogance')—and three daughters (*duhitṛ*), who also have significant names. The first is Arati, which literally means 'non-passion' (*a-rati*) and alludes precisely to lack of impulse, pleasure, joy, even enthusiasm. Sometimes, Arati is translated as Tedium, perhaps a slightly too specific rendering, although this connotation also exists. In relation to Dharma, Arati is, first of all, the metaphorical personification of lack of passion, and therefore of motivation in practice. It is also a less direct way of talking about lack of energy (*vīrya*). The second daughter is Ragā, 'Passion.' This name indicates egoistic desire, including desire linked to sensory satisfaction and compulsive attachment. The third and most famous is Tṛṣṇā (Taṇhā in Pāli), 'Thirst' or 'Greed.' This is yet another way to speak of attachment, especially since the two terms *tṛṣṇā* and *rāga* (from which the name Ragā comes) are often used interchangeably in Indian religious literature.

Hence, we have two different shades of meaning, Ragā and Tṛṣṇā, when we speak of attachment, and a name to indicate lack of commitment, disaffection, or a subtle form of aversion. In place of Arati, we might have expected something more intense, more evident, a term translatable as 'Angry' or something similar; likewise, instead of one of the two terms that indicate attachment, we might have expected Avidyā, 'Ignorance,' considering that the impurities mentioned above are based on delusion (*moha*), which in later versions of the list of impurities is actually replaced by the feminine term *avidyā* (in Pāli *avijjā*), 'ignorance' or 'nescience,' which would seem to be perfect for the name of one of Māra's daughters.

What could be the reason for using an equivalent term for 'attachment' twice, while never using *avidyā*, the awareness of which is fundamental to the Buddhist soteriological path and which is also the last impurity to disappear in its subtlest forms? In some texts, two other daughters of Māra are mentioned, namely Fear and Pride, who in their turn are two products of ignorance. Avidyā is not there.

In the definition of evil found in the earliest texts, ignorance is spoken of only indirectly, through the term *moha*, which, as we have said, appears in the list of *kleśa*s, collectively termed *kleśamāra*. But there is reason to believe that Buddhist texts did not immediately resort to *moha* as a synonym for *avidyā*, the distortion whereby, not knowing the true nature of things, one judges good that which is actually evil, beautiful that which is ugly, and so on. The notion of *moha* does not capture the dynamic character of *avidyā*, of which it is, if anything, one of the first effects. However, the fact remains that later, especially in scholasticism, the two terms *moha* and *avidyā* are understood as interchangeable. It may seem like a technical notation for insiders, but, as we will see, it is not of secondary importance to the subject we are about to introduce.

Māra is also metaphorically imagined as the head of an army. A famous episode in Buddhist literature witnesses the intervention of this army and the daughters of Māra when Siddhārtha Gotama is about to obtain *bodhi*, 'awakening,' and become a Buddha.[8] The army is composed of monsters, such as we would imagine in cartoons today. There are ten monsters in particular: 1) sensory pleasure; 2) frustration; 3) hunger and thirst; 4) desire; 5) laziness; 6) terror; 7) doubt; 8) conceit and ingratitude; 9) undeserved gain and honour; and finally, 10) self-exaltation and denigration of others. The last two are paired because of the common circumstance, even in everyday life, that when one speaks badly of another, it is usually to suggest their own superiority; this is a fairly well known and evident phenomenon. However, even here, in the army of Māra, ignorance does not appear.

This absence does not seem accidental at all. As we find at other points in the Pāli Canon, when something important is not mentioned, it is not because it is ignored, but because it has its own special status. Here, probably, an important aspect of the ontology of evil is underlined.

In order to try to understand what evil is according to Buddhism, we must say something about its essence. What is evil from an ontological point of view? What is the deep nature of evil?

A number of Indian religious texts, not only Buddhist ones, are devoted in large part to cosmology—a part that is broader than we may suppose and is usually neglected in Western Dharma teachings. All schools recognize that the cosmos is divided into three spheres or worlds. The first coincides with the Kāmadhātu or Kāmaloka, the sphere or world of desire (*kāma*): the world in which we live, based on giving and taking, on the desire to obtain, to remove, and so on. In this world, beings normally have a form and a physical body. The second sphere of existence, which is always corporeal, is called Rūpadhātu or Rūpaloka, the world of *rūpa*, which means 'shape/colour.' Non-human entities live here: a plurality of divine-like beings endowed with bodies. The third sphere is called Arūpadhātu, or Arūpaloka. This is the sphere of non-form/non-colour: the deities that live here (there are no hell beings) are bodiless.

Devaputramāra, or simply Māra—the above-mentioned personification of evil that also includes the other three aspects of evil, starting with *kleśamāra*—is defined as the lord of Kāmadhātu, our sphere of existence. It is important to underline, however, that this is not primarily a being, but a position, which, *mutatis mutandis*, is similar to that of a prime minister: he/she changes, but his/her position is relatively stable, at least so long as this type of 'state order' lasts. Or, in terms of a hospital, the position can be construed as that of a head physician, and so on. In traditional Buddhist cosmology, Māra, not unlike Śakra (Sakka in Pāli), the chief of the gods, primarily represents a function. One becomes Māra, and after having done this, the same individual later becomes something else. The one who becomes Māra assumes authority over the Kāmadhātu by karmic accumulation, due to causes and conditions. There is no definitive Māra; there is no absolute evil. Māra is a duty, we could say: a sort of empty box that needs to be occupied. And it is occupied, from time to time, by someone who has developed all the necessary and extremely negative karmic accumulations. Given that impermanence counts even when it comes to evil and that some good is achieved even in that condition, (s)he also then cedes that position.

Therefore, when we think of Māra, we must first acknowledge that this is not a reference to an eternal entity, always identical to itself, and that its power resides specifically in the sphere of common existence. Although he can also influence other spheres of existence, his absolute kingdom is the Kāmadhātu alone, the world we live in and know. He certainly has no power over unconditioned realities, such as *nirvāṇa* (Pāli *nibbāna*).

In the *Māratajjaniyasutta* (*Majjhima Nikāya* 50), a *sutta* in which he is the protagonist, Moggallāna—one of the most important disciples of the historical Buddha, said to be the most proficient in the practice of meditative absorptions—claims he was Māra in a past life.

The *sutta* tells the story of Moggallāna once having a very intense stomach ache. By means of his acquired powers, he realized that this was no common stomach ache: Māra had entered his stomach. On recognizing him, Moggallāna ordered him to leave. Māra has the following constraint: when he is recognized, he must necessarily go away. In this case, he did not leave immediately, but escaped from Moggallāna's body and stood before him. Māra was incredulous that this simple monk could recognize him, thinking that even the Buddha could not. Moggallāna explained that he recognized him as he himself had been Māra a long time ago. The *sutta* continues with Moggallāna recounting the story of when he was Māra. We will return to this later.

In at least two parts of the Pāli Canon, we find a *sutta* describing the moment when the Buddha acquiesced to death.[9] Despite the gravity of the story, the passage also has a subtly comic tone. The Buddha, already almost eighty years old, turns to Ānanda, his assistant monk, telling him that a Tathāgata 'could even live up to an aeon or what remains of an aeon' if he wanted to. Ānanda merely nods with satisfaction, not understanding that in this way, the Buddha was urging him to pray that he stay alive. The text reports only that Ānanda did not understand because he was confounded by Māra. The Buddha insists somewhat, but Ānanda still fails to understand. After the third time, the Buddha can no longer insist. If Ānanda had asked him to stay alive, the Buddha—it is implied—would have accepted. But he does not ask. At that point, Māra approaches and reminds the Buddha of an ancient promise of his, namely that once the Dharma was established, and the community of monks and community of nuns had learned to practice it correctly, he would abandon *saṃsāra*. The Buddha agrees with him. A storm breaks out in the sky. At that moment, the Buddha abandons his vital breaths; this is a way of saying that the processes leading to physical death have been activated. According to traditional Indian physiology, there are many types of breath in our body, of which there are ten main ones. However, death does not occur immediately; it takes a period of time that may last a few months, and it is said that the Buddha indeed died only after three months.

This passage is meaningful: once again, it is not a recognition of Māra as representing an 'absolute unconditioned authority,' but a recognition of Māra as the lord of nature. Māra rules over nature; he is the king of nature. The word 'nature' does not appear in the original text, but I think this conveys the intended idea: Māra controls all things governed by conditioned processes. Further, when the Buddha agrees to begin the process of physical death, abandoning his vital breaths, he is not granting death victory; he is simply recognizing that his physical body has performed its function and must be given back to the conditioned. The task of his body was to ensure that the Dharma was taught and that the community of monks and nuns had been properly educated; there is no longer any real reason for him to stay.

The position of Māra is part of *saṃsāra*; it is part of *this* world. The nature of an Awakened person, of a Buddha, is different in that the question of where (s)he is after death does not apply.[10] It is the only condition outside of time (*akālika*) and, as such, is indescribable. The description of the Buddha in terms of the categories that form part of the conditioned (*saṃskṛta*) does not apply, as Buddhists try to demonstrate by adopting the famous tetralemma—which, already known in the Pāli Canon, became famous with the Madhyamaka tradition, allowing something to be described as existent, non-existent, at once existent and non-existent, and at once neither existent nor non-existent. These four possibilities of description do not apply to the Tathāgata (nor to anything seen from the absolute point of view), but they apply to Māra. As long as there is *saṃsāra*, there is Māra; if there is no *saṃsāra*, there is no Māra. Māra is describable; the Tathāgata is indescribable.

This is a crucial point. From the Buddhist perspective, evil is not an ultimate dimension, ontologically comparable to *nirvāṇa*, to which it would thus be opposed. It is not irreducible and indescribable; it has no absolute value; it exists as a condition only as long as *saṃsāra* exists. Of evil, as of pain, we can determine the beginning and the end, the cause of its arising and its disappearance. It is a position, as we have seen, that is transiently occupied, and which could, in theory, be an 'empty box' at some point. It is a position within the sphere of the conditioned. It certainly does not have anything to do with the ultimate reality.

If we then return to the question of why *avidyā* does not appear in the list of Māra's daughters, it seems to me that the answer is because we are talking about 'products'; it is important to note that Māra and his children are products. Māra is never defined as *avidyā*, but only as something that arises from *avidyā*. Therefore, he is a product. We can define his beginning, his end, his causes; we can describe his arising and disappearance. When seen, he disappears;[11] when seen, he must come out into the open, thus losing his power. It goes without saying that it is necessary to see him repeatedly; it is not enough to see him just once, however important that may be. We will return to this point later on. Some texts emphasize Māra's sagacity and intelligence. In fact, his source, *avidyā*, is not a synonym for stupidity, but indicates intelligence used in an unwholesome way.

By way of further explanation, we can say that Māra is the entropic force inherent in anything that is conditioned. He is, first of all, the force that keeps coming, i.e. *saṃsāra*, into existence. As the personification of this force,

Māra strongly opposes leaving the *saṃsāra*. When he realizes that a monk is about to obtain awakening, he tries in every way to distract him. He does this in an archetypal way with the Buddha himself, and repeats it in several stories mentioned in the Canon. Every time someone escapes from *saṃsāra*, Māra is no longer able to grasp him/her; his power is exhausted. If the conditioned comes to an end, there is no longer room for Māra. Stories of monks or lay people dying soon after obtaining awakening are referred to in the Pāli Canon. Normally, the Buddha invites the monks to observe the dark clouds in the sky, or the flocks of birds that move rapidly in the air, and sees in them the troops of Māra that try in vain to grasp the mind of the awakened person. They cannot find him because he is now free; he has attained *nibbāna*.

The same conclusion occurs at the end of some *sutta*s that describe a liminal case. In the *Saṃyutta Nikāya,* some monks who are very close to achieving awakening believe that the only way to free themselves is to commit suicide. In the *Godhikasutta*, Māra, with admirable punctuality, goes so far as to inform the Buddha of what is about to happen. The Buddha, however, knowing the minds of these monks and that they are not depressed, but very close to awakening and that it is actually the bond with their bodies that prevents them from achieving it, knows that in their case suicide would not entail a negative karmic residue, and unexpectedly praises the gesture of these monks.[12]

We may consider a further two passages from this Nikāya. In the section dedicated to the six bases of the senses, there is a very short *sutta* that is useful for our discussion.[13]

> The Venerable Samiddhi approached the Blessed One … and said to him: 'Venerable sir, it is said, "Māra, Māra." In what way, Venerable Sir, might there be Māra or the description of Māra?'
> 'Where there is the eye, Samiddhi, where there are forms, eye-consciousness, thing to be cognized by eye-consciousness, there Māra exists or the description of Māra.
> 'Where there is the ear …, there Māra exists or the description of Māra.'[14]

We can describe evil in some way. It is connected with the sphere of our ordinary existence which, to put it briefly, is made up of causes and conditions. Where there are causes and conditions, and therefore where there is the possibility of knowing something conditionally, that is when there is an object and the eye that can see it, and so on; then there is Māra or, perhaps better, there is Māra's sphere of application, where he has power. If he appears, we can describe him. Where there are no eyes, no shapes, no visual focus, no things to know through visual focus, and so on, there is no Māra, nor can he be described. The same thing obtains for all the faculties.[15]

In a different section of the same text, there is another significant passage:[16]

> At Savatthi. Now on that occasion the Blessed One was instructing exhorting, inspiring, and gladdening the bhikkhus with a Dhamma talk concerning Nibbāna. And those bhikkhus were listening to the Dhamma with eager ears, attending to it as a matter of vital concern, applying their whole minds to it. Then it occurred to Māra the Evil One: 'This ascetic Gotama is instructing, exhorting, inspiring, and gladdening the bhikkhus ... who are applying their whole minds to it. Let me approach the ascetic Gotama in order to confound them.' Then Māra the Evil One manifested himself in the form of a farmer, carrying a large plough on his shoulder, holding a long goad stick, his hair dishevelled, wearing hempen garments, his feet smeared with mud. He approached the Blessed One and said to him: 'Maybe you've seen oxen, ascetic?'
>
> 'What are oxen to you, Evil One?'
>
> 'The eye is mine, ascetic, forms are mine, eye-contact and its base of consciousness are mine. Where can you go, ascetic, to escape from me? The ear is mine, ascetic, sounds are mine ... The nose is mine, ascetic, odours are mine ... The tongue is mine, ascetic, tastes are mine ... The body is mine, ascetic, tactile objects are mine ... The mind is mine, ascetic, mental phenomena are mine, mind-contact and its base of consciousness are mine. Where can you go, ascetic, to escape from me?'[17]

'Consciousness,' the above-mentioned focus, is a plausible and usual translation of the Pāli word *viññāṇa* (Skt. *vijñāna*). Let us say in passing that this rendering is somewhat misleading, because in contemporary Western languages, this usually refers to something else. Here, it is mainly the primary awareness.

> 'The eye is yours, Evil One, forms are yours, eye-contact and its base of consciousness are yours; but, Evil One, where there is no eye, no forms, no eye-contact and its base of consciousness—there is no place for you there, Evil One. The ear is yours… The nose is yours… The tongue… The mind is yours…'
>
> [Māra:]
> That of which they say 'It's mine,'
> And those who speak in terms of 'mine'—
> If your mind exists among these,
> You won't escape me, ascetic.

> [The Blessed One:]
> That which they speak of is not mine,
> I'm not one of those who speak [of mine].
> You should know thus, O Evil One:
> Even my path you will not see.
>
> Then Māra the Evil One … disappeared right there.[18]

This passage summarizes what has been said before. With the terms 'eye,' 'forms,' etc. we mean the conditioned sphere, namely the body, the senses, and the mind as a psychic capacity, not the mind as a reflection of an absolute dimension, as we also sometimes find in Buddhist texts, especially those of the Great Vehicle. Evil is not part of the absolute dimension. According to Buddhist tradition, there is no irreducible 'evil,' as opposed to 'good,' which may prevail sooner or later, as some thinkers of the last century suggest—thinkers such as Sergio Quinzio, for example, in his interesting book *La sconfitta di Dio* (*The Defeat of God*). Here the basic idea is that good is opposed to evil, and good does not necessarily win; it is an ongoing conflict.

In Buddhism, there is no concept of evil that is unable to be assimilated to good and that somehow confronts it, perhaps losing at times. Here, instead, there is a 'box' that may embody evil, but at a lower ontological level.

How does one defend oneself from Māra? The answer is, in a sense, simple: the practice of Dharma—more precisely, the eightfold path, the seven factors of awakening, the spiritual faculties, and so on. In the Pāli Canon, however, there are not many teachings on how to defend oneself from Māra in some specific way.[19] One of these teachings seems particularly interesting to me.

In *Majjhima Nikāya* 25, the Buddha trains the monks using a parable. He asks them to imagine a hunter who wants to catch deer. His technique is to sprinkle the ground with feed so that the animals come to eat and he can easily catch them. A first group of deer, at the sight of the readily available food, immediately enters the hunter's field of action, quickly becoming his prey. A second group, seeing the fate of the first, decides not to enter the hunter's domain and to totally refuse the food he has offered. The problem is that eventually, the seasons change; food is scarce, and the animals become very thin. They can no longer resist; they enter the hunter's domain and are captured. The third group develops a strategy. They think of hiding near the field strewn with food and making only occasional, quick raids. The hunter, however, is not unprepared; he understands the animals' plan and tries to discover their hiding place. He expands the range of space where he offers food and follows their trail. The animals do not notice that the hunter is so cunning, and do not bother to conceal their movements. The hunter defeats them with ease. The fourth group realizes that it is not enough to hide: they need to find a place inaccessible to the hunter. It could even be somewhere close and not as hidden, but it must be inaccessible. From that place it would be possible, if necessary, to go and eat when the hunter is not there and return in complete safely.

The Buddha explains that this is a metaphor for Māra, the hunter, and the monks, who are the deer. The field is none other than the objects of the senses, that is the shapes, sounds, and so on, down to mental objects (ideas, memories, etc.). Monks, and by extension all Dharma practitioners, can deceive Māra because they act like the fourth group of animals: they take refuge in something that Māra cannot reach, in something that is ontologically different from the sphere of Māra. Whether this 'something' is *vipassanā* contemplation (*vipaśyanā* in Sanskrit), absorption in the *jhāna* (*dhyāna* in Sanskrit), the practice of the *brahmavihāra*s (loving kindness, compassion, etc.), some other factor of awakening, or all of these combined, wisely employed, is relatively unimportant. But it must be something on a level beyond Māra's reach.

This is an interesting passage: it does not talk about specific practices, nor does it suggest the application of any certain element of the eightfold path or some particular meditation technique. It is more general; it invites us to reflect more broadly on how to behave with respect to the sphere of Māra, and tells us that we must take refuge in something else—which we can call Dharma, Buddha Dharma Saṅgha, or even simply 'practice.'

Let us now return to the *sutta* in which Moggallāna says that he was Māra in a previous life. Some very practical teachings are presented in the second part of this *sutta*, which we will now examine briefly.

In the previous *sutta*, a direct confrontation with Māra is described: evil appears and the practitioners take refuge in good. But evil is not necessarily so direct; it does not always attack us head-on, but through other people.

Moggallāna says that at the time he was Māra, the Buddha was called Kakusandha. He had two students, one of whom was very good at meditation, the other skilled in doctrine. It so happened that Sañjīva (Moggallāna's alter ego in a previous cosmic age), the one who was proficient in meditation, at one point became so absorbed in meditation that he seemed to be dead. Some farmers saw him under a tree and, assuming he was dead, decided to burn him. But he did not die because, thanks to the power of concentration, he had acquired supernatural powers. The peasants left while the fire was still burning. When it died down, Sañjīva got up and entered the village to beg. The peasants who had burned him cried out at the miracle. Respect, trust, and support for the monk community increased considerably. Māra was worried about the esteem and popularity of the monks, but he was unable to corrupt their minds, so he set out to poison the minds of the villagers, to whom the monks turned for alms. He did this by insinuating that the monks, who were not working, were parasites, shiftless freeloaders, and so on, and people began to believe this slander—spiritually immature people who could therefore be easily corrupted.

Kakusandha's teaching was: 'When people feel aversion towards you, instigated by Māra, practice the four "divine abodes," the *brahmavihāra*s,' which are loving kindness/friendship, compassion, altruistic joy, and equanimity. It does not matter what they say. To defend oneself from aversion, the practice of the four *brahmavihāra*s is fruitful.

Māra was forced to change strategy. He began to speak very well of the monks, to urge people to seek their company, to develop a climate of appreciation for the monks. Initially, we might interpret this as a kind of surrender on Māra's part; on the contrary, it was not. His attack was even more subtle and sophisticated. Kakusandha's teaching to the monks this time was: 'Practice the contemplation of impermanence.' Praise, success, etc., are thus to be seen in terms of the famous formula 'this is not me; it is not mine; it is not myself.' Otherwise, the risk is that 'I and mine' (*ahaṃ mama*) will return in the form of attachment to complacency. First, there was aversion, but aversion breeds aversion; on the contrary, complacency triggers attachment. Therefore, it is fruitful to work on the 'three signs' (*trilakṣaṇa*) of conditioned existence: dissatisfaction, impermanence, and insubstantiality.

As noted above, Māra, if recognized, disappears. It is helpful to reflect at least briefly on this crucial point.

There is an assumption, initially developed in a grammatical environment, that recurs very often in Indian philosophical texts and is more or less accepted by all schools: it is impossible for an agent to operate on itself. It is thus said: can a man climb his own shoulders? Can a sword cut itself? Can a finger point at itself?

Therefore, we wonder: can it be Māra who sees Māra? We have already stated that these are different ontological planes: Māra is on one side, but whoever sees him is on the other side. We contemplate evil over and over again, in its various forms—large, small, great, minor; since we are able to contemplate it, we do not belong to it. In fact, we did not belong to it previously either, even before we acknowledge its discrete existence, but the difference is more evident when we do acknowledge it: when contemplating what happens before our eyes, we realize that we do not belong to the reality we are contemplating.

We do not belong to evil, and evil is not part of us, both because *we can see* evil and because, as stated above, we take refuge in something that is not conditioned, or in the case of liberated individuals, we leave the conditioned at the moment of death: ergo, our nature is unconditional. Evil, as mentioned above, belongs to the sphere of the sense faculties.

As noted above, the Buddha grants Māra command over sight, hearing, and so on. But he tells him that he does not identify himself with any of this. He takes refuge in another dimension, in another reality, like the deer that take refuge in a place that is inaccessible to the hunter.

It may be helpful to think of Māra as a baby who is always seeking his mother, a hungry baby looking for his mother to feed him. Māra's mother is *avidyā*, ignorance. We have seen that Māra's daughters all more or less operate around attachment and aversion. Ignorance is not mentioned, but it has come up many times, and we have verified that attachment and aversion are not born by chance and are not *svayambhū*, 'self-born.' They derive from ignorance.

Māra can do his work so long as there is ignorance for him to feed on. As long as there is ignorance, he can grow roots, develop, and appear, but if there is no ignorance, Māra disappears, because he is deprived of nourishment.

According to what we seem to understand, the Buddhist vision—and certainly not only the Buddhist one—is that good cannot be assimilated to evil. In later Buddhism, there is a tenet that the mind of the Buddha cannot be negated by anything: it can only be hidden or covered and disappear from sight, similar to the spark of God, which, according to other traditions, is in each of us and it does not depend on our being good or bad; it is always there and always active. The Buddha nature is not a prize; good is not a prize; the natural tendency for good is not a prize. We may not notice it, we may not know it, but it is not a prize. It seems to be like this at least from a religious point of view, even a Buddhist one, though obviously it is explicitly stated as such only after a certain point in Buddhist tradition. In the canonical scriptures, there is more reticence on this topic, and the statements in this regard are more nuanced.

Some time ago, while walking through the streets of Naples, I noticed how beautiful it was. It is an extraordinary city: an effervescence of art, colour, and humanity combined with a natural location that finds few parallels in the world. I began to reflect on the importance of exposing oneself to beauty, then of exposing oneself to good, and that both beauty and good are connected to goodness. I have reflected, step by step, on the fundamental importance—the first step, I would say—of frequently exposing ourselves to good, and the good that we can find within ourselves. We can then see it in others, in things, in nature. But first of all, to value good, we must find it within ourselves. I thought of the drops mentioned in the *Dhammapada*, which fall one after another. If there is frequent exposure to good, hope never fails; everything is a gain. In Forcella, one of the most sadly notorious districts of Naples, Jorit Agoch, a brilliant street artist, painted an immense mural of San Gennaro on the side of a building—a modern painting, but using a technique that vaguely recalls the nearby Caravaggio on the Via dei Tribunali.[20] Looking at this painting, I understood that violence and decline can never prevail.

Just like frequent exposure to evil, which generates contempt, frequent exposure to good (the wholesome and the beautiful, which are its visible expressions) generates appreciation. Evil breeds mistrust; good breeds trust. But there is a difference, and it is that contempt results in despising even oneself and, when this happens, something new can begin. Frequent exposure to the good and the beautiful creates an inclination that helps souls turn to good, to seek it: it is a form of positive addiction. The good and the beautiful make their way into the soul, just like the evil and the ugly. And just as the evil and ugly generate mistrust, the beautiful and good generate trust; they induce improvement. In addition, they produce respect: respect for themselves. The ugly and evil conversely generate contempt for themselves, and that is where the germ of their own undoing can be found.

The contempt that evil inevitably experiences, even towards itself, is a sign of its limits. Good is greater; using a term borrowed from Indian logic, we could say that good pervades (*vyāp-*) evil. It continues to exist even in the presence of evil, and while—for reasons we have already mentioned—evil is measurable and has limits, good is unlimited. Evil is powerful (in Italian, *potente*), but I dare to say—and it may sound like a provocation—good is overwhelming (in Italian, *prepotente*). We must not underestimate the power of good.

There is a beautiful story that we find in a medieval Purāṇa—a non-Buddhist text, but still an Indian one—in which, at a certain point, the text refers to someone named Ajāmila, who had a son, Nārāyaṇa. Nārāyaṇa is also one of the names of Viṣṇu. The man was a very evil person; on the verge of death, he called out for his son: 'Nārāyaṇa!' His son does not arrive in time, and the man dies. The emissaries of the god of death, Yama, are there. They want to take Ajāmila's soul away, but the emissaries of Viṣṇu also arrive and prevent them from doing so by mentioning that he had pronounced the name of God. A debate erupts, and in the end, the emissaries of Viṣṇu win, because 'the use of the name Viṣṇu, be it to refer to another, as a joke, an interjection, or even as an offence, results in the destruction of any evil whatsoever.'[21]

This is not to say that everything is easy. In that case, the Pāli Canon would not be so full of teachings on right effort, which are greater in number than those on many other subjects. What I think these stories mean to teach us is that we are not alone in our work. All this emerges more clearly in the texts of the Mahāyāna, where there is clearer emphasis on the theme of the participation of the good in the efforts of each individual. But I would like to think that this is implicit also in ancient traditions. We are not alone in this work: the fruits arrive, the profit is sure to come, and it is easily greater than what we would have imagined.

Let's look at a passage from the *Milindapañha*, a text that reports a dialogue between Milinda, a Greek king from Bactria, and a Buddhist monk called Nāgasena. It is a very interesting dialogue, divided into four parts. In the second are perhaps the most useful elements from the point of view of meditation practice. The passage is titled 'Predominance of the Good.' Milinda asks a question, and Nāgasena answers:[22]

> The King said: 'Revered Nāgasena, which is the greater, merit or demerit?' 'Merit, sire, is the greater, demerit is a trifle.' 'In what way?' 'Sire, (someone) doing demerit is remorseful and says, "An evil deed was done by me"—therefore evil does not increase. But (someone), sire, doing merit, is not remorseful. Rapture is born of the absence of remorse, joy is borne of rapture, the body of one who is joyful is impassible, when the body is impassible, he experiences happiness, the mind of one who is happy is concentrated, and he who is concentrated comprehends as it really is—in this way merit increases.'[23]

This last expression, 'comprehends as it really is,' occurs many times in the canonical scriptures (*yathābhūtaṃ pajānāti*). This means that the practitioner does not consider things or entities as his own, his own ego, or his own self. (S)he knows them in their simplicity, as things that are born, endure, and die. By virtue of this disidentification, good increases, and appreciation, sharing, and happiness increase as well.

> 'If a man who has had his hands and feet cut off, sire, had given (merely) one handful of lotuses to the Lord, he will not go to the Downfall for ninety-one eons. It is for this reason that I say merit is the greater, demerit a trifle.'
>
> 'You are dexterous, revered Nāgasena.'[24]

This passage is particularly instructive because it describes the positive growth of good as linked to happiness. And it speaks of great results deriving even from a small action, even for a great sinner like a murderer.

The next step is also interesting—almost a paradox, since, according to numerous canonical texts, we know that according to Buddhism, a negative, harmful action that has been done unknowingly, unwittingly, does not bear karmic demerit. The king's question is: 'Is it worse to do evil by knowing it or to do evil by not knowing it?' According to standard Buddhist teachings, we would expect the answer to be, 'Not knowing it is much better than knowing it.' On the contrary, Nāgasena, surprisingly, says that it is much better to do harm by knowing it and adds that this is so because in this way the damage is minimized. Let's take a very trivial example. My house is infested with ants; I have to eradicate them. Of course, killing ants is a harmful action. In a way, it would be karmically negative. There is a way of doing it in a crueller, more destructive way, so to speak, and a way of doing it so as to minimize the damage. I think this is the point of the passage: here, the message is that if something painful must be done, such as punishing someone, eliminating parasites, etc., doing it while aware of the pain being caused allows us to minimize the damage.

I was having dinner with a friend from Milan. At one point, he said to me: 'I'm carrying out an investigation. What is evilness in your opinion? When can a person really be called evil?'

I report the outcome of our reflections. He went on to say: 'Someone told me that a really evil person is one who feels pleasure when others suffer, especially when he has not caused the suffering himself.' Various people he had asked earlier had come to this conclusion. It is not that he shared this conclusion; he merely reported it to me as a starting point.

We agreed that the category of evil is inconceivable from an absolute point of view. It exists only as an expression of discomfort. From a relative point of view, in line with common experience and with the linguistic conventions that represent it, we can define a wide range of behaviours as evil, ranging from simply creating obstacles to enjoying the suffering of others, especially if one has not personally caused it.

If what we have said so far is true, that evil does not ontologically belong to the sphere of the absolute, but rather to that of the relative; the fundamental discomfort is always and only a desperate need for love, more precisely the fear of being excluded from love because one is not worthy of it. At the basis of evil behaviour, there is always—paradoxically—the opposite of evilness: the search for good, a desperate need for love, a desire for unfulfilled love, a state of not being loved or the fear of not being loved, and feeling unworthy of love, a profound and radical insecurity triggered by the misperception of ourselves and our true nature.

The need for good, deeply rooted within us, can turn into a 'bottomless pit.' If we focus too sharply on our need for love, we realize that this need will never be satisfied; it will never be enough. And if we think about it, it is obvious why this is so. It will never be enough for us because it is the very infinity of good (only evil, we have said, is measurable), its elusiveness, that determines our dissatisfaction. And the difference with our imperfection scares and oppresses us. We would like to possess this infinite good, but we know we cannot.

We have said above that evil is describable, or at least, it is possible to identify it in something; it has its own sphere. There is also a formula that expresses its identification: '*this* is mine; *this* is me; *this* is myself.' As long as there is a 'this' and a 'that,' evil can be described. Good, on the other hand, as some Indian texts say, is *avāṅmanasagocara*, beyond words and beyond the mind. Again, it is the infinity of good that creates this chasm in a certain sense. Wanting to fill it is an unequal struggle; it will always be a desperate desire.

A different perspective might open up when we offer to 'give' love and not to 'take' it: we as a source. This is a radical inversion, similar to what David Steindl-Rast speaks of (1984), and according to which happiness is not the condition to be grateful for, but rather, gratefulness is what generates happiness.[25] When we are grateful for what we have, we share it. Some might object by saying that they have nothing or that they do not have enough, but this is in contrast with the fact that we were born as human beings and that therefore, as the eighth-century master Śāntideva reminds us in the *Bodhicaryāvatāra*, we have already obtained the greatest wealth.[26]

There is another perspective, an even higher one, which is that of abandonment: not as a receptacle, not as a source, but simply as a vehicle, a channel through which the flow of good can move in and out. Conceiving ourselves as a source of good is undoubtedly a step forward: we are no longer those who *must* have, but those who *can* give. But then there is another perspective, namely abandonment in faith: neither as a receptacle, nor as a source, but as a vehicle. Love in/love out. In a certain way, we do not have to do much except keep this channel open and unobstructed, so that good can freely move in and out.

Notes

1 A preliminary version of this paper was published in Italian in Sferra 2016. Unless otherwise indicated, the words in brackets are transliterated from Sanskrit.

2 See Rau 1959 and Hegarty 2018.

3 *māppamaññetha pāpassa na man taṃ āgamissati | udabindunipātena udakumbho pi pūrati | bālo pūrati pāpassa thokathokam pi ācinaṃ ||* (DhP 121). Transl. by Isabella Ranieri in Sferra 2021: 112.

4 *māppamaññetha puññassa na man taṃ āgamissati | udabindunipātena udakumbho pi pūrati | dhīro pūrati puññassa thokathokam pi ācinaṃ ||* (Dhp 122). Transl. by I. Ranieri in Sferra 2021: 112.

5 The complete list, which can be found in some Pāli texts (e.g., *Dhammasaṅganī* 1229 ff., *Vibhaṅga* 12, and *Visuddhimagga* 22.49.65), continues with 'pride' (*māna*), 'erroneous points of view' (*micchāditthi*), 'doubt' (*vicikicchā*), 'sloth' (*thīna*), 'excitement' (*uddhacca*), 'shamelessness' (*ahirika*), and 'recklessness' (*anottappa*). In Sanskrit sources, the prevailing list contains six factors, which, in addition to *lobha*, *doṣa*, and *moha*, include 'pride,' 'erroneous points of view,' and 'doubt' (see, for instance, *Dharmasaṃgraha* 67).

6 For more information about these two terms, *pāpa* and *puṇya*, see Harvey 2000: 18.

7 For some reflections on the theme of evil in traditional Indian culture (and in Buddhism), see Boyd 1971, Malalasekera 1974.2: 611–620 (particularly on Māra in Pāli sources), Gäb 2015, Herman 1993, Piano 1996: 202–215, and Hallisey 1999.

8 See, e.g., *Buddhacarita* chap. 13 and *Lalitavistara* chap. 21. For further information, see Gurugè 1991–1992 and Kinnard 2004.

9 See, for instance, *Dīgha Nikāya* 16.3.1ff (II 106ff.) and *Saṃyutta Nikāya* 51.10. (V 259–263).

10 See *Majjhima Nikāya* n. 72.

11 E.g., see *Saṃyutta Nikāya* 4.23 (IV 16).

12 See *Saṃyutta Nikāya* 4.23, 22.87 (III 119–124), 35.87 (IV 55–60), 54.9 (V 320–322).

13 *Saṃyutta Nikāya* 35.65 (IV 38–39, quoted with slight changes): *atha kho āyasmā samiddhi yena bhagavā ... pa ... bhagavantaṃ etad avoca—māro, māro ti vuccati. kittāvatā nu kho bhante māro vā assa mārapaññatti vā ti? yattha kho samiddhi atthi cakkhu atthi rūpā atthi cakkhuviññāṇaṃ, atthi cakkhuviññāṇaviññātabbā dhammā, atthi tattha māro vā mārapaññatti vā. atthi sotaṃ... atthi tattha māro vā mārapaññatti vā.*

14 Transl. Bodhi 2000, vol. 2: 1152–153.

15 See also Gethin 1997: 189–190.

16 *Kassakasutta, Saṃyutta Nikāya* 1.4.2.9 (I 114–115, quoted with slight changes): *sāvatthi nidānaṃ. tena kho pana samayena bhagavā bhikkhū nibbānapaṭisaṃyuttāya*

dhammiyā kathāya sandasseti samādapeti samuttejeti sampahaṃseti. te ca bhikkhū aṭṭhikatvā manasi katvā sabbacetaso samannāharitvā ohitasotā dhammaṃ suṇanti. atha kho mārassa pāpimato etad ahosi—ayaṃ kho samaṇo gotamo bhikkhū nibbāna-paṭisaṃyuttāya dhammiyā kathāya ... pa ... yaṃ nūnāhaṃ yena samaṇo gotamo tenupasaṅkameyyaṃ vicakkhukammāyā ti. atha kho māro pāpimā kassakavaṇṇaṃ abhinimminitvā mahantaṃ naṅgalaṃ khandhe karitvā dīghaṃ pācanayaṭṭhiṃ gahetvā haṭahaṭakeso sāṇasāṭīnivattho kaddamamakkhitehi pādehi yena bhagavā tenupasaṅkami. upasaṅkamitvā bhagavantaṃ etad avoca—api samaṇa balivadde addasā ? ti. kiṃ pana pāpima te balivaddehī? ti. mam eva samaṇa cakkhu mama rūpā, mama cakkhusamphassaviññāṇāyatanaṃ. kuhiṃ me samaṇa gantvā mokkhasi? mam eva samaṇa sotaṃ mama saddā ... pa ... mam eva samaṇa ghānaṃ mama gandhā. mam eva samaṇa jivhā mama rasā. mam eva samaṇa kāyo mama phoṭṭhabbo. mam eva samaṇa mano mama dhammā mama manosamphassaviññāṇāyatanaṃ. kuhiṃ me samaṇa gantvā mokkhasī? ti.

17 Transl. Bodhi 2000, vol. 1: 208.

18 *taveva pāpima cakkhu tava rūpā tava cakkhusamphassaviññāṇāyatanaṃ. yattha ca kho pāpima natthi cakkhu natthi rūpā natthi cakkhusamphassaviññāṇāyatanaṃ agati tava tattha pāpima. taveva pāpima sotaṃ tava ... taveva, pāpima, ghānaṃ ... taveva, pāpima, jivhā ... pe ... taveva, pāpima, mano ... pe ... yaṃ vadanti mama yidanti, ye vadanti mamanti ca, ettha ce te mano atthi, na me samaṇa mokkhasī ti. yaṃ vadanti na taṃ mayhaṃ, ye vadanti na te ahaṃ, evaṃ pāpima jānāhi, na me maggam pi dakkhasī ti. atha kho māro pāpimā ... pa ... vantaradhāyīti* (vol. 1: 115–116). Transl. Bodhi 2000: 208–209.

19 See, for instance, *Majjhima Nikāya* 49, and *Saṃyutta Nikāya* 4 and 5.

20 Photographic reproductions of this painting are available online. See, for instance: https://ecampania.it/event/napoli-san-gennaro-operaio-jorit/.

21 *Bhāgavatapurāṇa* 6.1.21 ff.

22 *rājā āha—bhante nāgasena, katarannu. kho bahutaraṃ puññaṃ vā apuññaṃ vā ? ti. puññaṃ kho mahārāja bahutaraṃ, apuññaṃ thokanti. kena kāraṇenā ? ti. apuññaṃ kho mahārāja karonto vippaṭisārī hoti pāpaṃ kammaṃ mayā katanti tena pāpaṃ na vaḍḍhati. puññaṃ kho mahārāja karonto avippaṭisārī hoti. avippaṭisārissa pāmojjaṃ jāyati pamūditassa pīti jāyati pītimanassa kāyo passamhati. passaṅkāyo sukhaṃ vedeti. sukhino cittaṃ samādhiyati. samāhito yathābhūtaṃ pajānāti tena kāraṇena vaḍḍhati* (ed. pp. 83–84).

23 Tr. Horner, vol. 1: 116.

24 *kho mahārāja chinnahatthapādo bhagavato ekaṃ uppalahatthaṃ datvā ekanavutikappāni vinipātaṃ na gacchissati. imināpi mahārāja kāraṇena bhaṇāmi puññaṃ bahutaraṃ apuññaṃ thokanti. kallo 'si bhante nāgasenā ti* (ed. p. 84). Transl. Horner, vol. 1: 116.

25 See the TED Talk of this Benedictine monk here: http://www.ted.com/talks/david_steindl_rast_want_to_be_happy_be_teful?language=it.

26 Cf. *Bodhicaryāvatāra* 1.4, 4: 15–18.

Bibliography

All references to Pāli texts are to the Pali Text Society editions.

Bodhi, Bhikkhu 2000. *The Connected Discourses of the Buddha. A New Translation of the Saṃyuttanikāya*. 2 vols. Somerville (MA): Wisdom Publications.

Boyd, James W. 1971. 'Symbols of Evil in Buddhism.' *The Journal of Asian Studies* 31.1: 63–75. https://doi.org/10.2307/2053052

Gäb, Sebastian 2015. 'Why Do We Suffer? Buddhism and the Problem of Evil.' *Philosophy Compass* 10.5: 345–353. https://doi.org/10.1111/phc3.12207

Gethin, Rupert 1997. 'Cosmology and Meditation: From the Aggañña-Sutta to the Mahāyāna.' *History of Religions* 36.3: 183–217. https://doi.org/10.1086/463464

Gurugè, A. W. P. 1991–1992. 'The Buddha's Encounters with Māra, the Tempter: their Representation in Literature and Art.' *Indologica Taurinensia* 17–18: 183–208.

Hallisey, Charles 1999. 'Chapter 2. Buddhism.' In Jacob Neusner ed. *Evil and Suffering*, Pilgrim Library of World Religions; Cleveland: Pilgrim Press, 36–66.

Harvey, Peter 2000. *An Introduction to Buddhist Ethics*. Foundations, Values and Issues, Cambridge University Press: Cambridge.

Hegarty, James 2018. 'The Dhammapada, the Mahābhārata and the Mānava Dharmaśāstra: a study in early South Asian intertextuality.' In Brodbeck Simon, Adam Bowles, and Alf Hiltebeitel eds. *The Churning of the Epics and Purāṇas. Proceedings of the Epics and Purāṇas Section at the 15th World Sanskrit Conference*, 209–239. New Delhi: Dev Publishers & Distributors.

Herman, A. L. 1993. *The Problem of Evil and Indian Thought*. Delhi: Motilal Banarsidass.

Horner, I. B. 1963. *Milinda's Questions*. London: Luzac & Company Ltd.

Kinnard, J. N. 2004. 'Māra.' In Buswell, Jr. R. E. ed. *Encyclopedia of Buddhism*, vol. 2, New York etc., pp. 512–513.

Malalasekera, G. P. 1974. *Dictionary of Pāli Proper Names*. 2 vols. The Pali Text Society, London: Routledge & Kegan Paul Ltd.

Piano, Stefano 1996. *Sanātana dharma. Un incontro con l'induismo*. Torino: San Paolo.

Rau, Wilhelm 1959. 'Bemerkungen und nicht-buddhistische Sanskrit-Parallelen zum Pāli-Dhammapada.' In Vogel Claus ed. *Jñānamuktāvalī. Commemoration volume in honour of Johannes Nobel on the occasion of his 70th birthday offered by pupils and colleagues*. New Delhi: Sarasvati-Vihara, International Academy of Indian Culture 38: 159–175.

Sferra, Francesco 2016. 'Il male secondo il buddhismo.' *Sati* 25.2: 42–71.

Sferra, Francesco transl. 2021 *Il Dhammapada. Sulle tracce del Buddha*. Roma: Ubiliber.

Steindl-Rast, David 1984. *Gratefulness, the Heart of Prayer: An Approach to Life in Fullness*. New York/Ramsey: Paulist Press.

Author Biography

Francesco Sferra (b. 1965) is Full Professor of Sanskrit Language and Literature at the University of Naples 'L'Orientale', Italy. His primary areas of expertise are connected to Sanskrit philology, history of Indian religions, tantric studies, and classical Indian philosophy. His works include the critical edition and translation of the longer *Ṣaḍaṅgayoga* by Anupamarakṣita with its commentary by Raviśrījñāna (2000), the *Sekoddeśaṭīkā* by Nāropā (2006) and (together with H. Isaacson) the *Sekanirdeśapañjikā* by Rāmapāla (2014). He is founder and co-editor of the series Manuscripta Buddhica (first vol. 2008).

PART II

THE DHARMA IN WORDS

Chapter 9

The Loveliness of the Ordinary

Christina Feldman

Several years ago, I resolved to renounce hurrying for a year. It was immediately obvious that hurrying had less to do with how quickly or slowly I moved, and more to do with agitation and preoccupation with being somewhere I was not. The blessing of this renunciation was to be increasingly aware of the loveliness of the ordinary. The journey of going places became as important as the arrival; instead of waiting for something to begin or end I discovered a deepening appreciation of attending to what was right before me. So much that had escaped my attention came alive—the warmth of the sun on my face, the sounds of life, the touch of my feet on the ground. A new found joy in the simple and ordinary connections, events and people in my life deepened.

Our lives can be filled with countless lost moments. In the haste of our lives, juggling the demands of family, work, friends and the needs of our own body and mind, connection with the present is replaced by preoccupation with the future. Lost in thought and busyness our attention is prone to simply slide over the surface of life. It is all too easy to simply miss the countless lovely moments in your day that make your heart sing. The sound of a child's laughter, the shape of a cloud, the coolness of a summer's breeze, the wildflower growing in the crack of a sidewalk, the beat of our own heart—you live and breathe amidst the miracle of life. For it to touch your heart you need to be present. The precious moments of calm and stillness your heart long for are born of your willingness to live the moment you are in.

Meditation practice shows the way to reclaim your capacity for profound, sensitive attentiveness and in turn to reclaim all the lost moments. Resting in an awakened heart you can deeply appreciate all that is joyful in our life, embrace that which is difficult and increasingly discover the loveliness of the ordinary.

In the moments and events of your life that are dramatic and intense you are likely to be immediately attentive. Excitement, pleasure, success, love and happiness are eagerly welcomed and are heroically pursued. Events that are painful, unpleasant, sorrowful are met with equally heroic efforts of avoidance and resistance. You may realize that it is only when all of your efforts of avoidance and distraction have been exhausted that you are willing to reluctantly attend to the difficult, often with the agenda of fixing or getting rid of all that disturbs your heart.

Intensity awakens us, offering a sense of vitality and richness that can be felt to be lacking in life. Once sitting on a train beside a young man whose face and body were marked with multiple body piercings, I asked him if it wasn't excruciating to have so much inflicted on his body. He answered: 'It is deeply painful, but it makes me feel so alive.' We can be intensity addicts. Busyness can be exhausting but offers apparent meaning, direction and identity. A rollercoaster ride, an exhilarating meditation, the excitement of a new love offers a longed-for wakefulness and sense of being fully alive. A broken heart, an illness, a grieving friend, an argument with a loved one bring pain and sorrow, but are also events that capture and enliven our attention. Wisdom teaches us that the home of this precious sensitivity, awareness, is not in the events of our lives, but in our own hearts.

There is so much in your life which is simply ordinary, neither exciting nor disturbing. Trees grow, birds fly, the sun shines, the rain falls. You go from morning to night breathing, walking and moving through your day meeting countless moments, people and events that you may barely notice. Within the ordinary the tendency is to disconnect, at times feel these moments are undeserving of our attention. The ordinary is dismissed as boring, lacking in richness, intensity and completeness. Accustomed to externalizing happiness and vitality, in the midst of any moment that is simply ordinary, neither dramatic nor intense, you may begin to detect an inner unease or discontent. The ordinary can seem to deprive us of purpose and consequently of identity. Non-doing appears at first deeply uncomfortable in its unfamiliarity, often becoming a springboard for the pursuit of some new, more exciting event or moment. In reality the ordinary moments in your life are doorways to a deeper wisdom, discovering the richness and vitality that live within our own hearts and a profound connection to life just as it is.

Awareness is designed to illuminate your life inwardly and outwardly. Awareness makes visible all that has lain in the shadows of your heart and life, shrouded in confusion, busyness or denial. The power of wise attention is to awaken the world. To understand anything deeply you need to be connected with it—this is the birthplace of sensitivity, peace and compassion. Each of us is asked to explore what it means to be consciously engaged with our life and a participant in the awakening of our world.

The path of awareness invites us to deeply question the inclination to externalize both happiness and unhappiness and the belief that the wakefulness of our heart depends upon intensity. In the exploration of what it means to feel truly alive, connected and awake you begin to understand that a meditative life is an invitation to awaken our capacity to be delighted, to see beneath the surface of all things and rest in the richness of an enlivened heart. Your capacity to be delighted and touched by life lives within your own heart. Honoring each moment unconditionally with your attention is to live in a sacred way, embracing the lovely, the difficult and the countless moments in your life which are neither pleasant nor unpleasant. In our capacity to be delighted we learn to discover the loveliness of the ordinary.

Awakening your capacity for sensitivity is to begin to appreciate the calm and ease of a heart that is not entranced by drama and intensity. No-one's life is endlessly exciting or painful, filled with an uninterrupted succession of high and low experiences. No-one has a mind that only ever enjoys lovely, uplifting thoughts or a body that is continuously bursting with health and vitality. None of us has a meditation practice that is continually exciting and rapturous. Your days have countless ordinary moments—sitting on the bus, shopping, preparing a meal, answering the telephone and walking from one place to another as you attend to all the ordinary tasks of your life. You move through a world meeting countless ordinary events, meeting numerous people who may barely touch your heart. These moments are not less worthy simply because they are lacking in intensity or drama. Learning to embrace the ordinary with a wholehearted sensitivity and attention, your world is illuminated and awakened. You learn what it means to listen more deeply, see more fully and sense an awakened heart that sees the special in the ordinary and the ordinary in the special.

Learning to attend wholeheartedly to the ordinary you begin to discover a heart that can rest in non-doing and deep receptivity. Stepping out of addiction to intensity, you find within all the ordinary moments of your life, a chance to pause, to breathe and sense glimmers of a profound calmness. The many sights, sounds, tastes and people you have overlooked because of their ordinariness are seen in a new way. You begin to be curious about all the ordinary encounters and activities we have ignored or neglected and discover their uniqueness and depth. Reclaiming the lost moments in our days, we are reclaiming our lives and our capacity to celebrate the loveliness of the ordinary; it is a place of deep ease and calm. The miracle of being alive is celebrated through the sensitivity and connectedness you cultivate.

Guided Meditation—Touching the Ordinary

Settle into a meditative posture that is relaxed and as ease filled as possible. Close your eyes and for a few moments rest your attention within your breathing, allowing yourself to calm and find your seat in this moment. Scan your attention through your whole body, sensing the spectrum of sensations and feelings that are present in this moment. Notice how your attention is drawn towards the sensations that are either pleasant or unpleasant. Be as aware as you can of how you respond to these sensations—the way in which you delight in the pleasant and how you might tighten around or resist the unpleasant. Moving your attention through your body sense the places where no sensation appears—areas you might describe as neutral—the touch of your lips together, the palms of your hands, your ears. Bring your attention to explore these areas and sense how the interest, sensitivity and calmness brings them to life, how they are seen in a new way. Sense what it means to rest within the ordinary, exploring the ease and peace to be found.

Expanding your attention to sense the range of sounds presenting themselves—notice the sounds that are pleasant and those that grate upon you. Sense the way you may be attracted to those you enjoy and resist those that are unpleasant. Notice the sounds of the ordinary—the hum of your refrigerator, the wind outside your window, the car passing on the street. Explore what it means to listen deeply to those sounds and to rest just in pure listening.

Bring your attention to notice the range of thoughts passing through your mind—planning, remembering, worrying—attend to them all equally with a calm, unbiased attentiveness that sees their arising and their passing. Sense what it might be to rest in the seeing, allowing the mind to do what a mind does, without taking hold of any of the thoughts that appear. Expand your awareness to receive everything that is present in this moment—your body, feelings, thoughts, sounds. Explore what it is to receive the moment, to rest in awareness. Sense the loveliness born of interest, connection and ease and the way that your world is awakened by the attention you bring. What would it mean to bring these qualities into our life; to attend wholeheartedly to all that we neglect or dismiss?

For Corrado—In honour of your many years of teaching and all the love and time you have committed to A.Me.Co. Love Christina

Author Biography

Christina Feldman has studied and taught Buddhist meditation since the early 1970s. She is co-founder of Gaia House in Devon, England, and is a guiding teacher at Spirit Rock in Woodacre, California (USA) and at the Insight Meditation Society (IMS) in Barre, Massachusetts (USA), where she founded Women's and Family retreats. She regularly leads retreats in Europe. She has written many books, such as *The Quest of the Warrior Woman: Women as Mystics, Healers and Guides* (1994); *The Buddhist Path to Simplicity: Spiritual Practice for Everyday Life* (2001a); *Way of Meditation* (2001b); *Boundless Heart: The Buddha's Path of Kindness, Compassion, Joy, and Equanimity* (2017); and *Mindfulness: Ancient Wisdom Meets Modern Psychology* (co-authored with Willem Kukyen, 2019).

Chapter 10

Ānāpānasati: A Brief Introduction[1]

Larry Rosenberg

Ānāpānasati is the meditation system expressly taught by the Buddha in which mindful breathing is used to develop both *samatha* (a serene and concentrated mind), and *vipassanā* (insightful seeing). In this clear and detailed teaching, the Buddha presents us with a meditation practice that uses conscious breathing to calm and stabilize the mind so it is fit to see into itself and to let go into freedom.

We are learning the art of allowing the breath to unfold without our imposing any controls. We let it happen rather than make it happen. Can we receive each in-breath, and each out-breath, just as it is—deep, shallow, pleasant, unpleasant, etc.? Can the quality of awareness be non-judgmental, not for or against what shows up? This practice, said to be the form of meditation used to bring the Buddha to full awakening, is based on the *Ānāpānasatisutta* (MN n. 118).

The first step is to take up our breathing as an exclusive object of attention. We focus our attention on the sensations produced as the lungs quite naturally, without interruption, fill up and empty themselves. At first, we pick up these sensations by stationing our attention at the nostrils, chest or abdomen. As our breath-awareness practice matures, this attention can be expanded to the body as a whole.

In the Buddha's words: 'Being sensitive to the whole body, the *yogi* breathes in; being sensitive to the whole body, the *yogi* breathes out.' It is important to note that what is being talked about are the raw sensations that come about through breathing, free of conceptualization or imagery of any kind. Of course, when you direct your attention to the breath, you may find that the mind prefers to be elsewhere. It has a mind of its own.

The practice is to gently keep returning to the breath each time you are distracted. Little by little the mind learns to settle down; it feels very steady, calm and peaceful. Even at this early stage in the training, we are also strongly encouraged to be mindful in the activities that make up our day. Keeping awareness of the breath alive can help ground us in these activities. The breath is always with us, helping to cut down on unnecessary thinking that so often distracts us from the here and now.

Concentrating on breathing in such a manner enables the mind to gather together all its scattered energies. The mind is now much steadier and clearer. We are now encouraged to enlarge the scope of awareness so it becomes more comprehensive. With awareness anchored in breathing we begin to include all bodily movements, the pleasant, unpleasant and neutral sensations that make up sensory experience and the wide variety of mind states that compose so much of our consciousness. We become increasingly familiar and at home with bodily life, emotions and the thought-process itself. We are learning the art of self-observation, all along being in touch with the fact that we are breathing in and out. The skills being developed are the ability to widen and deepen the capacity to receive our own experience with intimacy and a lack of bias. The breath becomes like a good friend, accompanying us every step along the way.

We are now able to practice *vipassanā* meditation. The mind is more able to bring the fullness of mental and physical life into focus. One of the primary meanings of *vipassanā* is *insight*—insight into the impermanent, empty nature of all formations. The *yogi* breathes in and out focusing on the impermanent nature of all formations. As we sit and breathe, we observe the arising and passing away of all mental and physical events. The mind empties itself of all its contents: the body discloses its transparent and constantly changing nature. Deep penetration into the law of impermanence can profoundly facilitate our ability to let go of the attachments that produce so much unnecessary anguish. A new dimension of living opens for us, as we learn to let go into freedom.

This brief sketch of one of the Buddha's most important meditation teachings is, of course, inadequate. I hope that the potential of breath awareness as a possible meditation practice becomes more and more apparent. If such a practice proves to be of some value, you can continue this practice for the rest of your life—until your last breath!

Notes

1 Corrado Pensa and I led many retreats together. We worked with great harmony and, I believe, effectiveness despite this not being his primary approach. He was familiar with this method, of course, and we were able to work gracefully together based on the needs of each student. For this reason, I want to dedicate this short essay to my dear friend Corrado.

Author Biography

Larry Rosenberg was Professor of Psychology at the University of Chicago and at Harvard Medical School. He is a senior teacher at the Insight Meditation Society in Barre, Massachusetts, and founder and resident teacher of the Cambridge Insight Meditation Centre in Cambridge, Massachusetts (USA). He is the author of *Breath by Breath: The Liberating Practice of Insight Meditation* (2004); *Living in the Light of Death: On the Art of Being Truly Alive* (2001, co-authored with D. Guy); and *Three Steps to Awakening: A Practice for Bringing Mindfulness to Life* (2013, co-authored with L. Zimmerman).

Chapter 11

Living in Mindfulness and Wisdom

Andrea Schnöller

It is not possible, personally speaking, to write or talk about *mindfulness* without mentioning Corrado Pensa. Writing on this subject for this particular volume immediately and inevitably brings about feelings of gratitude towards him and a need to acknowledge the person who has inspired me with his dedication and teaching, which is always given with remarkable tact, delicacy, intelligence, passion, clarity and love. Along with me, he has been able to rouse the sense of mindfulness and its ongoing cultivation in many students and readers.

1. Living in the Present Moment

I have only had the good fortune and opportunity to attend a few of Corrado Pensa's courses and retreats; regardless, I have never tired of reading and rereading his writings, both independently and in groups. Now, when I am teaching or perhaps writing on the subject, just mentioning the topic of mindfulness immediately brings to mind his advice, collected during my encounters with him. One suggestion that has left a profound mark on my path of mindfulness was given in Galbiate in 1990. It was my first intensive retreat with Corrado Pensa and we were seated together in meditation, collected and focused on the breath. I was entirely absorbed on the inhalation and exhalation, just as we had been instructed, when the voice guiding us, articulating every word, put forward an idea:

> The mind that adheres—that tries to adhere—to the breath is a mind that grows, that evolves. The quieter the mind is, the more it is able to listen, the more it is able to understand. In the quiet mind are the roots of intelligence and love. The mind that calmly and mindfully adheres to the real is a mind that transforms. All spirituality is nothing but a mind that transforms itself in order to bring about that fullness of being, which is far beyond anything our concepts and preconceptions tell us. The mind's growth and evolution are entrusted to the simplest of things—we go to the beginning of the nasal septum and observe what happens upon inhalation and exhalation with love and serene attention.

On that occasion, I immediately understood very clearly that all meditation was essentially a matter of *presence* and *listening*. This was the essential attitude with which one had to train regularly and with perseverance. At that same moment, the words of St. Francis uttered in Franco Zeffirelli's well-known film *Fratello Sole, Sorella Luna* (1972) also spontaneously surfaced in my mind:

> Every simple man carries a dream in his heart [...].
> If you wish, every day with your sweat,
> one stone after another, you will arrive high [...].
> In the simple life, you will find the path
> that shall bestow peace on your pure heart.
> And the simple joys are the most beautiful,
> they are the ones that, in the end, are the greatest.
> Step by step, every day with your sweat,
> one stone after another; you will arrive high.

I was also reminded of St. Francis by Carol Wilson's masterful words, reported by Corrado Pensa in a collection of his essays on Dharma practice entitled *L'intelligenza spirituale*:

> 'I spent many years in my life of meditation practice waiting, in a subtle way, for the definitive moment when I would awaken, once and for all.' [...] With this idealized waiting, however, '*we risk missing the essence of the practice*. For me, it has been a tremendous relief to see through this view and to put down the burden of unrealistic expectation. When we realize that our deepest meditation practice is a cultivation of attitude rather than a search for some special experience, our whole life opens up. *Every activity can become a vehicle for awakening*. Life is made up of moments. Mindfulness practice is simply a cultivation of *the ability*

> *to meet whatever is arising from moment to moment with fullness of presence and an open heart.*'[1]

In Éloi Leclerc's *Sagesse d'un pauvre*, I have read something similar. After the celebration of Pentecost in 1219, St. Francis left for the Holy Land, following the Crusaders. Arriving in Damietta, he obtained permission from the papal legate to go, at his own risk, to Sultan Melek-el-Kâmel, who received him with refined hospitality. In early 1220, he was in Acre and, it is believed, had the opportunity to visit the holy sites. Soon afterward, Francis returned to Italy, together with Brothers Pietro Cattani, Elias of Cortona, and Cesario da Spira. He was alarmed at the situation within the Order, learning that several friars no longer intended to follow his *Regola di vita*, which he had received as a "revelation" from the Lord. It was a time of profound crisis for the entire Order he had founded and also for Francis himself, who then resigned from the government of the fraternity and went to La Verna, where he withdrew into solitude, devoting himself entirely to fasting and prayer. Then, on Good Friday, immersed in this situation of conflict, discouragement and bewilderment, as he meditated on and contemplated the crucified Christ, he had a new surge of awareness, which he again defines as a "revelation" of God. Thanks to this intense inner experience, he regains perfect peace of heart, his usual serenity, joy and happiness. He then encounters Brother Tancredi, who had climbed all the way to La Verna to convince Francis to come down and join the friars for the Chapter of Pentecost (a gathering of all the friars that was celebrated every year at the Portiuncula of Santa Maria degli Angeli). Francis says to him, 'Yes; now I can come. I have found inner peace, gentleness and perfect happiness'. Indeed:

> The Lord has revealed to us
> that man arrives at complete self-knowledge
> and realizes the truth of himself,
> not when he pursues a noble ideal,
> however great and holy,
> but when he shows himself capable of embracing reality,
> all of reality,
> without excluding anything,
> just as it is,
> *with perfect inner peace.*[2]

These are words that Éloi Leclerc has taken the great liberty of attributing to St. Francis, but they also testify to the author's profound knowledge of both Francis and his writings.

It is well known that Francis' writings are concise and few in number, but for those who know how to read them, they reveal a tremendous inner depth. Anger, resentment and aversion, no matter towards whom or for what reason, were always forbidden from entering his life and spiritual quest. He 'was loved for his joy, his generous dedication, his universal heart. He was a mystic and a pilgrim who lived simply and in wonderful harmony with God, with others, with nature and with himself.'[3] Francis always and sincerely considered himself last and as being the servant of all. Faced with the reality of sin, both his own and those of others, yes, he feels great sorrow; but he is careful, and he always warns other people as well, not to become angry as a result of sin, either one's own or those of others. In his view, losing peace of heart is a sin decidedly more serious than any other for which one can blame oneself or somebody else. He expresses this clearly in an *admonition* addressed to his brothers, entitled 'Do Not Allow Yourself to Be Marred by the Sin of Others.' We read there, among other things, that the 'servant of God who does not become angry or upset about anything, lives *rightly* and *without anything of his own*. And blessed is he who keeps nothing for himself, rendering to Caesar what is Caesar's and to God what is God's.'[4] That is to say, it is right and proper to acknowledge one's own mistakes and errors, as well as those of others; and it is right to face the penalty or make amends. However, it matters much more and heals us to keep ourselves constantly open—with unwavering confidence, serenity and commitment—to truth and good, both towards ourselves and others.

Here, I am reminded of a passage from Corrado Pensa's book *La tranquilla passione*, where, referring to a cultivated, mature and adult awareness, he says:

> Passion for the work of mindfulness is comparable, once fully blossomed, to a great fire into which everything is put and in which everything, to the extent that we can be aware of it, contributes to its flame. And this is very different from what happens within someone who is not enlivened by a passion for inner work, where any thought, intention, sensation, feeling or emotion can become an independent force that controls us or a constantly changing purpose that absorbs us. On the contrary, in a life oriented according to mindfulness, the primary purpose of everything that arises in our mind is always the same: to become an

object of attention, to become fuel for the great fire. And therefore, in this sense, *everything helps us, everything is grace*.[5]

2. The Ingredients

Complete presence of mind, empathy, open-hearted listening, simplicity, total acceptance, compassion rather than judgment, inner peace and serenity in all circumstances are all *ingredients* that characterize a state of true awareness and lead, step by step, to clear vision. But it is quite evident that one could go on indefinitely listing the elements or inner attitudes suitable for mindfulness. Some have likened mindfulness to a *crystal-clear mirror*, in which everything is reflected for what it really is, without being subjected to the constant and unconscious backlash of our preconceived ideas, our personal tastes, our expectations, both individual and collective, which are so often short-sighted, self-centred, cowardly, partial and gratuitous. In order to live in full awareness, to know and cultivate with perseverance all its ingredients without neglecting any of them, it is essential to stop, to regain one's inner peace and serenity, to listen with equanimity to what we really experience, to first question ourselves and, only then, others. This is especially true when we find ourselves in conflict or suffering. If we do this with kindness and love, without accusing or degrading ourselves or those in our presence, we will discover that everything can be responded to in creative, enlightening and dynamic ways. And we realize that this is extremely positive for us and those around us. If being a *spotless mirror* means this, it is surely a metaphor to cultivate. It greatly helps us to understand the nature of consciousness and the preciousness of each of its ingredients:

> The nature of consciousness is to be just a mirror. The mirror has no choice of its own. Whatsoever comes in front of it is reflected—good or bad, beautiful or ugly—whatsoever. The mirror does not prefer, it does not judge, it has no condemnation. The nature of consciousness, at the source, is just mirrorlike. [...] In the root, mind is consciousness. If you stop making discriminations, if you stop making dual division—choosing this against that, liking this, disliking that—if you drop out of these divisions the mind again becomes a mirror, a pure consciousness. So the whole effort for a seeker is how to drop opinions, philosophies, preferences, judgments, choices. And this should not become a choice in itself—that's the problem.[6]

3. To Be in Love with the Real

'Meditation is a living relationship with the total Existence that surrounds you. If you can be *in love* with a situation, then you are in meditation.'[7] This is yet another suggestive statement by Osho. His images and statements are always stimulating, and they force us to reflect, to think, but most of all, to listen to what we are truly experiencing. He talks about meditation, but even more so about mindfulness. The practice of mindful presence is never a purely technical, cold or soulless exercise; it cannot be simply reduced to an exercise of willpower or skilful concentration. Instead, it expresses itself as a friendly, loving and compassionate presence towards the real. Even when we speak of *proper detachment,* it is an '*affectionate detachment*,' as Corrado Pensa often reminds us. This may sound like a contradiction, but it is what actually happens when we are truly present, with full and open awareness, to someone or something.

Consequently, when we encounter resistance to being totally present with compassion, love and affection in a situation, we must not stop asking ourselves, without harming ourselves: What does it mean *to be in love* with a situation? What does it entail? Are we really *in love with a situation* simply because we are enamoured with someone or something, gratified in its company or that it suits us? And if, after a short while, everything changes and we feel deeply disturbed, frustrated and disappointed, what has actually happened? Was ours truly a feeling of love?

4. An Ongoing Commitment

In his superb *Biografía del silencio*, Pablo d'Ors talks of his confrontation with the silence of mindfulness and meditation. He speaks of being profoundly struck, from the very beginning, by the simplicity of the method and even more so by the simplicity of the aim. But to transform this promising beginning into a steady and solid way of being, it was necessary to engage regularly and persistently with the work. If one does not involve themselves in this way, they risk continuing to dream and never getting anywhere. He writes:

> The simplicity of the method—*sitting, breathing, quieting one's thoughts …*—and, above all, the simplicity of its purpose—*reconciling man with what he is*—seduced me from the very beginning [...]; and I quickly understood that it was a matter of willingly accepting what was coming, whatever it was.[8]

However, in spite of this hopeful beginning:

> In the first few months, I meditated badly, very badly; keeping my back straight and my knees bent was not at all easy for me [...] The mental restlessness, which I felt immediately after the physical discomforts, did not constitute a lesser battle nor a more bearable obstacle for me. On the contrary—an endless boredom threatened me in many of my sittings, as I then began to call them.[9]

All this must be kept constantly and scrupulously in mind if we are not to run the risk of watering down and debasing the concept and practice of mindfulness. It should be kept in mind, especially when, returning from the training ground of our meditative sittings, we enter the thick of our daily relationships with others and our commitments. Indeed, the real opportunities to refine and strengthen our aptitude for mindfulness and open listening to reality are encountered primarily in our daily lives. It is there that we learn not to be bothered by events but rather to see and welcome them as opportunities for our human and spiritual growth as well as the growth of intelligence, wisdom and love.

5. An All-Pervasive Attitude

It is not my intention to list all the ingredients of mindfulness here. In particular, I do not intend to establish an order of importance. Let it suffice to repeat the words of St. Thomas Aquinas regarding the virtues: if only one is missing, all are missing. Mindfulness is, therefore, an attitude of the mind-heart destined to accompany us always and everywhere. As Francis of Assisi says, it is our friend and companion *in the encounter with reality, all reality, as it is, without excluding anything*. At the same time, we learn to recognize our resistances, but also our deepest aspirations and our unsuspected inner resources of goodness. This is how we bring to fruition the infinite opportunities that we are given, to establish ever more genuine, more generous and creative relationships in life, with all that exists.

It should be mentioned that there is a close relationship of interdependence between the righteous cultivation of mindfulness, which leads to profound vision, and "*peace of heart*," i.e. *esichìa*, *quies*, *samatha*, *samādhi*. These two attitudes proceed together, hand in hand; they mutually support and sustain each other along the way. On the one hand, *peace of heart* is the indispensable prerequisite to the correct practice of meditation and deep insight; on the other hand, it is also the most flavourful and precious fruit that ripens on the tree of mindfulness, over time becoming progressively larger and more stable. Indeed, as Patañjali attests in his earliest aphorisms on yoga, *samādhi* is the ultimate goal of the entire practice and inward search. It is also appropriate to frequently bring to mind another of his statements: that the most challenging *samādhi* to achieve is that of complete reconciliation with ourselves, just as we are. Only those at peace with themselves can indeed be at peace with others and with everything.

Peace of heart is an arduous achievement, and it is never final; it always needs to be resumed, cultivated and deepened. We should not be regretful or surprised when we find that the path to full awareness and inner peace is strewn with obstacles, resistance, setbacks and difficulties. It is an integral part of the inner journey, which is not entrusted to magic but to joyful, serene and persevering effort. Gandhi himself—the *mahātma*, the great soul—understood this perfectly, and he had learned to delight in and rejoice inwardly over the small steps he took day after day with jovial perseverance:

> God is the universal Spirit of truth that pervades everything. But in order to see face to face the universal Spirit of truth that pervades everything, we must be able to love the meanest being in creation as ourselves. And the one who aspires to this cannot afford to keep away from any field of life. Self-identification with all that lives, however, is impossible without self-purification. Without self-purification the observance of the law of *ahiṃsā* remains a dream, empty: and God can never be understood by one who is not totally pure in heart [...]. To achieve perfect purity, one must become absolutely free from passion in thought, speech and action. To rise above the opposing currents of love and hate, attachment and repulsion. I know that I do not yet possess this threefold purity, despite the tenacious and unremitting effort to achieve it. I am but a poor soul struggling and pining to be totally good, totally true and totally nonviolent in thought, word and deed; but I never reach the ideal *that I know to be true*. It is a painful ascent, but this pain is a positive joy for me. Each step upward makes me feel stronger and ready for the next.[10]

6. In Service of Unity and Peace

To conclude these limited reflections on mindfulness, I would like to quote another brief but striking passage from the letter that the apostle Paul addressed to the Christians of Ephesus. Admittedly, today it is no longer considered a letter written or dictated by Paul but is attributed to an anonymous disciple. Furthermore, it was not written in the 1960s but is dated between

90–100 C.E. Apart from these clarifications, it nevertheless reflects Paul's central proclamation, both in his preaching and authentic writings. Chapter 4, verses 1–3, of the Epistle to the Ephesians reads:

> As a prisoner for the Lord, I (Paul) urge you to live a life worthy of the calling you have received. Be completely humble and gentle; be patient, bearing with one another in love. Seek to preserve, through the *peace* that unites you, that *unity* which comes from the Spirit. (Eph 4: 1–3)

This means that if one wants to be a disciple of Jesus, they must be willing to invest all of their resources and energies in the service of *peace* and *unity*. God is *peace* and *unity*; consequently, one who intends to enter a full and filial communion with him must place themselves necessarily and entirely in the service of peace and unity. 'Blessed are those who are not violent: God will give them the promised land' (Mt. 5:5). This is their vocation, the natural consequence of *their being called*. It is an announcement that resurfaces again and again in the letter, but also in all of Paul's other recognized authentic writings. Immediately at the beginning of the letter, a hymn is quoted, taken in all probability from the liturgical repertoire of a Christian community in Asia Minor. In this hymn, God is praised and celebrated for the '*secret design of his will*.' The author attributes knowledge of this secret plan to a powerful event, which is hesitantly called a "*revelation*"—a revelation brought about by the contemplation of the crucified and risen Jesus, who breaks down every wall of separation and division—reconciling all things within oneself, with each other and with God:

> This is the richness of God's grace.
> He has given it to us abundantly.
> He has given us full wisdom
> and full intelligence.
> He has made known to us
> the secret plan of his will.
> That which from the beginning
> generously
> he had decided to accomplish
> through Christ.
> Thus God leads history
> to its fulfilment.
> He brings all things together,
> those in heaven and those on earth
> under one head,
> the Christ.

By virtue of this divine revelation, the reference to *unity* and *peace* becomes, for the disciple of Jesus, the supreme criterion of discernment also in relation to the maturity of his mindfulness. That which unites people with one another, but also with every other reality in the universe, and fosters understanding and concord, moves in the line of right awareness. That which divides, separates, wounds, implies instead the presence of another spirit, if only that of our meagreness, fragility, ignorance and fear; and at other times, unfortunately, of our narrow-mindedness, greed, arrogance and pettiness.

Regarding this last aspect of mindfulness, which deserves decidedly more substantial, detailed and in-depth consideration, it is worth referring, in conclusion, to a short but enriching collection of reflections on verse 32 of the *Dhammapada,* which the author and well-known Buddhist monk, Ajahan Sumedho, entitled *Mindfulness:The Path to Deathlessness.*[11] *Dhammapada* 32 reads as follows:

> The renunciate who loves to keep vigil
> and shuns distraction
> is protected. He cannot go back;
> he goes straight toward liberation.

However, I would like to end with a prayer attributed to St. Francis, since I have mentioned him several times:

> Lord, make me an instrument of your peace.
> Where there is hatred, let me sow love;
> where there is offense, pardon;
> where there is discord, union;
> where there is doubt, faith;
> where there is error, truth;
> where there is despair, hope;
> where there is sadness, joy;
> and where there is darkness, light.
> Grant that I may not so much seek
> to be consoled as to console;
> to be understood as to understand;
> to be loved as to love.
> For it is in giving that we receive;
> it is in forgiving that we are forgiven;
> and it is in dying that we are born to eternal life.

Notes

1 Wilson 1999: 35, reported by Pensa 2002: 10.
2 Leclerc 2007: 10.
3 Francesco Papa 2015: 10.
4 Cf. *Fonti Francescane* 1983: 160.
5 Cf. C. Pensa 1994: 13.
6 Osho 1997.
7 Osho 2000.
8 Translated from the Italian rendering, Pablo d'Ors 2014: 9.
9 Translated from the Italian rendering, Pablo d'Ors 2014: 11.
10 Quoted in *Young India* 9/4, 1925. Cf. also the Italian rendering in Gandhi 1963: 86.
11 Sumedho 2012.

Bibliography

d'Ors, Pablo 2014. *Biografia del silenzio*. Milano: Vita e Pensiero.

Fonti Francescane. Scritti e biografie di San Francesco d'Assisi. Cronache e altre testimonianze del primo secolo francescano. Scritti e biografie di santa Chiara d'Assisi. 1983. Padova: Edizioni Messaggero.

Francesco Papa (Jorge Mario Bergoglio) 2015. *Laudato si'. Lettera enciclica sulla cura della casa comune*. Roma: Libreria Editrice Vaticana.

Gandhi, Mohandas K. 1925. *Young India* 9/4.

Gandhi, Mohandes K. 1963. *Antiche come le montagne. La verità e non violenza sono antiche come le montagne*. Milano: Edizioni di Comunità.

Leclerc, Éloi 2007. *La sapienza di un povero*. Milano: Ed. Biblioteca Francescana.

Osho 1997. *Hsin Hsin Ming—The Book of Nothing: Discourses on the Faith-Mind of Sosan*. Poona: Rebel Publishing House.

Osho 2000. *The Revolution: Talks on Kabir*. Mumbai: Jaico Publishing House.

Pensa, Corrado 1994. *La tranquilla passione*. Roma: Ubaldini.

Pensa, Corrado 2002. *L'intelligenza spirituale*. Roma: Ubaldini.

Sumedho, Ajahn 2012. *Mindfulness: The Path to Deathlessness: The Meditation Teaching of Ajahn Sumedho*. Malaysia: Bolden Trade (Amaravati Publications).

Wilson, Carol 1999. 'Do I Want to Be Comfortable or Do I Want to Be Free.' In *Inquiring Mind*, 15.2 (https://www.inquiringmind.com/authors/carol-wilson/).

Zeffirelli, Franco 1972. *Brother Sun, Sister Moon (Fratello Sole, Sorella Luna)*. [Film]. Paramount Pictures.

Author biography

Andrea Schnöller resides at the Sanctuary of the Madonna del Sasso above Locarno, Italy. He is part of the Swiss Capuchin community. He holds regular evening meditation courses in Ticino. He founded an association for meditation and spiritual growth called the 'Ponte sul Guado', in the Chiese Valley, Trento. He completed journalism studies at the Catholic University of Milan and psychology studies at the Center for Psychology and Transactional Analysis in Milan. For several years he followed yoga and meditation courses, including *vipassanā* retreats, with Corrado Pensa, and introductory courses to Christian meditation with Father Antonio Gentili, with whom he published *Dio nel silenzio*, Ancora (2009).

Index of Names

'Bri gung spyan snga Grags pa 'byung gnas 127

Agoch, Jorit 158, 163
Agostini, Giulio 9
Aitken, Baker Robert xiii
Ajāmila 158, 159
Ambedkar, Bhimrao Ramji 31, 34, 37, 48, 50, 51
Amritananda, Bhikkhu 48, 50, 51
Anālayo, Achan xiii, xxi 9, 13, 21
Ānanda 15, 17, 150
Ānandabodhendra Sarasvatī 59
Anuruddha 20
Appleton, Naomi xxi
Arati (daughter of Māra) 147
Ariyadhamma, Nauyane 10
Aśoka 41, 50
Aśvaghoṣa 35
Atreya, Bhikhan Lal 59, 60

Bahadur Rana, Deva 38
Bahadur Sris, Rim 42
Bareau, André xiii
Batchelor, Martine and Stephen xiii, xvii
Baumann, Martin xx
Becatti, Giovanni 96
Bechert, Heinz 9, 48
Beltz, Johannes 48
Bergonzi, Mauro xx
Bernhard, Franz 9, 10
Beyer, Stephan 135
Bhāskarakaṇṭha 58, 59, 76, 77
Bhattacharya, Sivaprasad 59, 60, 61, 62
Bhikkhu, Bodhi 9, 19, 23, 24, 25, 26, 102, 104, 105, 106, 109, 112, 113, 115, 116, 117, 118, 119, 120
Blancke, Kristin 136
Bosson, James 136
Braham, Achan xiii
Braun, Erik 111, 119
Brewer, Judson Alyn 10
Bronkhorst, Johannes 116
Brough, John 9
bTsun pa chos legs 128, 137
Buddhaghosa 8, 14
Buffetrille, Katia 136
Burnouf, Eugène xiii

Cabezón, José xx
Caesar 180
Capa, Robert 86
Cartier-Bresson, Henri 85, 93, 96
Cattani, Pietro 179
Cesario da Spira 179
Chah, Achan xii
Chang, Garma C. C. 136
Chao, Emily 96
Charbonneaux, Jean 96
Chögyam, Trungpa xii, 126, 135
Chos dbang rgyal mtshan 128, 129, 137

Choudhary, Vasudev 39, 44
Cone, Margaret 9, 18, 24
Cornell, Timothy J. 96
Cousins, Lance Selwyn xiii, 23, 111
Cox, Collet 23
Crosby, Kate 23

Dalai Lama 91
Darpa (son of Māra) 147
Dasgupta, Surendranath 59, 60
Davenport, John T. 136
Davidson, Ronald M. 62, 63, 64
Davis, Jake H. 10
de La Vallée Poussin, Louis xiii
De Rossi Filibeck, Elena 137
De Simini, Florinda xx, xxi
Deleanu, Florin 10
Dennis, Dannah 49
Devaputramāra 146, 149
Dhammadinnā, Bhikkhunī 9
Dhammadīpa, Bhikkhu 10
Dhammajoti, Bhikkhu K. L. 10
Dharmapala, Anagārika xi, 31
Ditrich, Tamara 115
Divanji, Prahalad C. 59, 60, 61, 62, 76
d'Ors, Pablo 182,187
Dowman, Keith 61, 62, 63, 64
Dreyfus, Georges 112
Dutt, Nalinaksha xiii, 10

Eimer, Helmut 136
Elias of Cortona 179
Epstein, Mark 96
Evola, Julius xi, xx

Feldman, Christina xiii, xvi
Fitzgerald, Timothy 52
Frauwallner, Erich xiii
Fujikura, Tatsuro 38

Gäb, Sebastian 162
Gaborieau, Marc 49
Gamble, Ruth 126
Gāndhī, Mohāndās Karamchand 184, 187
Ganeri, Jonardon 76
Gao, Minglu 96
Gauḍapāda 60
Gellner, David 31, 32, 35, 45, 48, 49, 51
Geoffrey, Samuel 115
Gethin, Rupert 15, 19, 23, 100, 101, 111, 114, 115, 116, 120, 162
Ginsberg, Allen 126
Gling ras pa Padma rdo rje 126, 136
Gñānārāma, Mātara Sri 10
Gnoli, Raniero xv, 62
Goldstein, Joseph xiii, 10, 111
rGod tshang pa mgon po rdo rje 124, 127, 133, 137
Gombrich, Richard F. 48
Gotami, Kisa 46
Grandazzi, Alexandre 96
Griffiths, Paul 113, 120
Gross, Philippe L. 96
gTsang pa rgya ras Ye shes rdo rje 126, 136
gTsang smyon Heruka 125, 135, 136, 137
Guarisco, Elio 136
Guenther, Herbert 135, 138
Guneratne, Arjun 41, 50
Gurugè, A. W. P. 162

Hachhethu, Krishna 49
Halbfass, Wilhelm xx
Hallisey, Charles 162
Hangen, Susan I. 43, 49
Hansen, Mette Halskov 96
Harrison, Paul xxi
Harṣa (son of Māra) 147
Hartmann, Jens-Uwe 45, 48, 49
Harvey, Peter xxi, 162
Hegarty, James 162
Helffer, Mireille 135
Herman, A. L. 162
Hookham, Shenpen xvi

Horner, Isaline B. 163
Hsü, Immanuel C. Y. 96

Jackson, Roger 135
Jesus 185, 186
Jiyu-Kennett, Houn xii
Johnson, Will 10
Jondhale, Surendra 48
Jones, Dhivan Thomas 9

Kabat-Zinn, Jon xiii, 111, 114
Kakusandha 155, 156
Kalhaṇa 62
Kallaṭa 60, 62, 77
Kapleau, Philip xiii
Kapstein, Matthew 135
King, Winston 116
Kinnard, J. N. 162
Kloppenborg, Ria xxi, 32, 48
Ko brag pa bSod nams rgyal mtshan 127, 128, 129, 130, 137, 138
Kornfield, Jack xiii, xvi, 111
Koselleck, Reinhart 92, 96
Krauskopff, Gisèle 36, 37, 40, 41, 50
Kr̥ṣṇācārya 124
Kṣemarāja 62
Kuan Tse-Fu 10, 25, 115, 117, 118
Kudo, Noriyuki 9
Kumārajīva 8
Kunreuther, Laura 45, 49
Kværne, Per 135, 141

Lamotte, Étienne xiii
Lavaṇa 63
Law, Bimale C. 23
Leclerc, Éloi 179, 180
Lecomte-Tilouine, Marie 36, 49, 50
Leve, Lauren 30, 32, 34, 35, 46, 46, 48, 50
Lévi, Sylvain xiii
LeVine, Sarah 31, 32, 35, 45, 48, 49, 51
Lhalungpa, Lobsang 138
Li, Lincoln 96
Liebenson, Narayan xvi
Lok Darshan, Bajracharya 36
Lopez, Donald Sewell xxi

Magar, Tulsi Regmi 39
Maha Boowa, Achan xii
Mahānāma 16, 21, 23, 26, 106, 118
Mainkar 59, 60, 76
Maitrīpā 124
Māra 146, 147, 148, 149, 150, 151, 152, 153, 154, 155, 156, 157, 161, 164
Mañjuśrī 128
Martin, Dan 136
Marx, Karl 34, 89
Masefield, Peter 24
Mazocchi, Luciano xvii
McDonald, Michele xvi
McMahan, David L. xx, xi, 48
Melek-el-Kâmel (sultan) 179
Milarepa 126, 127, 128
Milinda 159
Miller, Willa Blythe 136
Moggallāna 149, 150, 155

Nāgasena 159, 160, 162
Narayan Panjiyar, Tej 39, 40
Nārāyaṇa 158
Nāropa 127
Nigaṇṭha Nātaputta 16, 17, 24
Norman, Kenneth Roy xx, xi, 22, 23, 24
Nyanaponika Thera 104, 111, 112, 119

Obeyesekere, Gananath 48
Olcott, Henry Steel 31
Oldenberg, Hermann xiii
Osho 187
Ostaseski, Frank xiii

Pa-Auk, Tawya Sayadaw 10
Palumbo, Antonello 10
Papachristou, Neva xvi, xx, 109, 118, 119, 120
Pāsādika, Bhikkhu 9

Patañjali 184
Paul (apostle) 184, 185
Petech, Luciano xv
Pfaff-Czarnecka, Joanna 33, 49
Piano, Stefano 162
Pigg, Stacy Leigh 38
Pizzi, Franco 136
Prebish, Charles xx

Quinzio, Sergio 154

Ragā (daughter of Māra) 147
Rāhula 109, 119
Rāma 62, 68, 71, 72, 73, 77
Ranieri, Isabella 162
Rau, Wilhelm 162
Rhys Davids, Thomas William xiii, 23
Roerich, George N. 136
Roland, Martin 96
Ronkin, Noa 23
Rosenberg, Larry xiii, xvi
Rother, Larry 96

Sa skya paṇḍita Kun dga' rgyal mtshan 127
Said, Edward W. 96
Śakra 149
Salzberg, Sharon xiii, 111
Sañjīva 155, 156
Śaṅkara 60, 77
Sāṅkṛtyāyana, Rahul xiii
Śāntideva 161
Saraha 124, 126, 128, 136
Sarasvatī 42
Sāriputta 15, 20
Śāstrī Paṇśīkar, Wāsudev Laxman 58, 78
Sayādaw, Ledi 110, 111
Sayādaw, Mahāsī 111, 112, 119
Sayādaw, Mingun 110
Schaeffer, Kurtis 135, 136
Schlemmer, Grégoire 49
Schnöller, Andrea xvii
Shakya, Dharma Ratna 51
Shakya, Keshab Man 35
Shapiro, S. I. 96
Sharf, Robert 111, 112, 113, 115
Shneiderman, Sara 49
Siddhārtha Gotama 44, 148, 153
Singh, Ramanand Prasad 39, 40, 41, 50
Skilling, Peter 9
Slaje, Walter 58, 59, 60, 61, 62, 63, 76, 77, 78
Somānanda 60
Stache-Rosen, Valentina 9
Stagg, Christopher 136
Stcherbatsky, Theodore xiii
Stearns, Cyrus 127
Stein, Rolf A. 135
Steindl-Rast, David 161, 163
Stephan, Peter 63
Sujata, Victoria 135, 136
Sujato, Achan xiii
Sumedho, Achan 13, 186, 187
Suzuki, Shunryu xii, xvi

Thapa Magar, M. S. 35, 38, 41
Thich Nhat Hahn xii, 111
Thomas Aquinas 183
Timalsina, Sthaneshwar 61
Toffin, Gérard 49
Torella, Raffaele 76
Triratna Manandhar 45
Tṛṣṇā (daughter of Māra) 147
Tucci, Giuseppe xiii, xv, xvi, 15, 16, 135

U Ba, Khin xii, 111, 119
U Pandita, Sayadaw xii, xvi
Upāli 16

Vasiṣṭha 59, 63, 64, 66, 67, 71, 72
Vasugupta 60, 62
Vekerdi, Jozsef 135
Vetter, Tilmann 116, 120
Vibhrama (son of Māra) 147

Villard, Francois 96
Viṣṇu 158, 159
von Almen, Fred xvi
von Hinüber, Oskar 23
von Rospatt, Alexander 49

Wallace, Alan 113, 115, 119, 120
Walther, Marco 136
Whelpton, John 33
White, David G. 61, 62, 63, 64
Wille, Klaus 9
Wilson, Carol xvi, 178, 187
Wynne, Alexander 116, 117

Xiaoping, Deng 86

Yama 159
Yang dgon pa rGyal mtshan dpal bzang po 124, 127, 137
Yimou, Zhang 87

Zedong, Mao 89
Zeffirelli, Franco 178
Zelliott, Eleanor 48, 56

Index of Texts (Sanskrit, Pāli and Prakrit)

Abhidhammapiṭaka 14, 15, 101
Āhuneyyasutta 26
Alagaddūpamasutta 62
Ambalaṭṭhikārāhulovādasutta 109
Ānāpānasatisutta 115, 174
Aṅguttaranikāya (AN) 4, 17, 24, 104, 106, 115, 116, 118
Atthasālinī (Dhammasaṅganī-aṭṭhakathā) 23

Bhāgavatapurāṇa 163
Bodhicaryāvatāra 161, 163
Brahmacariyasutta 24
Buddhacarita 162

Cūḷasuññatasutta 17

Dhammacakkappavattanasutta 107
Dhammasaṅgaṇi (Dhs) 23, 162
Dhammapada (Dhp) 3, 5, 9, 10, 144, 168, 162, 186
Dharmasaṃgraha 162
Dīghanikāya (DN) 9, 10, 23, 24, 25, 115, 116, 120, 162
Dutiyaanuruddhasutta 20

Ekottarikāgama 7

Godhikasutta 152

Kammanirodhasutta 26
Kandarakasutta 3, 4, 25
Kassakasutta 162
Kāyagatāsatisutta 6, 7, 115
Kāyasakkhīsutta 22
Khemasutta 23
Kīṭāgirisutta 19

Laghuyogavāsiṣṭha (Yogavāsiṣṭhasāra) 61
Lalitavistara 162
Laṅkāvatārasūtra 59
Līnatthapakāsinī I (DN-pṭ: Dīghanikāya-purāṇaṭīkā) 23

Madhupiṇḍikasutta 119
Madhyamāgama (MĀ) 4, 7
Mahābhārata 144
Mahācundasutta 19, 20
Mahāmāluṅkyaputtasutta 62
Mahānidānasutta 25
Mahāpadānasutta 16, 24
Mahāpadesasutta 23
Mahāparinibbānasutta 23
Mahāsatipaṭṭhānasutta 101
Majjhimanikāya (MN) 6, 7, 9, 10, 13, 17, 23, 24, 25, 62, 103, 108, 109, 115, 116, 118, 119, 120, 154, 162, 163, 174
Mañjuśrīnāmasaṃgīti 128
Manorathapūraṇī (Mp) 26
Manusmṛti 176

Māratajjaniyasutta 149
Milindapañha 24, 101, 159
Mokṣopāya (MU) 58, 59
Mokṣopāyaṭīkā (MṬ[VIa]) 59, 78
Mūlakasutta 25

Papañcasūdanī (Ps) 10, 24
Paramatthadīpanī (It-a: Itivuttaka-aṭṭhakathā) 24
Paramatthadīpanī (Th-a: Theragāthā-aṭṭhakathā) 24
Pariyogāhaṇañāṇaniddesa 21
Paṭhamanakuhanasutta 24
Paṭhamapācīnaninnasutta 18
Paṭiccasamuppādasutta 26
Paṭisambhidāmagga (Paṭis) 14, 16, 17, 18, 21, 22, 23, 24, 25, 26
Paṭisambhidāmaggapariyogāhaṇa 22
Peṭakopadesa 26
Puggalapaññatti (Pp) 16
Puttasutta 25

Rājataraṅgiṇī (RT) 62

Sabbāsavasutta 103
Saddhammappakāsinī (Paṭis-a: Paṭisambhidāmagga-aṭṭhakathā) 23, 26
Saḷāyanasaṃyutta 26
Saṃyuktāgama (SĀ) 9, 10
Saṃyuttanikāya (SN) 4, 9, 10, 15, 23, 24, 25, 26, 100, 107, 112, 116, 117, 118, 152, 162, 163
Sāratthapakāsinī (SPk: Saṃyuttanikāya-aṭṭhakathā) 24
*Śāriputrābhidharma 8
Satipaṭṭhānasaṃyutta 112
Satipaṭṭhānasutta 6, 7, 101
Śivasūtravimarśinī (ŚSV) 62
Suññatalokasutta 15
Suttapiṭaka 14, 15, 100

Theragāthā (Th) 24

Udāna (Ud) 105, 112, 118

Vāsiṣṭhamahārāmāyaṇatātparyaprakāśa 59
Vibhaṅga (Vibh) 9, 16, 23, 24, 101, 115, 162
Visuddhimagga (Vism) 8, 10, 14, 115, 116, 162

Yogavāsiṣṭha (YV) 58, 59, 60, 61, 63, 76, 77, 78

Christian Texts

Epistle to the Ephesians 185

Francis of Assisi prayer 186
Franciscan sources 180

Matthew (Gospel) 185

Tibetan Texts

Collected Sayings of Grags pa ’byung gnas 127, 136
Collected Songs of Ko brag pa 127, 138
Collected Songs of the Venerable Master rGyal ba yang dgon (rGyal ba yang dgon chos rje’I mgur ’bum) 128
Ocean of bKa’ brgyud songs (bKa’ brgyud mgur tsho)
Opening the Eyes of Faith (Dad pa’i mig byed) 125, 135
rGyal ba yang dgon chos rje’i mgur ’bum 128, 133, 137

Index of Terms

Abhidhamma 15, 16, 107, 117
absorptions. See *jhāna*
aggregates. See *khanda*
altruistic joy (*muditā*). See *brahmavihāra*
ānāpānasati 101, 174
anattā xix, 21, 22, 105, 106
anicca xxix, 21, 22, 46, 107, 117, 149, 156, 175
anussaraṇa 18
anussati 101
arūpadhātu 149
arūpaloka 149
asceticisism 65, 126, 130
attachment. See *upādāna*
attā 106
attraction. See *taṇhā*
attention. See *manasikāra*
aversion (*dosa*). See defilements
awakening 3, 5, 8, 30, 38, 47, 102, 104, 117, 148, 152, 154, 174, 178

bliss 118, 130, 131, 132
brahmavihāra 155, 156
  karuṇā 59, 65
  mettā xix, 155, 156
  muditā 156
  upekkhā xix, 75, 78, 112, 114, 116, 120, 156, 181
Brahmins/Brahmans 40, 41, 42, 43, 45, 50, 65, 71, 75, 76

cessation. See *nirodha*
Christian/Christianity xi, xiii, xvii, xix, 30, 31, 33, 93, 147, 184, 185
citta 59, 67, 69, 70, 101, 108, 113, 163
compassion (*karuṇā*). See *brahmavihāra*
concentration. See *samādhi* and *samatha*
cosmology (Buddhist) 148, 149, 156

Death 19, 21, 22, 46, 130, 132, 146, 150, 151, 157, 158, 159
defilements (*kilesa*; Sanskrit *kleśa*) 68, 146, 148
  avijjā (S. *avidyā*) 15, 16, 17, 26, 38, 103, 108, 110, 147, 148, 151, 157, 186
  dosa (S. *doṣa*) 15, 103, 108, 119, 131, 132, 146, 147, 156, 157, 180
  lobha 74, 103, 147, 162, 186
  moha 146, 147, 148, 162
delusion (*moha*). See defilements
deities 84, 89, 91, 149
Dependent origination. See *paṭiccasamuppāda*
dhamma (physical and mental processes) 15, 16, 101, 108
dukkha (S. *duḥkha*) xi, xix, 16, 21, 24, 25, 66, 67, 69, 101, 102, 105, 106, 110, 114, 146, 151, 160

effort. See *sammāvāyāma*
emptiness 15, 17, 18, 65, 128, 131
equanimity (*upekkhā*). See *brahmavihāra*

freedom xvii, 31, 71
feelings. See *vedanā*

God 36, 42, 51, 154, 157, 159, 179, 180, 184, 185
goodness xiv, 158, 183
greed (*lobha*). See defilements

happiness 3, 4, 5, 6, 8, 74, 106, 124, 159, 160, 161, 170, 171, 179
hindrance 4, 15, 16, 22, 117, 118
Hinduism 31, 33, 34, 36, 39, 42, 46, 48

identification 87, 161, 184
ignorance (*avijjā*). See defilements
immaterial spheres. See *arūpadhātu* and *arūpaloka*
impermanence. See *anicca*
insight. See *vipassanā*

jhāna (S. *dhyana*) 4, 5, 6, 8, 9, 10, 15, 20, 22, 71, 102, 111, 112, 116, 120, 149, 155
joy. See *pīti*

kaya (S. *kaya*) 19, 22, 25, 101, 108

liberation xi, 4, 5, 9, 14, 16, 17, 18, 20, 22, 23, 25, 37, 58, 62, 63, 65, 114, 186
loving-kindness (*mettā*). See *brahmavihāra*

Mahāsāṅghika 7, 8
Mahāyāna 32, 83, 159
manasikāra 103, 104
meditation (early Buddhist) 3, 5, 8
mind. See *citta*
modernist (Buddhist) 32, 37

nirodha 106, 113
nibbana (S. *nirvāṇa*) 18, 19, 20, 22, 24, 25, 62, 64, 101, 102, 113, 118, 131, 132, 149, 152, 153, 162
non-self. See *anattā*

pain. See *dukkha*
Pāli Canon xx, 30, 51, 62, 99, 107, 111, 112, 118, 144, 146, 148, 150, 151, 152, 154, 159
path (eightfold) xix, 18, 24, 75, 102, 107, 109, 154, 155
paññā (S. *prajñā*) 16, 19, 25, 26, 69, 75, 105, 106, 107, 110, 116, 183,
paṭiccasamuppāda 5, 6, 26, 83, 110, 119
pīti (S. *prīti*) 3, 4, 5, 6, 7, 8, 9, 15, 71, 116, 130, 131, 147, 159, 163

rebirth 17, 18
recollection. See *anussaraṇa* and *anussati*
repulsion. See *taṇhā*
rituals xi, 30, 32, 33, 37, 39, 40, 43, 44, 45, 46, 47, 51, 65

samādhi 4, 5, 8, 9, 16, 17, 18, 20, 107, 111, 113, 116, 155, 183, 184
samatha 102, 112, 174, 183
sammāvāyāma 102, 107, 159
saṃsāra 26, 37, 64, 69, 70, 75, 130, 131, 132, 146, 150, 151, 152
Saṅgha vii, xv, xvi, 32, 115, 155
saṅkhāra 15, 21
Sarvāstivāda 7, 8, 10
khanda 5, 117
satipaṭṭhāna 7, 101, 104, 108, 113, 115, 116, 117
self xiv, xvii, 15, 45, 74, 88, 89, 93, 94, 106, 148, 159, 184

sensation. See *vedanā*
serenity 75, 179, 180, 181. See also tranquility
suffering. See *dukkha*

taṇhā (S. *tṛṣṇā*) 110, 119, 147, 184
Tathāgata 23, 24, 150, 151
Theravāda Buddhism x, xvii, xxi, 8, 14, 29, 30, 31, 32, 33, 34, 35, 36, 39, 43, 45, 46, 48, 50, 51, 83, 88, 100, 115
tranquility (*passaddhi*) 4, 5, 6, 9, 75, 116
transmigration. See *saṃsāra*

upādāna 9, 59, 66, 108, 110, 119, 156, 157, 175, 184

vipassana (S. *vipaśyanā*) xvi, xvii, 5, 10, 21, 26, 32, 45, 48, 51, 89, 102, 105, 110, 111, 112, 113, 114, 115, 116, 119, 155, 174, 175, 184
vedanā 16, 25, 101, 108, 110

wisdom. See *paññā*

yoga xvi, xviii, 61, 63, 101, 113, 128, 132, 184

www.ingramcontent.com/pod-product-compliance
Lightning Source LLC
Chambersburg PA
CBHW062024220426
43662CB00010B/1457
* 9 7 8 1 8 0 0 5 0 3 3 1 1 *